ON THE ROCK

TWENTY-FIVE YEARS IN ALCATRAZ

The prison story of Alvin Karpis

as told to Robert Livesey

Mississauga, Canada

First published in 1980 by
Musson Book Company
30 Lesmill Road, Don Mills,
Ontario, Canada.

1981
Paperjacks Ltd.
330 Steelcase Road, Markham,
Ontario, Canada.

American paperback editions
1984, 1986, 1987,
Mosaic Press
P.O. Box 1032, Oakville,
Ontario, Canada.

2001
L.B.S. Inc. Publications,
P.O. Box 84001,
1235 Trafalgar Road,
Oakville, Ontario, Canada. L6H 3J0

ISBN 0-919788-05-X

Canadian Cataloguing in Publication Data

Karpis, Alvin, 1908-1979
  On the rock

ISBN 0-88962-262-0

1. Karpis, Alvin, 1908-1979 2. Prisoners –
California – Biography. 3. Crime and criminals –
California – Biography. I. Livesey, Robert, 1940-
II. Title.

HV6248.K37A3   365'.97946'0924   C80-094372-4

Every effort has been made to locate and acknowledge the sources of the photographs used in this book. We regret any instance where we have been unable to acknowledge the source of a particular photograph.

Credits/United Press International
        The Canadian Broadcasting Corporation
        The National Maritime Museum of San Francisco
        Cameron & Co., San Francisco

Jacket design/Peter Maher

Printed and bound in Canada
ISBN 09-919788-05-X Paperback

Acknowledgments

I am grateful to Joy Watson who typed and helped prepare the manuscript; Bo Janek who ably contributed to the reproduction of the photographs; and Don Loney for his excellent job of editing.

I am also indebted to Howard Aster and Mike Walsh who acted as agents for the book; Bernie Beauchamp, the executor of the Karpowicz estate; Gianni Tomasi for the introduction to Karpis; the employees of the U.S. Parks Service for their hospitality and cooperation while I toured Alcatraz Island; the guards and prisoners of Alcatraz; and particularly Alvin Karpis for sharing with everyone so openly his prison experience.

Foreword

Albin Karpowicz was born in Montreal, Canada, in 1908. He grew up in Topeka, Kansas, where an elementary schoolteacher changed his name to Alvin Karpis which he kept for the rest of his life.

Karpis began robbing stores and warehouses in Kansas during his teens; he reputedly stole his first gun when he was only ten years old. His first sentence was thirty days on a Florida chain gang for illegally "riding the rails". At eighteen he was given a five-to-ten-year sentence for a warehouse robbery; he and an inmate, Lawrence Devol, escaped from the reformatory in Hutchinson, Kansas, in the spring of 1929 but were arrested in Kansas City. Karpis was transferred to the Kansas State Penitentiary where he worked hard in the coal mines. He was released in the spring of 1931.

In the fall of 1931 Karpis married Dorothy Slayman but the time he spent with her was short. Karpis teamed up with Freddie Barker whom he met in Lansing (the State Penitentiary) and the Karpis-Barker gang set out on its own crime wave robbing banks, stores, and warehouses across the Midwest. The gang also successfully carried off two kidnappings: the first victim was William Hamm, Jr., a bachelor who was president of the Hamm Brewing Co. of St. Paul, Minnesota. The ransom paid was $100,000. The second victim was Edward Bremer, president of the Commercial State Bank at St. Paul. A $200,000 ransom was delivered but the bills were marked and the gang had difficulty distributing the money.

The Bremer kidnapping took place in 1934. By this time the FBI was "coming down hard" on the nation's desperadoes who were Karpis's friends and associates: Freddie and Ma Barker were killed in a one-sided shoot-out at a cottage in Florida; the FBI gunned down Dillinger outside a Chicago movie theatre; Baby Face Nelson was killed by G-men in a shoot-out on a Chicago street in the fall of 1934; Pretty Boy Floyd was killed in a raid on a farm in Ohio. Karpis was barely able to keep a step ahead of the FBI but in the fall of 1935 the Karpis gang pulled off a western-style train holdup in a Cleveland station. Karpis was forced to move around the country and finally, in 1936, the FBI closed in on Karpis and his partner, Freddie Hunter, and arrested them in New Orleans. Public Enemy Number One, "Old Creepy" as the FBI called him, received a life sentence to be served at Alcatraz, the island prison in the bay of San Francisco.

In 1962 Karpis was transferred to McNeil Island Penitentiary at Puget Sound, Washington. He was released in 1969 and deported to Canada. Alvin Karpis died in 1979.

1

New Orleans
May 1, 1936

"Alvin Karpis, you're under arrest! Don't take your hands off that steering wheel!"

Reflex snaps my head in the direction of the voice and I am looking into the business end of a .351 automatic rifle held next to my temple.

The street is in chaos. Machine guns, rifles, shotguns, and pistols dance in disorder. I look up to see two men lying over the hood of a car with machine guns pointing directly at me. In the confusion, my partner, Freddie Hunter, opens the right-hand door and slips out of the car we just entered a few seconds previously. He crosses the green grass between Jefferson Parkway and the sidewalk and starts walking down the pavement. No one sees him leave, all eyes are on me as I am ordered from the driver's seat.

Suddenly a voice from above shouts, "Watch out, that man is getting away!" Four FBI agents overlooking the scene from an upstairs apartment spot Freddie. One of the agents on the street runs down to where Freddie stands, looking as innocent as the situation will allow, and herds him back with the barrel of a machine gun.

FBI agents rush in every direction and crowds of curious civilians gather. I am given a half-dozen contradictory orders by as many panic-stricken agents.

"Put up your hands!"
"Don't move!"
"Sit down on the running board!"

"Come over here!"

"Put down your hands!"

A rifle is stuck in my back. I can feel the barrel shaking against my backbone. One of the agents, holding a machine gun with a fifty-shot drum on it, steps in front of me. He is the only cool head in the entire circus of cops. He looks me up and down and asks calmly, "Karpis, have you got a gun on you?"

"No."

"Are you sure?"

"Yes, I'm sure!"

"Alright then, I'd better put the safety on this machine gun before it goes off by accident," he says with a side glance at the gathering crowd of citizens.

"Who's the boss of this outfit?" I respond.

"He'll be here soon. Why?"

"Well somebody better tell this guy behind me to take it easy—the way he's shaking he's liable to shoot right through me and hit you."

I feel the barrel grind into my back. "I'll show you who's the boss when we get you downtown, you son of a bitch." The threat bounces off the back of my head.

I start to turn my head to the right and have just got out a "Go fuck yourself!" when I notice someone peeping around the corner of a building. My hesitation causes the others to follow my stare and we are all gazing at the half-hidden form. Several agents begin shouting at it.

"It's O.K.! Come on Chief! We got him! You can come out now!" With this encouragement, the figure moves from its secure position and starts toward us—in his left hand is a .45 automatic. Its companion is in the hand of a second man who hurries along only a step behind the first, walking in his shadow. I "make" the first man immediately. I've seen many newspaper photos of him: it is J. Edgar Hoover, Director of the FBI.

The second man, slight and blond, is Clyde Tolson; he is never too far from J. Edgar Hoover. The pair are often referred to as "The Goldust Twins" after a pair of colored kids who are pictured on a cleaning powder. Tolson and

Hoover live together, eat together, are always seen together. There are many rumours in Washington circles that they're homosexuals, supported by stories of Hoover appearing at parties in "drag". I don't know if such stories are true but I do think it's strange that the only woman Hoover has ever been seen with in public is Ginger Rogers's mother, who, when questioned by an inquisitive press, denied emphatically any romantic attachment between them.

Hoover brags to the press and the government that he, at great personal danger, "put the cuffs on Karpis". What bullshit!

We climb the broad stone steps of the old post office which now houses the FBI field offices in New Orleans. Once inside the office, Hoover sits down at a desk and looks darkly at me. He pauses dramatically and then asks, "Well Karpis, do you feel better now that it's all over?"

"I'm just sorry to be caught," I reply honestly and think to myself, I wish I could have another five-year run.

Buchanan, the ex-chief of police of Waco, Texas, standing beside me, interrupts my thoughts: "It could have been a lot worse! We were going to shoot that goddamn place apart when you surprised us by walking out the front door onto Canal Street. Lucky for you we had to change our plans rapidly. There were twenty-six of us armed with every weapon from machine guns to those new gas shells that burn your hands with phosporous if you try to throw them back out."

As he speaks, Buchanan slips off his suit jacket to reveal what looks like a heavy sandwich board around his neck. "We had our execution squad out"—he unbuckles the bulletproof vest as he continues—"rough, tough veterans who know their business. Them two hobos standing in front of the apartment when you came out was Gus Haman and Doc White, two of the Texas Rangers who gunned down Bonnie and Clyde. Clarence Hurt, the ex-chief of police of Oklahoma City, was there too. They're all men recruited 'cause of their reputations in shoot-outs.

"You did alright in this Karpis. We knew you was in

that ground floor apartment. Another few minutes and it would have been filled with gas and bullets. We weren't goin' in til we knew you was all dead. Us guys don't play at being policemen—we planned to pull your bodies out, not take you alive. We had you set up as well as we set up Bonnie and Clyde until you walked out unexpectedly. Count yourself a lucky son of a bitch you're still alive."

"Now I want to ask you a few questions," Hoover cuts in, attempting to take advantage of the moment. "Did you have any guns in the car?"

"Yes," I answer, "two rifles wrapped up in a blanket in the turtleback. Also, there's a briefcase with a .45 automatic inside."

"Did you have any guns in the apartment?"

"I left a .45 automatic under the cushion of the couch. I don't know of any others."

"But you do own some machine guns, don't you?"

"Yes," I admit.

"Where are they?" Hoover's eyes seem to brighten a little.

"In Cleveland, with some friends."

Now his eyes are glowing and he turns to Tolson, who stands by with gaping mouth, as if to say, "You see, this is how to interrogate a criminal." Then he turns back to me. "Good, now who are these friends and where do they live?"

My reply turns out the light in his eye, as he shifts from smirk to scowl.

"Look I know you guys are going to beat my ears off when you find out I'm not going to tell you anything so get with it. It will clear the air a little and then we will understand each other better 'cause then you'll know you won't find out a fuckin' thing from me."

"We don't do that sort of thing," protests Hoover in a deflated tone.

"Don't hand me that bullshit!" I retort.

"We want you to sign a waiver so we can take you to St. Paul," he announces, seeming to change the subject. "Otherwise you'll have to be put in jail here in New Orleans until we get a court order and extradition papers from the governor."

"Let me talk to a lawyer first," I shout.

"Not now, but if you cooperate and sign the waiver we'll let you call a lawyer when you get to St. Paul," bargains Hoover.

I sign the paper.

"Extra, Extra, Public Enemy Number One caught in New Orleans today," shouts the young paper boy on the streetcar island, as the Canal Street traffic flows past him on both sides. "Old Creepy arrested by Hoover!"

He thrusts his head into the open window of a car that stops for a red light. The occupants of the car show no interest in the paper he wags under their noses. The kid looks from the stern face of J. Edgar Hoover to my own blue eyes fixed on his. Suddenly he realizes who we are, bounces back from the car and turns in search of someone to share his excitement. Before he can point us out, the light changes and we are gone in the direction of the airport.

We're approaching St. Louis, where we're scheduled to land for gas, when Connelley sits down beside me. I'm shackled and handcuffed to my seat.

"You son of a bitch," he begins, "we don't know what to do with you. Most of the states where you are wanted for murder don't have the death penalty or, if they do now, they didn't when you were robbing banks in them.

"We might hand you over to Missouri where you shot that sheriff. They want your blood bad. Or we might take you to Chicago where you killed that policeman." He continues to probe, watching for the change in my expression or the nervous gesture that might indicate he is close to a vulnerable area.

"Go ahead and take me to Chicago. I didn't do that job."

"Don't give me that goddamn bullshit. Bolton told us all about it. We know you pulled the trigger."

"O.K. Let him testify to that," I calmly suggest.

"Hell, he won't testify to that because he was in on it himself," Connelley admits. Then, realizing he has just thrown the game, adds an attempt to break even. "But we know it was you."

I feel the chartered government plane banking as it approaches the St. Louis airport. It's a new TWA airliner and this is its first official assignment. It was flown to New Orleans to bring me back to St. Paul. Myself, Hoover, Tolson, Connelley, Buchanan and various agents are the only ones on board.

We hit the runway with a bump, come to a stop and taxi to the buildings. Six cars screech out of the night and form a circle around the plane like the spokes of a wheel; they turn their headlights out across the flat airfield, spotlighting the need for the heavy security.

Over 10,000 people, who have heard news of my capture over the radio and that the special FBI plane taking me to St. Paul will land for gas in St. Louis, are gathered along the fence surrounding the airstrip.

We hit rough weather. The plane bounces up and down 300 feet at a time over air pockets. We're ready to turn around when suddenly the winds become calmer and through a layer of ground fog we descend on St. Paul.

The plane taxies directly into a large hanger filled with cars and agents assembled to greet and protect me. There are men high in the rafters, armed with machine guns, while others scurry about on the floor.

Ever since the underworld tried to take Frank Nash away from the FBI in the Union Station Massacre they are extra careful with big name criminals.

In the FBI offices in St. Paul I'm chained to the radiator by the window. Hoover stands in the middle of the room surrounded by a dozen agents.

"Alright," he announces, "I'm going back to Washington now. If you try to pull a fast one, I've given orders to have you really worked over!"

"What about my lawyer?" I remind him of his promise in New Orleans and the deal we made.

"Why you son of a bitch! After all the trouble you caused me and I'm going to let you have a lawyer? You won't get a lawyer until you've signed a confession."

A long silence follows his departure. Finally one of the agents tiptoes to the door and peers out. "He's gone! He's gone!"

Another uncomfortable silence. No one speaks. No one moves.

Then one of the agents begins to pace the room. He walks around a desk two or three times and stops in front of me. He is husky and about five-foot four-inches tall. Nervous, dark eyes twitch in the center of a sallow complexion. His hair, dark and straight, is combed back above two little jug ears. This is McKee, trusted only by his superiors because they know he will follow every order and report on the behaviour of the agents under him.

He suddenly slams his briefcase down on the desk, takes a .45 out from under his jacket and locks it in the filing cabinet. Ten slow minutes pass without anyone speaking. I give a disinterested glance out the window which seems to rub McKee the wrong way. He growls at me, "Well Karpis, if you ain't going to say nothing you son of a bitch, I am. I'm in charge of this operation. You fuck around up here and give me the wrong answers and you ain't goin' to have no teeth left!"

Thus begins my interrogation. I was arrested on a Friday but it is Wednesday before I'm allowed to sleep. Between physical abuse and keeping me awake, the FBI expects to get confessions and information.

St. Paul, Minnesota
July 24, 1936

"Does the defendant wish to say anything to the court before the sentence is passed?"

I am about to be sentenced in connection with the William Hamm Jr. kidnapping which occurred more than three years ago. None of the $100,000 ransom has ever been recovered. The star witness for the government is Byron Bolton, a former associate of mine who has turned against myself and the others who are to be sentenced today. He is also the main witness in the Bremer kidnapping for which I am under indictment as well. In that case the ransom was $200,000.

Ironically, a few months after the Hamm snatch, members of the notorious Touhy mob of Chicago were tried for the Hamm caper but the jury acquitted them. At the time Hoover was furious. He announced that although they had beaten the rap, they were guilty and the FBI put the case down as solved. It has been reopened for our benefit almost three years later. We were indicted in the month of April, 1936, just a few weeks before the statute of limitations would have run out.

Judge Joyce, of the U.S. District Court at St. Paul, Minnesota, looks down at me from the bench waiting for an answer to his question. He's so frail a good wind would blow him right off his bench. I think of what an awesome power he has.

I shoot a quick glance at the jug-eared Sam McKee and catch the smug look of victory on his face. That does it! I decide to risk the wrath of the judge.

Only a few minutes before "Old Fitz" tried to tell Judge Joyce that Bolton had given false testimony against Jack Peifer during Peifer's trial. The frail white figure behind the bench had surged to life and read the riot act to "Old Fitz" much to the delight of the spectators, FBI agents, U.S. marshals and news media crammed into the tiny courtroom.

"Never mind Peifer! Have you anything to say for yourself?" he had asked and then handed "Old Fitz" a life sentence.

We all entered a plea of guilty except Peifer who had chosen a trial and, due to the evidence given by Bolton, had been found guilty. I know that the judge has to be aware of the acquittal of the Touhy mob on the same charge.

"Your Honor, I have nothing to say for myself but I would like to say that Mr. Peifer is entirely innocent and that

Bolton's testimony is mostly false. Peifer had nothing to do with this crime, knew nothing about it, and did not receive one cent of the money.''

I wait for the scolding that "Old Fitz" received but the judge looks thoughtful, not angry. He clears his throat. "I am going to postpone sentencing Mr. Peifer for one week while I look into the matter more closely and allow him to remain free on $100,000 bond," announces the judge, and then proceeds to give me a life sentence just as he had to Fitzgerald.

I'm taken quickly from the courtroom surrounded by marshals and FBI agents. Descending in the elevator, McKee is furious. "You son of a bitch!" he shouts, "What in the hell do you think you're doing? Just wait until the director hears about what you did in that courtroom!"

Back in my cell, I punch the breeze with the FBI agent guarding me until it is almost time for the shift to change. He informs me that I'll be leaving for Leavenworth in the morning. I go to bed, but not to sleep. I want to sort out my thoughts.

My first thoughts are about Peifer—I wonder if he will hang around to see how much time he gets. I recall him telling me once that he would rather be dead than go to the penitentiary for as much as one year. A jail sentence for six months, yes; but a penitentiary sentence, never!

The long months of interrogation are over now, but a few images remain. I recall how ridiculous McKee looked the day he rolled up his sleeve and, flexing his muscle, said: "Feel that Karpis! I think I could whip you in a fight."

Then there was the day a thin ghostly figure walked into the interrogation room. McKee introduced him as, "Sam Hardy, the guy that worked up the case against those guys who robbed the bank in Redwood Falls, Minnesota, in the fall of 1933, and put them in the state prison."

My interest was immediately aroused and I looked at the hero of the department—he was a hardshell Baptist from down south and, dressed in a black suit and hat, he looked like a minister.

"You must have had a real tough time with that case," I said. "If I remember right, the guys who robbed that bank knew that the sheriff in those parts had bought a plane in case of bank robbers. He and his son took to the air and traced a car speeding down the dry gravel road at sixty or seventy miles per hour, landed in front of the car, and stopped it with shotguns, only to discover it was a group of college kids. The robbers disappeared with the loot. If you caught them later, I think you did a hell of a good job!"

"The three of them are in the state prison right now," Sam Hardy brags. "They should have put me on your case Karpis, you would have been caught years ago."

I had a hard time keeping a straight face in front of that fool. I was the one who had robbed that bank. I had never known the three men now serving time in the state prison. My friends and I got a lot of money out of it because we hit the bank when a new shipment of government money had arrived to be distributed to smaller banks in the area.

Next, I remember the face of the U.S. assistant attorney general as he offered me a deal.

After my arrest, Hoover flew back to Washington where reporters asked: "Now that the fourth and last of the big name public enemies is captured, who is next?" (Only three men, along with myself ever held the title of Public Enemy Number One: Dillinger, Baby Face Nelson, and Pretty Boy Floyd—they all died violently.)

"Old Man Politics!" Hoover had foolishly blurted out, referring to the many crooked politicians found in every city I ever worked and who help protect people like myself.

Immediately the Washington politicians were on Hoover's back and he needed my testimony to back up his rash statement. He gave orders to get my cooperation at any cost, so the assistant attorney general came to see me, asking me to help and guaranteeing that he would square all the beefs against me and see that I receive only a fifteen-year sentence. "You'll be free on a deportation parole in five years," he concluded.

When I gave him my answer he exploded and, as he stomped away from my cell, he swore he would be present at my execution and would remind me of the opportunity I turned down.

The news that I will leave for Leavenworth in the morning means only one thing. Leavenworth will be a brief stop on the way to Alcatraz. The mysterious Alcatraz, the superprison built to house the most dangerous and hardened criminals in the United States. I try to sort out all that I've read, heard or been told about it.

In November, 1932, Roosevelt was elected President and Homer S. Cummings of New England became Attorney General. Cummings received congressional approval to build a maximum security prison in Alaska. After selecting a small island off the southeast coast of Alaska, he was returning home via San Francisco. Steaming through the Golden Gate, his eye caught huge brilliant letters that read U.S. Army Disciplinary Barracks on a wall surrounding part of a prison on Alcatraz Island. He became intrigued with the possibilities and immediately made arrangements with the army to sublease the place for five years in order to house the public enemies while the Alaska prison was being planned and constructed.

In a radio address on October 12, 1933, U.S. Attorney General Cummings spoke about "The Recurring Problem of Crime": "For some time I have desired to obtain a place of confinement to which could be sent our more dangerous, intractable criminals. You can appreciate, therefore, with what pleasure I make public the fact that such a place has been found. By negotiation with the War Department we have obtained the use of Alcatraz Prison, located on a precipitous island in San Francisco Bay, more than a mile from shore. The current is swift and escapes are practically impossible. It has secure cells for 600 persons. It is in excellent condition and admirably fitted for the purpose I had in mind. Here may be isolated the criminals of the vicious and irredeemable type so that their evil influence may not be extended to other prisoners who are disposed to rehabilitate themselves."

In midsummer of 1934, the first group of convicts arrived at Alcatraz from the federal prison located on McNeil Island in the waters of Puget Sound. Their number and identification were kept secret which only increased speculation in the media.

Next a transfer arrived from Atlanta which included "Scarface" Al Capone. A few weeks later came big news of a special train hauling several prison cars, each loaded with cons from Leavenworth. The prison cars were loaded directly onto a barge and the barge taken to Alcatraz Island. Among others on the shipment was "Machine Gun" Kelly.

Next came news of a mutiny by the cons which was crushed but followed by a hunger strike led by Harmon Waley, one of the George Weyhauser kidnappers, and John Chase, who was given a life sentence and sent directly from court to Alcatraz in connection with the slaying of two FBI agents, Hollis and Cowley, by Baby Face Nelson, in a fast shoot-out during the fall of 1934 on a highway outside Chicago.

The place is getting rough. People are always different in prison than they are on the outside. I've been in two other prisons. If conditions are as harsh as the newspapers describe them, I wonder how the cons are affected? How are they reacting? Are they taking it out on each other?

Since I was scooped up by the FBI on May 1, 1936, and put in jail here in St. Paul, two big news items have broken in regard to Alcatraz. First, Al Capone has been stabbed, but not seriously wounded, with a pair of barber shears by a con from Texas named Jimmy Lucas. According to the papers, Capone had been assigned to work in the shower area which was located near the barbershop where Lucas was an inmate barber. Capone was rushed to hospital but authorities refused to say what precipitated the encounter.

I put the incident down to jealousy and resentment. Only ten percent of any prison population are ever really capable thieves or criminals, the rest are born losers who spend two-thirds of their lives behind bars on minor infractions. A successful mobster such as Capone would be resented by the scum in any prison.

The second headline is that a con who was a notorious mail robber has been shot and killed by a screw while allegedly attempting to escape. Dutch Bowers was said to be climbing over the barbed-wire storm fence around the perimeter of the island when a guard yelled for him to stop. I have never heard of him before and wonder why he is "notorious" as well as why he would try to climb a fence in broad daylight in front of a tower guard. This mystery will soon be cleared up when I arrive at Alcatraz.

I doze off, dreaming of Alcatraz until the agent on the 8:00 to 4:00 P.M. shift wakes me. "Come on Karpis, get up. Your breakfast will be here in a few minutes and you want to eat plenty because McKee is so burned up over your statement in court yesterday, he's apt to starve you on the way to Leavenworth."

Then, sitting down on the chair outside my cell, he asks in a friendly tone, "Ready for the trip?"

"Yah, I suppose so." Then I ask, "Say, can you tell me whether or not Harry Sawyer, Doc Barker, Volney Davis and Harry Campbell are out in Alcatraz?"

He smiles before replying. "All of them are there but I'm not sure of Davis because he was writing his life's story for the FBI when taken from here to Leavenworth and it was on the understanding he would remain in Leavenworth until the story was complete." He seems amused at the expression on my face because he laughs and remarks, "Don't worry, the story is confidential and not for publication."

"Everyone is waiting downstairs," announce the two marshals to the FBI agent outside my cell.

"Even McKee?" I ask and all three of them laugh with me. When we step out of the elevator downstairs McKee is waiting along with four marshals and two FBI agents. Bristling with self-importance, he orders, "Turn over what money you have in your possession right now."

He is referring to the $5 which I am allowed while in jail for commissary purposes such as candy and cigarettes. As I run out of money, I can ask for another $5 from my funds which are kept in the jail office. I reach into my pocket and, keeping my eye on McKee to watch his reaction, pull out a roll of bills and some change.

"Jesus H. Christ!" he splutters. Then, after counting it

and discovering it totals more than $475, he explodes. "See there! See there!" he storms. "See why we insisted that only the FBI be in charge of this guy while he was in jail. Christ, it's a wonder he didn't manage to escape if he could get this much money."

"Well, as you said," interjects one of the marshals calmly, "no one but you FBI agents has had access to him since he was arrested—the marshal's office was ordered by Hoover to take a hands-off policy throughout the whole affair."

That stops McKee dead. You can see the tiny wheels turning in his confused head. Should he or should he not report this incident to the director? Who gave me the money and how?

Of course, the money had been passed to me by my attorney during one of his visits to ensure that I had funds if the opportunity to escape presented itself, but McKee probably suspects every one of his agents.

2

Leavenworth, Kansas City, Missouri
July 26, 1936

Every prison has a "dressing-in" procedure. Leavenworth's is similar to most prisons I have been in. We are registered in a large ledger and I become Leavenworth-49368.

Two screws carrying billy clubs similar to those carried by harness bulls on the outside escort me through a barred gate into a large rotunda with a high ceiling. The cell houses all seem to open onto this and we cross the rotunda to a hallway on the other side. As we start down the hallway, I see the main dining room ahead filled with cons having breakfast. We take a quick left through a doorway leading outside the building

We turn into the building which houses the "dress-in" area on the ground floor where several benches sit parallel to the three shower heads which jut from the wall.

"Strip and shower!"

As I wash, my clothes are taken to a counter and the shoes and belt cut up in search of blades or narcotics. When I emerge from the shower, a con stands by with a can of blue ointment and a small wooden paddle. He quickly smears the stuff under my armpits and on the hair around my balls and prick. After I don the prison uniform I'm marched, blankets in arms, to the office of a Mr. Morrison, Deputy Warden. In the hallway outside sit a dozen young cons, waiting to go before him on disciplinary charges. The door opens and his secretary, a guy dressed in white, says, "The deputy wants Karpis to come in right away."

The deputy warden, already seated back of a large desk in his shirt sleeves, wears a beautiful pearl-grey Stetson that had to cost $50. His shirt, obviously tailor-made, is also a soft grey material and open at the throat. His grey hair is immaculately groomed and the skin of his face has felt many a massage. One finger is decorated with a diamond that could easily go to two-and-a-half carats, set in a very expensive piece of workmanship. Altogether he looks more like the owner of a Nevada nightclub than a deputy warden. I see the amusement in his eyes as he realizes the effect his appearance has on me and he smiles as he begins.

"Karpis, convicts don't usually sit down when they are in front of me but put your blankets on the floor and take a seat. We have direct orders from Washington regarding you. They want you housed in isolation until you are transferred to Alcatraz. As far as I am concerned you have not yet violated any of the prison rules and should therefore be treated as a first-class prisoner but I have no say in the matter.

"Make the best of the circumstances. If, at any time while you are here, you feel that you are being mistreated or abused I want you to ask for me personally, and make it clear when you do, that it is at my request. Any questions?"

"Yes, how long will it be before I am on my way to Alcatraz?"

"Just as quickly as we can get you put through a physical and psychiatric examination along with the intelligence test. No more than ten days."

"This way Karpis," announces the screw outside the office and I walk past the riveted eyes of the cons on the bench to a barred and heavily screened door. He pushes a button and as it is unlocked from the other side I hear one of the kids on the bench whisper, "Boy, he sure don't look like no public enemy to me!"

Once inside the isolation unit, I'm face to face with a puzzled-looking screw and two cons. No one speaks for about thirty seconds, and then the screw asks, "Are you Karpis?"

"Yes, I am."

"Okay, put down your blankets and strip off!"

My clothing is minutely searched and handed back to me piece by piece. First the shorts, then the undershirt, next the socks, the shirt, the trousers and finally by the time I get the shoes I'm already dressed and ready for the next step.

"Bring your blankets and come with me!" I follow him down a corridor with cells on both sides, facing one another. Some of the cells are completely sealed shut by heavy wooden doors while others are open revealing bars and a heavy mesh screen. An occupant stands in each doorway watching me. These are the select occupants of Leavenworth's isolation block, the most hardened and troublesome cons in the prison. At the end of the gauntlet of eyes through which I pass, directly in front of me, is a door leading outside the building. When I'm only two cells from the door, the screw stops and, turning to the left, opens a cell door. As I step back out of his way, I discover something I should have already known—the two cons trailed us so silently down the corridor I did not even know they were behind me. They are this screw's watchdogs, both of them are black.

I ran into a similar situation in the Kansas State Pen, at Lansing, Kansas, only seven miles from here when I was thrown into isolation after assaulting a guard. That was back in 1931.

"Karpis, this is your cell. While you're here I've been told that we're not to give you a hard way to go as long as you behave. We're leaving all the outside wooden doors open, unless the cell is being used as a hole, so that the air can circulate in this heat.

"You guys can talk in low voices up til seven o'clock but from then til breakfast you're to remain quiet. The rules state that the light in your cell must stay on all night and all day, but it is on a long drop cord so you can wrap a newspaper around it at night and put it at the other end of the cell if you want. That way the light won't bother you while you're sleeping.

"Anything you need or want, tell one of the orderlies that you want to see me." With that he locks the door and all three of them disappear down the hallway.

Tossing the blankets on the bed, I look around me. The

cell is twelve or fifteen feet long and about six feet wide. At the far end high up toward the ceiling is a small window, too high to see out of. A small table with a pitcher full of syrup on it sits against one wall. Further along, a set of radio headphones are plugged into a jack but the radio is not on right now. A toilet and a wash basin are crammed in a corner of the cell next to the door. A roll of toilet paper on the floor by the toilet and a gallon can on the floor by the table complete the decor, except for a cotton pillow and mattress on the bed.

I'm sleepy from being up all night on the train and relieved because this is the first time I've been left alone and unwatched. Since my arrest two months before, I've constantly had an FBI agent outside my cell in St. Paul. And yet, I can't shake off the eerie feeling that eyes are watching me still.

A short while later my door opens and the two black watchdogs hand me bed sheets, a pillow case, some matches, a bar of soap, an aluminum cup, an aluminum plate, a spoon, a couple of books of cigarette papers and a bag of Country Gentleman smoking tobacco. The screw, who unlocks the door for them, remarks, "The radio comes on at 6:00 P.M. and goes off at 10.30 P.M. If you damage the headphones accidently or otherwise you will be expected to pay for them."

I quickly make the bed but I feel that same sensation that someone is observing me. Glancing toward the door, I understand why. Crouched in the doorway of the cell opposite me, a dark shape is staring at me. The light in his cell is dim so I barely see his silhouette but, sure as hell, he is there, silent and watchful.

"Oh, to hell with it. All I want is some sleep," I tell myself.

The unlocking of my door awakens me. "Okay Karpis, it's chow time. Get your plate and come to the door."

"I'll pass on dinner. I'm too sleepy to eat." I wake for the second time, drenched in sweat and wonder what time it is. I hear a door open and the jingle-jangle of metal lids on food containers announcing it is chow time again. The portable steam table rolls down the corridor, stopping at each cell. As the orderlies fill the plates, the screw relocks the doors. Mine finally opens, my plate is taken and returned with a vegetable salad, navy beans and bread pudding on the same plate with four slices of bread. The gallon can is half-filled with ice over which cold tea is poured.

"Anything left on your plate just flush it down the crapper."

Jesus! I look at the conglomeration on my plate. It has merged into one soggy mess. I nibble at the beans. Cold! I notice a few shreds of coconut in the pudding and pick them out. Rancid! I walk over to the toilet and dump the whole mess. I have bread, syrup, and iced tea for supper.

The shift changes. I remember the screw said the radio comes on at six o'clock so I lie on the bed with the headphones on. Suddenly a bugle sounds, jolting me out of my bed. The silent watcher in the cell across from me is in his doorway. "That's for the count," he volunteers. "No talking while the count is on." He is being helpful. The screw comes by looking in each cell. In less than ten minutes the bugle sounds the "all clear".

"They'll go into supper now and then from the dining room to the yard," explains the stranger across the corridor. I nod that I understand and go back to the headphones.

I'm in a sort of daydream, when the radio comes on with such volume it startles me before it's turned down. The first program is the evening news, and the first item is about me. "Alvin Karpis, captured Public Enemy Number One, was taken to Leavenworth today and will be held incommunicado in solitary confinement until he is sent to Alcatraz." The announcer goes on to rehash my criminal life and then adds, "The director of prisons claims that the twenty-seven-year-old Karpis will not be kept in Leavenworth long enough to remember his number before proceeding to Alcatraz."

It sounds like he's talking about someone else. It's ten years since I listened through headphones to a radio. Me and another kid in Chicago had put together a crystal set but we were always pulling in at least three stations at once. I hang the phones on the rack and get myself a drink of iced tea from the gallon can.

As I glance out of my cell door, I see a strange sight. The con across the corridor is squatting in front of his cell door completely naked! He wears only a green celluloid eye shade. It's humid, so there is some logic in his behaviour. I pour myself some tea and walk to my cell door. He speaks to me in a quiet but very clear voice.

"Karpis, if you want any cigarettes, toothpaste or gum, I can let you have some until you can order some from the commissary." I'm surprised to hear I'll be allowed commissary in isolation.

"I'm sure you have a lot of friends in here who would be glad to help, but no one can send you anything from general population." I still haven't replied when he continues, "Another thing, you might not think so but you are real lucky to be in isolation rather than population where half those bastards would be trying to make parole at your expense."

Jumping Jesus! I've decided I'm locked up with a naked screwball when a voice from a cell to the left of him chimes in, "Karpis, as a rule this character and I seldom agree on anything but I'll have to admit he's right about that. By the way, Doc Barker and me were kids together in Joplin, Missouri. When you get to Alcatraz say 'hello' for me. I'm Jimmy Wren."

I robbed banks with Doc Barker and his brothers for years. Doc is in Alcatraz and his brother Lloyd is here in Leavenworth on a bum rap. Freddie Barker and Ma Barker were massacred when the FBI caught up to them in a Florida hideout. I thank the nude con across from me for his offer and begin asking Jimmy if he knows this guy or that one around Joplin.

I discover Jimmy Wren has been in isolation now for almost eight years for cutting up a fellow con with a shiv. He left more than forty slashes on his victim in one of those prison romance feuds which are the cause of most of the violence in prisons. On the outside, homosexuals are usually pictured as weak and humorous, but in a prison they are the most aggressive and dangerous inhabitants. The victim managed to live, was transferred to the medical center at Springfield, Missouri, and then paroled—but he was a scarred mess for the rest of his life.

Seven o'clock comes and with it silence. I listen to the radio until it goes off and then try to sleep. Between the humidity and my worries about the future, I toss restlessly during the night. I arise at dawn, take a piss and taste the iced tea. I spit it out. It is as warm as the piss I just let out! To pass the time before breakfast, I wash and clean the toilet bowl and wash basin then give myself a whore's bath with one end of the towel and dry off with the other end.

I look across the way to see if my neighbour is awake and am shocked at what I see. He sits, naked, at a table looking through, of all things, a microscope. Then an even stranger thing happens. He jumps up from his work abruptly, walks toward the wall of his cell and disappears. Instantly I hear what sounds like the singing of thousands of birds rising to a frenzied pitch. For a second I think I'm having a strange dream, but a closer look reveals a curtained doorway between his cell and the next one on the right. He soon reappears with several birds perched on his shoulders and two on top of his head. They're each of a different hue—red, green, and pale orange.

"Karpis, what do you think of my pets? Surprised? I have close to two hundred of them, all canaries, and they all came from the original two I started with many years ago." My strange neighbour, standing in the nude decorated with colorful canaries, is Bob Stroud, who has been in isolation here for around twenty years. He originally "took a fall" out of Alaska for murder and later was given the death penalty for killing a screw here in Leavenworth. At the last moment President Wilson commuted the sentence to life imprisonment in solitary confinement. Many years later he is to become famous as "The Birdman of Alcatraz"! Of course he never kept any birds at Alcatraz, only at Leavenworth. On this early morning of July in 1936, as I stare at him across the corridor, I wonder who and what he is.

I'm allowed in the exercise yard back of solitary once a day. It's here that I meet the mysterious occupant of the end cell next to mine. He never enters into any of our conversations but now he stands in the window of his cell which faces onto the exercise yard where I'm playing handball by myself with a tennis ball.

"Karpis, I guess you know that you are going to be sent to Alcatraz."

"Sure it's only a matter of time, are you going there too?"

"Hell no! I just came from there a couple of months ago."

This is Gordon Alcorn (AZ-114) who I read about in the newspapers when he was sent to Alcatraz for the Boettcher kidnapping and who, like myself, was born in Canada. His partner Sanky committed suicide in Chicago where Alcorn was finally cornered, after shooting his way out of Denver. They kidnapped the son of a wealthy brewer in Denver who announced he would "not pay one cent" until his son was released. They turned the kid loose and the old man kept his word paying off the ransom. The kid was kept on a turkey ranch by Sanky's wife who is now charged in connection with the crime. Alcorn tells me he has been transferred here to testify on behalf of Sanky's widow.

Stroud waves me up to my door and begins doing something I've not seen since the Kansas State Reformatory. He's asking me with his fingers if I talk and understand the hand language used by the deaf and dumb to communicate. I can, and our silent conversation begins.

"Were you talking with Alcorn while out in the yard?"

"Yes."

"He is a no good bastard. The government has brought him back to testify against Sanky's wife in Denver!"

"He told me he was here to testify *for* her."

"Never, but never, does the government hold a defense witness here in isolation!" Stroud is highly excited and his fingers are going so rapidly I'm having difficulty keeping up with him!

"Besides that, for the first couple of weeks Alcorn was

here the FBI called on him every day for hours at a time. I've seen many similar instances over the years I've been here. Believe me, Alcorn is a stoolie!"

I never speak to Alcorn again.

All day my thoughts are on Jack Peifer and how he is making out in court today. Peifer is the banker for many of the big-time bank robbers. He holds money for many prisoners now in Alcatraz and he has $30,000 of mine. Many cons will be upset to see him get a long sentence because it is understood that a sudden death or a long prison sentence wipes the books clean. I wait impatiently for the radio to come on with the news of the trial. Finally, it begins and the first news item is the one I'm waiting to hear.

"In police circles, suicide by a prisoner is regarded as a confession of guilt. This morning, Jack Peifer made a liar out of Alvin Karpis, former public enemy, by committing suicide in the Ramsey County Jail at St. Paul, Minnesota.

"Peifer had just received a thirty-year prison term for his part in the Hamm kidnapping which occurred in 1933, and which netted a $100,000 ransom.

"Karpis had attempted to convince the judge that Peifer was not guilty. Peifer died a few hours after swallowing poison of some sort. An autopsy will no doubt reveal exactly what kind of poison."

The newscast has not even finished when several of the guys in solitary begin shouting simultaneously, "Hey, Karpis, did you hear that?"

"Yes, yes," is my reply, "but I want you guys to know that he really was innocent." This brings bursts of loud laughter from them and even the screw gives a sort of cackle.

When the news about Peifer is over, I slowly hang up my earphones. Jack had always confided that he would never do a long prison term so I have to admire him for his constancy, but I regret the loss of my $30,000 which went with him. He's as guilty as the rest of us, but I tried to save my money.

"Put all the belongings you want to keep in this pillow case Karpis—you and a lot of other guys are leaving tonight for

Alcatraz," I'm told by the screw. "Come out in just your shorts." We stop in front of Dimmenza's cell and the screw shouts, "You too, you dago bastard!"

It is all taken in stride, though, because Phil is a likeable guy. We're taken to a wing of the administration building where we are the last to arrive. The room is filled with cons putting on clothing from paper bags; only two bags remained unopened—one for me and one for Phil Dimmenza. In the bag is a pair of pants, a shirt, a pair of sneakers, a comb, a handkerchief, a toothbrush, and a coat.

Jumping Jesus! It's really "old home" week as I look around. "Old Fitz," who was sentenced with me, and Harry Campbell are here as well as Herb Farmer, Dick Galatas, and Fritz Malloy, all given two years and ten thousand dollar fines for conspiracy in connection with the Union Station Massacre. In that shoot-out FBI agents, police, and Frank Nash all ended up dead after a desperate attempt to take Nash from custody while he was being returned to Leavenworth where he had escaped. Vern Miller and Pretty Boy Floyd had led the attack with machine guns blazing.

There sits Harry Fleisher, leader of the notorious Purple Gang of Detroit. Beside him is his deadly younger brother Sam Fleisher, Joey Stein, and Jake Selbin who is the "bank roller" for the gang. They all fell on a beef connected with selling liquor that had not been licensed by the U.S. government.

I recognize a couple of other guys from pictures in newspapers—Fred Reese and Jim Sparger—two members of the Ozark Mountain Boys who took many a bank in their time. The FBI surrounded a cottage in a tourist court Sparger was hiding in and told him to come out naked with his hands high. His reply was a hail of pistol bullets but they were soon drowned out by the steel-blanketed rifle bullets of the FBI smashing through the walls of the cottage. He was hit many times and passed out. How he lived through that pulverizing is a miracle but here he stands with a forty-five-year bit for bank robbery. Other members of the mob were in jail at Muskogee, Oklahoma, when they captured the jailer. After equipping themselves with machine guns and rifles from the jail's armory, they were just starting out of the building when they met the chief of detectives on his way in. He reached for his pistol but was killed instantly by about twenty slugs from a fifty-shot drum on one of the Thompson submachine guns. The gang was eventually surrounded in a log cabin up in the Arbuckle Mountains of Oklahoma. During the shoot-out which followed Don Heady was killed, Leonard Short committed suicide, and the other two surrendered. The FBI made a clean sweep of the Ozark Mountain Boys that day.

Another member of our group is a racketeer named Charley Yanowsky, out of New York. He has only a five-year bit, but is lucky to be alive. An FBI agent put a pistol against his head and pulled the trigger. Instead of penetrating his skull the bullet followed a path between the scalp and the skull, to stay lodged in his head.

Twenty of us line up, double file, shackled by an ankle to the guy beside us, handcuffed individually, and march out of the building onto a railroad car inside the prison walls. The windows of the train are screened and barred; about three feet inside the car at each end is a barred door. Outside each door sits a screw with a twelve-gauge riot gun. Once we are inside our jail on wheels, it begins to roll. The large back gate of the prison opens to allow the prison switch engine to pull us out and onto another railroad track where a regular switch engine waits. At Lawrence, Kansas, our prison car is attached to the back of the Overland Limited, a crack train of the Union Pacific, which carries us to the Coast.

We stop for five minutes at Topeka, Kansas; I recognize the town where I spent most of my boyhood. Between here and the Rockies is familiar territory to me because as a kid I rode the freight trains for kicks. I relive many an adventure on the rails and in hot cars on U.S. 40 as I cross the Kansas prairies. We travel from Colorado Springs to Denver and due north to Cheyenne, Wyoming, then westward until we reach Ogden, Utah, where we switch to the Southern Pacific. We cross the Great Salt Lake via the Lucien Causeway with

Utah, Nevada, and a chunk of California yet ahead. We begin the descent at Colfax, California, and soon reach our destination.

At Richmond, California, the car is shunted onto a long pier which stretches into the bay. We are hustled from the train and ordered down a steep fifteen-foot iron-rung ladder at the bottom of which waits a launch with the name *McDowell* on it. We descend carefully, two at a time, my 128-pound body shackled to the 200-pound Italian who was my neighbour in isolation. "Jesus," I think, "I hope this dago doesn't slip or we'll go down like the Titanic!"

Alcatraz
Thursday, August 6, 1936

"Take a good look you bastards!" screams a large, six-foot, red-faced monster in a brass-buttoned, blue uniform decorated with five stars and four bars of gold cloth. He refers to the dozens of screws armed with riot guns, heavy Browning automatic .30-.06 rifles, and Thompson submachine guns, who line the catwalk joining a lonely gun tower on steel stilts in the water to a large three-storey building on the island proper.

"Them guns you see aimed at you ain't nothin' to what we can come up with. Remember this, if any of you sons of a bitches start thinkin' of gettin' away from here. You're sent here 'cause they're afraid of you in them other prisons, but we ain't!"

Following this friendly reception, we're loaded into two long panel trucks on the dock to take us up the winding road leading to the top of the rocky island. The windows of the building connected to the gun tower are filled with the curious heads of wives and children of the screws. They look down on us from their high perches with the appetite of vultures and one of the kids, hyped up over the publicity involved with my transfer, shouts:

"Daddy, kill Public Enemy Number One right now and get the reward!"

As we slide off the benches and out of the panel truck, there is no place to go but straight ahead into a narrow hallway where we line up while one of the screws unlocks and removes the shackles from our swollen ankles.

"Warden, I think this is going to turn out to be the worst lot so far." The screw who threatened us down on the dock is speaking to a sharply dressed man in his sixties who sits at a small desk. This is J. J. Johnston, Warden of Alcatraz.

"Every shipment is the worst lot, Mr. Simpson, and don't forget it!" replies the white-haired little warden. He wears costly gold-rimmed glasses that perch on a mottled and blue-veined nose. "It cost him a lot of dough to get a nose like that, the most expensive kind of booze over a lot of years," I think to myself.

The guessing game of who the warden of Alcatraz would be had been a daily event in the newspapers. All the foremost penologists, such as Lawes, of "20,000 years in Sing-Sing" fame, and Fenton of Nebraska, had their names connected with the new supersecurity prison. Imagine my surprise when, during a "hurry up" trip to Reno, Nevada, I had walked into the backroom of the Rex Club, owned by Graham and McKay, to find the boys discussing the new warden of Alcatraz.

Graham and McKay were responsible for legislation legalizing gambling, prostitution, and quick divorces in Nevada. They owned large slices of property around town including the Bank Club and, until it burned to the ground, The Willows. They later built the Cal-Neva on the shores of Lake Tahoe with the insurance money from The Willows. They were on a first name basis with major politicians and major criminals. I sat down with a drink while they filled me in.

President Roosevelt had been fuming over the reluctance of many judges to agree to his famous "100 Days" legislation and to get control of the courts he needed a democrat named to the federal judgeship vacancy in southern California. However, he needed the senior senator in southern California, Hiram Johnson, a republican, to agree to his nominee. A deal had to be made—a protégé of Hiram's had to be named warden of Alcatraz and also had to be assured a federal post for life.

The new warden, badly in need of a job, was J. J. Johnston, who was forced to resign as warden of San Quentin following a financial scandal. What I learned in the back room of the Rex Club was announced to the media and public a few weeks later. His appointment was accompanied with glowing reports of what a wise choice the attorney general and director of prisons had made.

Under the watchful eyes of Warden Johnston I become AZ-325, indicating I am the 325th person to enter this federal penitentiary.

"Follow me!" orders a screw and I follow him into a large room with a high ceiling and many individual shower stalls. Benches run parallel to the stalls and on the benches lie bundles of clothing. The screw I am following stops beside the bundle with AZ-325 on the front. "Undress and get into the shower!"

Unlike Leavenworth, there are individual stalls and a guard assigned to each prisoner. As we shower, the guard assigned to each man stands in front of the stall and watches. I start to turn off the water when a voice halts my hand in midair. "Who the hell told you that you could come out of that shower? Get back in there and stay put until I tell you to come out!"

For a second I think the voice is talking to me, but then realize instantly that it is one of the guards a few stalls down. I decide to wait for my orders. "That's all," I'm told eventually.

I dry myself and reach for the underwear on the bench beside the bundle of clothing. "No one told you to dress! Wait until I tell you!"

About this moment a white figure appears at the top of a long staircase which leads from the floor above. He reminds me of a French waiter in an expensive restaurant as he carefully balances an aluminum bowl in the palm of his hand and descends softly with his nose in the air. By now everyone is out of the shower and standing naked in a row.

"Bend over and touch your toes!" The figure in white reaches the bottom step, struts behind us, and proceeds up the line of bent over cons, sticking his finger up the ass of each prisoner. In the aluminum bowl are a few dozen rubber finger gloves and he uses a new one for each asshole he investigates in search of contraband. The attendant finishes his job and starts up the stairs.

"O.K., get dressed!" All the clothing is size XL. Mine would fit a six-footer with a forty-inch waist. If they were trousers rather than coveralls they would fall around my ankles. The "long johns" of heavy wool seem out of place for sunny California. Once we dress an officer begins to lay down the rules to the line of uniformly clad cons.

"We have a silent system here! At no time are you to talk or make a noise while in the cell house or mess hall at Alcatraz!

"You convicts are now going to the dining room to eat. When you finish eating, put your silverware on your food tray and sit with your arms folded across your chest until you are ordered to leave.

"Take as much or as little as you wish to eat but finish everything on your plate. If you fail to eat everything you take, you will end up in the hole eating bread and water once a day. It is now 10:00 A.M., and you will eat again at midday.

"A book of rules is in your cell. Read them carefully and, when in doubt, ask the cell-house guard. O.K., let's go!"

We follow him up a flight of stairs and through a locked gate into the cell house where we make a sharp right turn and, within ten steps, stop. On our right is another barred and locked door leading to the dining hall; on our left is "Broadway," the central corridor which runs through the cellblocks.

Steel cages, the size of cupboards, line each side of Broadway and on top of the rows of tiny cells is a second and a third tier of similar cells. Monkeys in a zoo have more space than these cages afford.

Across each end of the cell house a catwalk gun cage high off the floor is manned by armed guards who view the entire cell house safely from behind heavy bars. The guards who come into direct contact with cons never carry guns, only billy sticks equipped with gas grenades.

The dining room door is unlocked for us. We march under one of the gun cages and down the middle of a large room with twelve tables on our right and twelve more on our left. Each table holds ten cons, five on each side facing each other, although they are empty this time of the morning. Directly in front of us at the other end of the dining hall is a shining steam table manned by five or six convicts serving the food. They dress in denim trousers and white shirts and are framed behind by a large barred gateway, also locked, leading to the kitchen area. The cons fill our trays with grilled pork sausages, creamed gravy, mashed potatoes, string beans, and apple sauce.

As we walk down the center of the dining hall, I notice another gun cage to my left on a catwalk which runs along the exterior of the building enabling armed guards outside to watch us through windows spaced about four feet apart. Above us, on the huge concrete beams supporting the ceiling, hang cannisters of nauseating gas which can be automatically released in case of a riot.

As I take my seat, I see that a window has been cut through the wall high above the doorway we entered from the cell house enabling the screw on the cell-house catwalk to view the entire mess hall. Everyone is sitting with backs rigid and arms folded over their chests to indicate they are finished eating. A shrill blast on a whistle brings us to our feet and we parade from the mess hall back to the cell house through the same door we entered.

After the cell in Leavenworth, this one seems like a small box. It is eight feet by five and one-half feet with an eight-foot ceiling on which is mounted a twenty-watt light bulb. The bunk is made up for me with two white sheets and a blanket as well as two more blankets folded military style across the foot of the bed. The bunk hangs by chains from the wall and folds up against the wall when necessary. The mattress and pillow are cotton. The toilet is at the end of the bunk beside a small wash basin in the center of the back wall.

Under the basin a heavy mesh screen a foot off the floor encloses a ventilator eight inches wide and six inches high. Eighteen inches from the ceiling a shelf of one-inch plank, one foot wide, sits against the back wall supported by three metal pegs, one in the center of the back wall and one from each side wall of the cell. On the shelf I find the following items: a safety razor, an aluminum cup for drinking water, a second one with a cake of Williams shaving soap in it, a shaving brush, a mirror made of highly polished metal, a toothbrush, a container full of toothpowder, a bar of playmate soap, a comb, a pair of nail clippers, a sack of Stud smoking tobacco, a corncob pipe, a roll of toilet paper, a can of brown shoe polish, a green celluloid eye shade, a wisk broom for sweeping out the cell, and the rule book we were told to read. In the middle of the wall, opposite the bed, a steel table and seat fold against the wall when not in use. On the underside of the long shelf are several clothes hooks. It never occurs to me as I look around this minute cell in 1936 that I will still be here in 1962, nearly twenty-six years later.

It is the toilet paper I use first because, after the long trip, I need to sit on the "crapper". I look across the corridor to see most of the guys doing the same thing. It's a strange situation for all of us, taking a shit while staring at someone else a few feet away doing likewise, but just one of the things we will have to become used to.

The cell house is one huge building which houses four cellblocks, each three tiers tall. Between the third tier and the roof of the cell house is an air space large enough to allow a fourth layer of cells if they ever wish to build one. Only the two inside cellblocks (cellblocks B and C) are remodeled with tool-proof steel bars and the modern locking devices for the doors. The two outside cellblocks (cellblocks A and D) are not in regular use but are both used as "the hole" when the officials wish to segregate prisoners.

At the end of each cellblock is the mechanism which rolls open the cell doors automatically. All the doors on one tier can be activated at the same time, or the guard may choose to open only one cell or a group of cells. We are on

Fish Row, the cells reserved for new arrivals on the bottom tiers of Broadway at the administrative end of the cell house near the visiting area. I notice all the cells on Broadway are facing other cells filled with cons. There is much more privacy in the outside cells which face the unused A and D blocks. "Once I learn what makes this place tick, I'll get an outside cell," I promise myself as I finish my shit. Then I hear cell doors opening and a rough voice shouts, "Cell-house orderlies!"

A few minutes later an old associate pops up in front of my cell—Alfred Bates (AZ-137)—who "took a fall" with Machine Gun Kelly (AZ-117) and Harvey Bailey (AZ-139) over the Urschel kidnapping of 1933 which brought a 200 G ransom. The last time I saw Bates was shortly after that caper when he brought fourty Gs to Minneapolis to have it changed to "cool money".

"Hello, Ray." All my close friends and associates use the alias "Ray" when addressing me on the outside. Although I am Alvin Karpis, Public Enemy Number One to the officials and most of the other cons, I am always called Ray by my friends, even after twenty-six years in Alcatraz. Of course I am registered under my real name, Albin Karpowicz.

Bates works in the prison library: he hands me a catalogue and card. "Look through the catalogue and fill out the card with your selections. I'll be back tomorrow morning to collect the card," he says mechanically.

"What kind of place is this?" I ask, noting how different he looks in prison clothing. It isn't just the clothing, he seems to be under a great strain.

"It's more like an insane asylum than a prison," he whispers in a hollow voice and moves on to the next cell. A few minutes later, I hear a voice shout, "Orderlies all in!"

Again the banging of steel on steel punctuates the order and then everything is silent. No one is seen in the cell house and nothing is heard.

"At the sound of the bell stand up at the front of your cell until after the count!" The clash of steel doors echoes through the cell house. Cell doors rack open for the main population returning from the work areas. When they all drag themselves up onto the second and third tiers and inside the cells which have their names and numbers posted on the front, the doors rack shut again with a jarring crash. Immediately the bell rings and the count begins. It takes only a few minutes for the guards to count each con standing inside his barred door and shout the numbers down to a central checking point. When the count is complete the "all clear" whistle sounds.

The cell doors open with the same unnerving noise which is already pounding in my head. A whistle blows and all the cons except for us "fish" step out of their cages. At the sound of a second whistle, they shuffle toward the dining hall. It is uncanny. Not one word is spoken. They move like sleepwalkers.

Only after the main line has wound its way, like a slow colorless serpent down the tiers and up Broadway to the dining room, do they open our cells on Fish Row and we follow on the tail end, reaching the steam table just as the last of the general population is served.

I take very little to eat, gobble it down, and sit back to look over the scene—approximately 250 men but all one hears is the clattering of forks on dull aluminum trays. Never have I seen such a sight. Talk about a group of zombies!

I recognize fellows I knew on the outside but they are only pale imitations of their former selves: Machine Gun Kelly, Volney Davis (AZ-271), Harry Sawyer (AZ-299), Francis Keating (AZ-130), Doc Barker (AZ-268), and Tommy Holden (AZ-138). Color and life are drained from them all. Looking around again, I pick out "Scarface" Al Capone (AZ-85), much thinner and far more sallow than the last time I saw him. Like the rest, Capone seems to be in a daze. "How in the hell could these guys reach this state?" I wonder to myself.

Guards survey the scene from the gun cages outside the windows. I feel they will enjoy mowing us down, if they are given an excuse. The guard in the gun cage over the doorway into the mess hall is more alert than any of the others. He holds a riot gun, pointed directly at our table, a warm and deliberate reception for us "fish".

Nine negroes sit at their own table. Unlike the state pen where I did time, segregation is in full force at Alcatraz. They even have a complete tier of cells to themselves, right above Fish Row, twenty-seven cells tied up for the use of only nine blacks. They are a quiet, subservient lot, unlike those to follow by the hundreds in later years.

At the shrill blast of a whistle we arise simultaneously. Table by table, the mess hall empties as the cons return to stand in front of their designated cell doors. Another blast of the whistle and we all step into our cages. The doors roll shut behind us in one loud bang. The bell rings for the count and again we stand by our doors until the blast on the whistle indicates the count is over. I slide slowly down onto my bunk. Never have I seen a prison like this one.

After supper I hear a voice gradually become clearer as it gets nearer. A con stops at each cell to find out if you want to write. If so, he hands you three sheets of tablet paper, an envelope, and a pencil. If for some reason you don't use all the paper, it is returned along with your letter and pencil.

Another con makes the rounds of B block with a board that holds razor blades—each blade has a number beside it. I take AZ-325. "Your shaving nights are Monday, Wednesday, and Friday. I'll be back in fifteen minutes to collect the blade."

C block shaves on Tuesday, Thursday, and Saturday. There is only cold water in the cells.

Daylight Saving Time is still in force. It won't be dark until "lights out" (9:30 P.M.). The place is so quiet I hear the wall clock ticking at the other end of the cell house. Hard to believe that there are about 250 other cons in this building with me. The only noise is the occasional toilet flushing or tap running. The screw counts us every hour and then spends his time sneaking around on the various tiers trying to catch someone whispering or passing something between cells.

I open the rule book we were told to read. The rules have little to do with Alcatraz. They apply to other federal prisons. It mentions such things as radio headphones and commissary which do not exist here.

I'm pleased when the lights go out. I've had lights day and night for several months, first in the St. Paul jail, then in Leavenworth isolation and finally on the train. My last thought before I fall asleep for my first night in Alcatraz is that if I have to kill a dozen people to get out of here, it will be just too bad for whoever they might be.

3

Alcatraz
Friday, August 7, 1936

The shrill ring of the bell shocks me into my first morning at Alcatraz. The icy water in the wash basin burns against my skin. I hate this place already. I hate the count bell when it rings to make us face out into the dull grey cell house at 7:30 A.M. I hate the hollow clanging of metal doors being rolled open. I hate the slow moving chow line as it inches toward the breakfast steam table and I hate the insipid pile of cooked cereal dumped on my tray without milk or sugar. I don't want to finish it but if I leave any of the crap on my plate, I can easily end up in the hole on "bread and water". The coffee helps to wash the mush down.

The mess hall is an uneasy place. The eyes of the screws flick nervously across the section of tables assigned to them, ready to pounce abruptly on violators breaking the rule of silence. The cons eat mechanically, utensils scraping on tin trays with irritating repetitiveness, like metallic raindrops sprinkling the dining room. Coverall-clad cons and blue-uniformed screws are both aware of an unspoken contest, each watches the movements of his opponents with tense anticipation.

My armpits are soaked and my hand shakes as I try to steady the aluminum cup against my lips. Nerves are a bad sign in prison. What's wrong with me? Has the place got to me already?

I go through the slow monotonous routine of counts, locks, and bells as I return to my cell and see the main line off to their work areas. We "fish" remain in our cells facing the greatest obstacle confronting any prisoner—time! Confined to a few feet of space, without distractions such as radios or the possibility of a conversation with your neighbour because of the watchful eyes of the screws patrolling the cell house.

Bates slips by under the pretext of asking what magazines I would like from the library and whispers, "Be careful who you talk to in this joint!" I stare at him in disbelief. He smiles, "You'll see." Then turning sharply he disappears down Broadway in the direction of the mess hall.

"Damn," I think to myself, "how can this be? Stool pigeons among the 250 most dangerous prisoners in America?"

One of the cons who is a cell-house orderly passes the front of my cage following a long-handled push-broom. He hesitates, then speaks rapidly from the corner of his mouth. "Karpis, Doc told me to tell you he'll be seeing you on the yard as soon as they let you out there. In the meantime he says to be careful who you talk to and what you say!"

There it is again! Now I'm curious to get out on the yard and find out from Doc Barker and other former associates just what the score is around here.

Saturday, August 8, 1936

Finally I pick out my old friend Harvey Bailey in the mess hall. He looks as dignified as ever.

The last time I saw him was July of 1932, after we had robbed the bank together in Fort Scott, Kansas. Bailey was picked up at a golf club in Kansas City, along with Holden and Keating. In Bailey's wallet was a $500, First World War Liberty Bond stolen from the bank. In 1932, bank robbery was still a "state beef" so he was sent to Lansing, Kansas, the "state pen".

Bailey might just have something cooking on the back burner, I think to myself. He beat Lansing on Memorial Day, 1933, along with three other guys less than a year after his arrest. Hopefully, I got here just in time to leave this place.

Asleep on an army cot in the back yard of the Shannon ranch near Paradise, Texas, Bailey was taken by surprise when the FBI and some detectives from Fort Worth, Texas, raided it. They were not looking for Bailey at all. Shannon was the stepfather of Kitty Kelly, wife of Machine Gun Kelly. They had used the ranch to hold Urschel, an Oklahoma oil millionaire, for whom they collected $200,000 ransom. Kitty, Machine Gun, and their partner Bates, who warned me yesterday to beware of stool pigeons in Alcatraz, had left the ranch a few days before. Seven hundred of the two thousand dollars found on Bailey was ransom money, so although he had not participated in the kidnapping, he was convicted and sent here to Alcatraz.

Sunday, August 9, 1936

We shower in the same room we were brought to when we arrived at Alcatraz but there is no longer a guard assigned to each prisoner. The atmosphere in the crowded room is far more relaxed and playful as we are brought, tier by tier, down to the basement for our weekly shower. Some of the stalls have single occupants, others are shared. I wait my turn in the naked conglomeration of cons then, as I am sitting on a bench drying off, two kids come over. Both are in their early twenties.

"Hi, Karpis!" I merely look at them, remembering the warnings from Bates and Doc. Sensing my unwillingness to talk, one of them continues as I pull on my socks.

"We're friends of Doc's. I'm Hard-Rock, this is Whoop-em-up."

"For Christ's sake!" I think. "What the hell gives?"

"I'm from Oklahoma," explains Whoop-em-up. "I work with Doc down in the mat shop." Before he has a chance to continue, a screw interrupts. He's a mean looking bastard with a badly battered face. "Obviously an ex-pug," I think to myself.

"That will be enough! You guys get the hell away from this guy and stay away from him!"

Hard-Rock immediately walks away but Whoop-em-up

simply stares at the scarred facial tissue of the screw for a few seconds then replies, "You punch-drunk bastard, go fuck yourself!" Whoop-em-up is on his way to the hole immediately. The guard's nickname, I discover later, is "Punch-drunk" Pepper!

I'm not back in my cell ten minutes when my door flies open. I stick my head out and look in both directions up and down Broadway. No one in sight. Then the cell-house screw appears from around the corner where he operates the levers which open the cell doors and motions me to approach. "The deputy warden, Mr. Shuttleworth, wants to talk to you!"

Two thoughts flash through my mind. The first is that I'm on my way to the hole because of the incident provoked by Whoop-em-up down in the shower room. The second is that the deputy warden is the same Shuttleworth from St. Paul who was taken off the "White Bear" resort area patrol when he was deputy sheriff because he was a pain in the ass to everyone involved in the slot-machine rackets, especially the crooked sheriff. As I walk down Broadway my nerves are jangling—I'm ready to go into a tirade about being persecuted.

At the end of Broadway, I turn the corner in the direction of a solitary desk. Behind the desk is a swivel chair and in the chair a stern looking individual dressed in civilian clothing, shuffling papers. He has large pouches under his eyes and a very bad complexion. By now I'm ready to explode but his first words take me off guard—they are friendly.

"Karpis, I'm Charles Shuttleworth, the deputy warden of Alcatraz. I'm from St. Paul, like yourself, and I know one of your attorneys very well. Tom Newman has been a good friend of mine for years. Did he ever mention me?"

"As a matter of fact, he did," I respond, recovering from his affability. "He said I would likely run into 'the Major' out here."

"That's me! That's me!" he beams. Shuttleworth is a Major in the National Guard and extremely proud of his rank.

"I've got news for you. We were going to keep you on Fish Row for ninety days but I notice in your commitment papers that tomorrow is your birthday so, the warden and I have agreed to give you a birthday present. Instead of remaining in your cell on Fish Row, we're going to assign you to the laundry where you can work with a number of your friends from the outside. Move up to gallery three today, you start work in the morning!"

As I return down Broadway, I'm less apprehensive. Shuttleworth obviously believes he's doing me a favour and probably is. But I'm going to be twenty-eight years old tomorrow and I chuckle at my "birthday present". I've never worked before in my life although throughout the depression years I always had at least $10,000 for spending money. In the past five years, I stole millions of dollars and my "birthday present" is to work for the government for free.

Monday, August 10, 1936

I eat with a different group at breakfast this morning because of my move from Fish Row to a third-gallery cell above, also facing onto Broadway. Now I'm anxiously awaiting the bell which will send me to work with the rest of the population. I'll find out what exists beyond the thick metal door leading out of the cell house.

The whistle! My door opens. I join the line along the third tier moving toward the end of the cell house. Down three flights of steps. Past the dining hall entrance at the end of Broadway. Almost to D block, the isolation unit. A right turn and out the door.

Fresh air! Clear sky!

Down some steps between the outside wall of the dining hall and the wall surrounding the yard, through the electronic metal detector, down another dozen steps, into the yard. High above, armed guards hover on catwalks.

Doc Barker greets me with an outstretched hand. Machine Gun Kelly, Harry Sawyer, Keating, Harvey Bailey say a few hurried greetings during a ten-minute smoke break as guys begin to sort themselves into their assigned work details. Each industry on the island has its own lineup.

The yard itself is small. The central area is like a squared-off version of an old Roman arena. The years ahead are to be filled with many dangerous contests played to the death in this cement stadium surrounded by walls and towers. It almost appears as if the architect foresaw the dramatic potential of the yard because along the outside wall of the three-storey building which houses the kitchen and the hospital, and which makes up one side of the yard, he has built in a "spectators' gallery" of cement steps overlooking "the pit" area.

We line up by number which puts me at the tail end of the laundry line. Next to me is Loeb Cossack (AZ-313), a former attorney out of Los Angeles convicted of conspiring with an outfit of bank robbers known as the Mutt and Jeff Gang.

Another whistle! The first line starts to move. The garment-factory workers are swallowed up by an opening cut through the base of the wall facing San Francisco. We're next. As I file through the gate, I give my number to the screw stationed there, then turn, to find myself on the edge of a high rocky cliff. Far below, the waters of the bay. Shimmering on the horizon, the Pacific Ocean, where one day will be built the Golden Gate Bridge.

A steep set of steps leads sharply down the cliff which is dotted with convicts picking their way carefully to the bottom. Halfway down we pass through a second electronic stool pigeon. Then, another dangerous flight of stairs cut from the cliff's side. A right turn. Straight ahead a city block. On my right stands the big laundry, two storeys high; behind it, high on the cliff, the grey line of convicts following us to work still trails through the gate in the wall surrounding the yard.

Richtner is the officer in charge of the laundry. Also in the laundry are about a half-dozen civilian supervisors hired by the government. Ours turns out to be a young, clean-cut guy named Jimmy Halstead who tells me, "Karpis, go ahead and visit around this morning but don't keep anyone from doing their work."

In less than two minutes, Keating, Machine Gun Kelly and I are in a huddle. Talking is permitted in the industries. Why it's against the rules up on the hill is a mystery to me.

"What the hell kind of place is this?" are my first words. Both begin to laugh. Finally, Keating replies, "You simply won't believe it!"

Kelly breaks in with, "But don't worry, they're going to move us all out to some other place."

"What other place?"

He's quite vague on this important point but continues, "Don't get into any serious trouble around here. Once we get to the other joint we'll have a much better chance to lam."

"Interesting news, if it's true," I think to myself but make a note to check with Doc Barker and Harvey Bailey before I resign myself to tolerating the conditions around Alcatraz in hopes of being transferred. "Speaking of lams, how about that guy that got killed trying to get away?" I ask.

"Joe Bowers?" Keating asks.

"Yeah, that's the guy. What happened?"

The memory of the incident turns Keating sour as he recalls it. "Hell, he wasn't trying to get away! He was a 'bug'! They had him working on the incinerator and he used to feed the seagulls from the garbage they brought down for him to burn."

"The incinerator's at the bottom of the stairs you took coming out of the yard to work this morning," cuts in Machine Gun.

"He'd throw the stuff in the air for the gulls to grab on the fly," continues Keating. "Joe was a bit simple and he loved to watch them snatch it in midair.

"This one day he was throwing it up for them when some of the food landed on top of the storm fence. It was the last of the stuff. Without thinking, he climbed the fence to get it so he could throw it for them again. He got it and was on his way back down when the tower screw turned and saw Joe on the fence.

"That tower stands right over top of the incinerator; when he levelled down on Joe, he couldn't miss! He killed him with one shot!"

"It was that bastard Chandler in the road tower," adds Kelly. "Everyone knew Joe was crazy. It was a murder, not an escape!"

"Maybe it was just a mistake," I suggest, thinking Kelly is going to extremes.

"No! It was no accident!" Keating comes to Kelly's aid. "Joe had flattened a screw right at the mess-hall door as he was going to eat one day. The screw was counting us as we went in and had a habit of pushing his pencil into each con's chest as he passed. Like I said, Joe wasn't too bright and kinda crazy. He flattened the screw with one punch. I think maybe that's why he died!"

During the balance of the day, I poke around the laundry meeting some of the other personalities working here. Elmer Farmer (AZ-299), doing twenty years for conspiracy when we kidnapped Bremer is an old friend of mine. I also recognize old Limpy Cleaver (AZ-78) sweating over the mangle. Limpy is so old, he used to own a livery stable in Chicago. He is feeding the laundry into the mangle at such a speed the two young cons at the other end are grumbling as it pours out on top of them. Because he's illiterate, the tough sixty-year-old hoodlum has nothing to do when he gets back to his cell in the evenings but fall asleep; therefore, he tires himself out by putting all his energy into his work during the day.

Caught in a clump of weeds out on the far west side of Chicago after grabbing 100 Gs in a train robbery, Limpy was surrounded by cops who riddled the bushes with submachine guns. He was torn apart by about sixteen slugs but survived to be sentenced to twenty-five years at Alcatraz. I learn that one day when a written notice was sent around to the cells Limpy, not wishing to admit he couldn't read or write, asked the guy in the next cell what it said, claiming, "I left my glasses down in the laundry."

"Everyone is to get an electric razor; it says to leave your cup, razor, and brush on your pillow to be picked up," explained his neighbour without cracking a smile. Limpy dutifully left his shaving utensils out as he went to work.

His is a happy ending. He survives the bullet wounds and Alcatraz to return to Chicago where some racket guys set him up with a bar in the stockyard area.

Four of the workers in the laundry are members of the infamous New York Mob doing twenty-five years each for the Falls River, Massachusetts, mail truck holdup which netted them over $150,000 in cash. They have also been indicted for the kidnapping of the nephew of O'Connell, a powerful democratic boss of Albany, New York. They stole over a million dollars in the New England states before taking this "fall". The head of the mob is Carl Rettich (AZ-254); the others are Tom Duggan (AZ-256), Joe Fisher (AZ-253), John McGlone (AZ-252), and Charlie Harrigan (AZ-255) who had an eye shot out in a barroom fight.

Carl is good-naturedly referred to as "search and seizure" because he is always ready to discuss how he made legal history when he won his case in the Supreme Court on search and seizure involving his yacht *The Mozaltov* confiscated by the coast guard during prohibition days.

By 4:00 P.M., I'm preparing myself for the return trip back to the cell house which almost killed me at noon. I take note of the incinerator and remember the fate of Joe Bowers as I pass the road tower. I puff and pant my way up the first flight of steep steps. I'm in trouble when I reach the electronic stool pigeon and I still have another long stairway ahead. It's as bad as mountain climbing.

Trembling with exhaustion, I finally stagger through the gate onto the yard. The wind whips in from the Pacific at thirty miles an hour, snaps against the building and twists back into the yard. The force and violence of its biting attack takes my breath away and, light as I am, almost lifts me off the ground; I back across the yard stooped over to avoid its lashes.

Exhausted, I fall asleep early, wondering if the laundry

is the best place to be working or if there is another work area which has better potential for escape.

Tuesday, August 11, 1936

"See that son of a bitch over there!"

"Yeah," I confirm, following the direction of Doc's nod to a paranoid individual standing alone, deserted in the crowded yard. The number on his coveralls is AZ-284. He keeps his back close to the wall at all times and stands directly under one of the armed guards on the catwalk.

"That's Rufe Persful! He was a shotgun guard at Tucker Farm. That bastard's shot many a con in his time."

In Arkansas, at Tucker Farm State Penitentiary, it's the custom to have chosen convicts act as guards over the other convicts. They are issued shotguns and rewarded for their cruelty and brutality toward their fellow inmates. Sometimes, as in the case of Persful, they even kill them.

"What the hell is he doing here?"

"On his last bit he went too far! A snuff-dipping son of a bitch of a screw who couldn't read or write was in charge of the shotgun cons and was screwing a young cunt in the joint where they kept the broads across the road from Tucker. Her name was Mary Eaton. I heard she used to be a streetwalker around Hot Springs and Little Rock. The screw finally knocked her up but, instead of giving the poor kid a couple of bucks and putting her on a train or bus to Chicago, the louse told Persful to knock her off. Rufe blew her apart with his goddamn shotgun and claimed she was trying to lam.

"He thought it would be that easy but the doctor blew the whistle on her being knocked-up. Now Rufe is doing twenty-five years with the G for a mail caper.

"There's a lot of guys around here who were in Tucker under that bastard. I don't know how he's lived this long but I don't give him much longer before someone does him in!"

Watching the twitching fingers and restless movements of Rufe Persful, I know that he has come to the same conclusion as Doc about his future around Alcatraz. He avoids any unnecessary contact with other cons and keeps himself in the protective shadow of the screws on the walls at all times.

Persful works down on the dock. One day, fearing for his life, he desperately grabs a fire axe and deliberately chops off the fingers of his own hand. There's a strange gleam in his eyes as he glares defiantly at the convicts and guards who crowd around him with open mouths. The blood spouts in curved arcs from the stubs at the end of his arm onto the ground where he kneels. It splashes crazily, freckling the severed fingers lying there, still twitching nervously in the dirt. They are the same fingers that once pulled the trigger on a shotgun.

His spectacular stunt convinces the authorities that he's insane. They transfer him to the safety of the medical center in Springfield.

The whistle blows ending the ten-minute smoke break. It's time to line up and get down to work. Doc throws me a parting word. "This place is lousy with stool pigeons and rats like Persful! Even Volney Davis wrote his whole life history for the FBI!"

All the fresh water for Alcatraz is brought from the mainland, so the laundry industry is no winning proposition financially for the government. We do the army laundry and also the linen and blankets from the transport ships that come into the harbour.

My job is simple. A matter of sorting the clean laundry into large clothes bins by matching the laundry number on the clothes with the bin numbers. I keep to myself all morning, thinking over Doc's remark about Volney Davis. It seems to match what the FBI agent in St. Paul told me.

Saturday, August 15, 1936

I'm anxious and excited as work ends for the week. Now I can get on the yard. Saturday afternoons and Sunday mornings are yard days which means the entire general population is loose in the cement arena. "The Yard" at Alcatraz is more than an exercise area, it is an experience—often a dangerous experience, sometimes a fatal experience—always an unpredictable one.

At this time of the year the yard is always cold and the wind increases steadily in velocity as the afternoon grows late. The sand and dirt swirls around the clustered figures in the cold courtyard as we sit on the steps trying to roll and light our smokes. There's always a ball game in progress and the danger of being hit by a fastball or dumped on your ass by an anxious outfielder trying to snare it keeps everyone alert. At the other end of the yard are two handball courts and two horseshoe pits getting plenty of action.

Today is our private reunion of bank robbers, kidnappers, and murderers. Fish Row is allowed out so the guys who accompanied me on the train from Leavenworth have their first opportunity to greet old friends as I have done for the past week. It's a who's who of 1930-crime figures as we converge enthusiastically: Doc Barker, "Old Fitz," Harry Sawyer, Herb Farmer, Elmer Farmer (no relation to Herb), Harry Campbell, Dick Galatas, Fritz Malloy, Tommy Holden, Harvey Bailey. I notice Volney Davis is not around.

Other groups eye us up and down buzzing among themselves. Guys from the same part of the nation tend to cling together in their respective "families" dotted around the yard. The New York Mob forms one clique, the Californians are by themselves, and the Okies and Texans remain aloof from the others. No animosity exists between these geographic groupings, they seem to form from some innate sense of security or comradeship.

Capone is not on the yard. When I ask about him, I'm told he prefers to remain in the shower room where he practices his tenor banjo at noon and on weekends. Down there he can hold private conversations with his friends and associates without interference.

A lot of old touches and scores are cut up and many an "if" story told. Before I know it, the whistle blows and our time in the yard is over.

Sunday, August 16, 1936

At first I'm convinced I'm hearing things, but there is no doubt. From somewhere in the cell house we are being serenaded by a string band. The boos and catcalls from other cons tell me I'm not the only one hearing it. Their violent reaction confuses me because the music is a welcome change.

Peering out from behind the bars of my cage, I see the reason for their reaction. It is not the music they are booing but one of the musicians. "Scarface" Al Capone leads the group of cons in the string band—Capone has bought instruments for those unable to afford them. The catcalls resounding through the cell house are for Capone, not the quality of the music.

"Jealous-assed white trash!" is my reaction. The majority of the population in any prison is made up of losers from the gutter of society. Most of them aren't even wanted at their own homes when they are released. They resent anyone who has had prosperity on the outside. With all due respect for the many great guys I met while doing time, the worst punishment of any prison is not the confinement, the work, the cruelty of guards, or the lack of women but the "garbage" you are forced to live with—your fellow inmates.

My sympathy is with Capone and his efforts to give a pleasant interlude to an ungrateful cell house.

Sunday Evening

Not even 5:30 P.M. yet! What to do till "lights out"? I wish there was a commissary at Alcatraz as there is at all the other federal prisons. A candy bar or something sweet would help a lot.

I browse through some late editions of *Time* and *Newsweek*, but there are missing pages and, in some cases, holes in the pages. Censorship! Any mention of crime has been removed.

Looking out across the grey cell house from my vantage point on the third gallery, I see the cons in the cells across from me and below on the second tiers. They are either reading, writing a letter, or just sitting on the edge of their bunks smoking. Many of them stare hypnotically at one spot on the cell wall opposite them.

Restlessly I try walking up and down in my cell but it makes me dizzy turning around so often. I sit down and try to read again but it's no use.

My mind keeps going back to all I have learned about this place in a week. Escape seems impossible. Many of the guys who I thought would be working on escape plans have resigned themselves to waiting for the day they are to be transferred to a less secure prison.

It will still be sunlight when the lights go off at 9:30 P.M. Weird place! I wonder how the others survive here? A bed, three meals a day, a job, three shaves a week (fortunately for me I don't have much of a beard), one shower a week on Sunday afternoon, one letter a week to relatives, some books and magazines, the uniform with your number stamped on it. How long is this going to last?

I decide to take my time and not make any definite judgements until I've been here awhile. I don't want my mind racing like a squirrel on a treadmill in a wire cage. If it does, I might go crazy in this monotonous madhouse!

Machine Gun Kelly is one member of a committee of the better-known criminals in Alcatraz who meets me on the yard one day shortly after my arrival and attempts to caution me about being too friendly with the "common" criminals on the island. I tell him bluntly, "Go fuck yourself! I'll talk to whoever I want. There's only one way you spell 'Big Shot' in my dictionary, 'S-H-I-T'!"

Ironically, Kelly spends most of his time down in the laundry entertaining new arrivals at Alcatraz with stories of his past adventures. This lasts until the new cons grow bored and begin avoiding him. But there are always new sets of ears arriving from outside who listen eagerly, for awhile.

Those of us who work near Kelly in the laundry tire of his tales of robbing and shooting but we're a captive audience due to our close proximity on the job. It is none of my business, so I just ignore the situation, until one day he captures my interest.

We have two smoke periods a day during working hours, between 10:00 A.M. and 10:30 A.M. and in the afternoon between 2:15 P.M. and 3:00 P.M. It is the afternoon break and I'm only half listening to Machine Gun Kelly as he entertains some new arrivals. Suddenly, my ears perk up and I'm intrigued with every word. He is describing the holdup of a Federal Reserve Bank messenger and his two armed guards as they walk from the main post office in Chicago toward the Federal Reserve Bank.

"The messenger handled a push cart that held a dozen or so bags of registered mail, with the guards trailing behind him. It was almost midnight in late September of 1933, still fairly warm for the time of year. Even at that late hour, Jackson Boulevard was filled with traffic from the 'world fair'. Sally Rand was 'wowing' them with her 'fan dance' at one of the spots inside called 'The Streets of Paris'.

"The caper turned into a nightmare. Before it was over, one policeman was dead and the holdup car wrecked. We were forced to steal another car from a passer-by."

As Kelly continues with his story, he's in all his glory and a young inmate sits directly in front of him, with his mouth wide open, but not as wide open as mine.

"Oh, we lost the Hudson and all the equipment in it but even though it cost us a lot of money to have it armor-plated, bulletproof glass put in, and equipped with shortwave radios, we really didn't mind so much because none of us got hurt and we got a real good score out of that one."

A real good score? There was not one dime in those bags. All the envelopes had contained were cheques from the banks along with letters telling on what day they would need the money in order to meet payrolls of their customers and in what denominations the money was to be sent.

I'm flabbergasted! It was our outfit who attempted that miserable fiasco. A diamond was shot right out of the ring that Doc wore on one of his little fingers and the chewed-up mounting that the diamond had been in is still imbedded deep in his finger. But here sits Machine Gun Kelly claiming it was his caper.

He tells the story to so many new arrivals over the years that when he dies of a heart attack in Leavenworth in the mid-fifties, *Time Magazine*, while writing him up, tells of Machine Gun Kelly being one of the guys on the "Reserve Bank Caper" and mentions another caper that I know for a fact he had nothing to do with. I can only surmise that one of his listeners, after getting out, repeated the stories to the news media.

I can't get over what a real bullshitter Kelly has turned out to be!

Thursday Laundry

George Thompson (AZ-249) arrives in the laundry. I learn that he is obtaining a radio crystal set each evening from a screw. Now I have a direct line to the news of the day.

Saturday, On The Yard

Doc is waiting for me at the foot of the steps. "Let's go this way."

Up and down. Up and down the yard we walk all afternoon. Luckily neither of us is hit by a fastball because we are so intent on our conversation, the yard, the cons, the walls, and the screws disappear. The intensity of the conversation takes our minds away from Alcatraz. I am being offered a chance to fill in on a pretty rough attempt to beat the place.

"I want to think it over before I give you my answer," I tell Doc. "Also, I want to know who else is involved."

"Oh, they're guys from Oklahoma." Doc always assumes if a guy is from Oklahoma, he is alright.

"Look Doc, there are guys from Oklahoma I want no part of on a thing like this."

He shoots me a knowing glance. "Ray, if you have Volney in mind, don't worry, he won't ever be in on anything I'm in on. The biggest mistake I ever made in my life was when I asked you to put up money to get that bastard out after we fell together. Freddie was right about that motherfucker all along."

A wild gleam jumps into Doc's eyes as he tirades against his former friend Volney Davis; it subsides as he concludes, "Don't ever tell Volney one bit of your business, he turned out to be poison!"

Sunday Morning

I'm having spells of nervous tension more and more frequently. Even at this moment my coveralls are damp around the armpits. A bad sign!

As I hit the yard, Doc is not waiting for me as usual. It only takes me a moment to locate him—he's walking with Ralph Roe (AZ-260) and Ted Cole (AZ-258). One of the tower guards is watching them pretty close so I stay clear. They're together all morning until the whistle blows.

Sunday Afternoon, Bath Line

I'm drying off with my towel when a big "dago" walks up to me. "Karpis, I'm Frank Del Bono, a friend of Capone's. He wants to talk to you."

"Tell Al I'll let him know in the next few days when I'll be able to get together with him."

Del Bono (AZ-150) walks away without responding, goes directly to Capone who is standing near the clothing issue door facing into the shower room. He says a few words, Capone looks in my direction, smiles, nods his head "okay".

I'm in deep thought over Capone's invitation as I finish dressing and, picking up my clothing, head for the clothing bins labelled socks, underwear, coveralls, and towels. A heavy voice startles me.

"Aren't you forgetting something, Karpis?" I look up at the big grinning screw who points to my feet with the clipboard he holds in one hand.

"Damn!" I forgot to walk through the long shallow tank filled with disinfectant solution designed to prevent the spread of athlete's foot. Dropping the soiled clothing to the floor I begin to take off my shoes and socks again.

"Even if you somehow got past me unnoticed, they would have come to your cell and brought you back because your name and number wouldn't be checked off my list."

I smile inwardly. You can make a clandestine appointment with Al Capone without this screw noticing but you can't neglect to walk through his goddamn disinfectant tank.

I'm only back in my cell a few minutes when once again we are given a Sunday serenade. This time however it is not Capone's string band but gunfire. The shooting is continuous and comes from the direction of the yard. I can hear pistols, rifles, riot guns, and Thompson machine guns all in one harmonious tune. As the death music continues, cons around the cell house add vocals to it by booing and cursing louder than they did the week before against Capone.

Across the cell house, George Thompson smiles and motions for me to take it easy, that it is nothing to get excited about. "Just target practice by the screws for our benefit," he tells me in sign language. It continues for fifteen minutes then stops as suddenly as it began.

As I fall asleep, I'm wondering why Capone wants to talk with me. We have little in common. Doc stated it simply one day on the yard. "Capone's okay. There's nothing wrong with him but he's not like us. He's a racket guy, not a thief." Doc also told me the truth about the stabbing of Capone by the little punk who now works in the laundry with me, Jimmy Lucas (AZ-224).

Lucas and Capone had nothing in common. Capone, from Chicago was wealthy and successful, Lucas was poor, Texas white trash. Capone had made some remarks about Lucas being a pervert, which he is: Lucas was seeking prison notoriety from the day he arrived at Alcatraz. Both were working down in the basement—Capone, in the shower room, Lucas in the barbershop. One day the personality clash broke into open violence.

Capone sat in the big shower room leaning against one of the thick concrete pillars, practicing on his tenor banjo.

Lucas slipped up on him from behind, barber shears poised in his uplifted hand and buried them in Capone. The Italian grunted with pain, stood up with the shears still protruding from his back, turned around on the wide-eyed Lucas, picked him off the ground with his large powerful hands and threw him against the cement pillar. Lucas's frail frame smashed against the pillar almost breaking his back before he slid down to a crumpled heap on the floor.

Capone's wound turned out to be as superficial as Lucas's cheaply won notoriety.

Monday Morning

Strange ghostly figures line the roadway on the inside of the storm fence topped with barbed wire. The roadway leads to the laundry about a city block away and is overshadowed by three gun towers. The road tower, from which Joe Bowers was shot, is directly above; another is on top of the factory buildings across the street from the laundry; the third stands high atop the cliff overlooking the industries as well as the yard. All are interlinked with the main cell house by a network of catwalks.

Man-sized silhouette targets, manufactured from heavy cardboard and held upright on individual poles, stand shoulder to shoulder along the slow march to the industries. Each is riddled, some with jagged holes where buckshot from riot guns tore through limbs and trunks, others punctured by small neat bullet holes and still others almost toppled over by steady bursts of machine-gun fire. A sample of their nickle's worth of psychology. I get the message. "Try getting into the water and this is what you'll look like before you even get over the fence."

Arrangements have been made. While waiting my turn in the basement to get my hair cut, I slip into the shower room to meet with Capone. Our privacy is ensured by Del Bono and some other Italians who keep watch outside.

"He sure as hell don't look like the Capone I knew back around Cicero," I think to myself as I shake hands with the pale, shrunken figure. His gut is gone along with his $300 suits and he looks bleached from being indoors rather than on the yard.

However, the thinned down, Alcatraz version of Capone is as crafty and calculating in his colorless coveralls as he was in Chicago. Calm and controlled, he makes the purpose of our meeting clear immediately. Without newspapers or outside contacts his only source of information is new arrivals like myself who know the same people he knows. Capone is friendly and hospitable but puzzled over events on the outside which he thinks I can explain. His first question is "Why was Frank Nitti shot by that detective?"

Nitti had been shot through the neck in the syndicate offices in Chicago by a detective, Walter Lang. I remember the evening because I was on my way to Reno, with a large amount of hot money to exchange. Some of the racket guys had accompanied me to the airport to ensure I had no trouble leaving town. The manager at the airport warned us there was a lot of heat around that night because Nitti had been shot.

I spoke with Nitti the next spring after he had recovered. He swam on a private beach along the shore of Lake Michigan only a few houses away from the summer home belonging to the ex-mayor of Cicero which I was using as a hangout.

"Nitti told me the guy shot him over a personal grudge," I tell Capone. "Something left over from years before."

"Did he tell you what it was about?"

"I didn't ask."

"Do you know why Willie 'Three-fingers' was executed?" asks Capone methodically.

I laugh. Willie "Three-fingers" Jack White was the victim of a gangland killing.

"Whenever someone in your outfit is killed," I reply, "you guys always claim he was caught talking to the FBI. Sure enough! 'Three-fingers' was said to be talking to Pervis. Hell! Pervis was almost on your payroll. He wouldn't chase you guys like he did Dillinger."

I don't mention to Capone that Zeigler, who was a member of the syndicate's execution squad, and who helped us snatch Bremer, had to leave suddenly for St. Louis after receiving a phone call. We were holding Bremer at the time and when Zeigler returned a few days later, it was right after Willie "Three-fingers" was eliminated.

Zeigler worked with us on the kidnapping of Hamm as well. He had first joined the ranks of organized crime after raping a twelve-year-old girl and had engineered the infamous St. Valentine's Day Massacre for the Capone outfit.

Eventually the mob had put out orders that none of their members were to get involved with us thieves because it was bad for business. When the FBI started tailing Zeigler over the Bremer kidnapping, his involvement was obvious and he met the same fate he had dished out to "Three-fingers". The organization terminated his employment.

There is much I could tell Capone but I don't know how he'll take it so the best rule is silence. However, he seems well satisfied when our conversation ends and thanks me for the news from outside. As I return to the cell house, I'm contrasting the man to whom I just spoke with the Capone I used to see around the speakeasies in Chicago.

During the depression Capone dispensed life and death at a whim yet hundreds hailed him as a saint as they joined his "soup lines". His personal armoured car was always flanked fore and aft by other vehicles loaded with machine guns and bodyguards.

In Alcatraz, he's a fish out of water, he knows nothing of prison life. For example, he is allowed to subscribe to various magazines and like any prisoner he is permitted to send the magazines to other inmates after he reads them. Ironically Capone, who gave orders to eliminate hundreds of lives, is now confined to rubbing out names on his magazine list when he becomes displeased or annoyed with fellow cons.

"It's kinda sad," I conclude.

I'm accosted on the yard by a wild looking character who I first take to be one of the many "bugs" running loose in the joint. The number on his coveralls is AZ-230.

"Hey, you're Karpis, ain't you?"
"Yeah."

"You stole my wife's car!"

Wow, this one's far gone, I think to myself as he continues. "It was a green '34 Pontiac. You used it to get away from that hotel in Atlantic City."

His words snap me back to Atlantic City, January, 1935, gunfire flashing, me, caught in my underwear, cops surrounding the hotel, my girlfriend shot in her leg and left behind, eight-months pregnant with my son. Our car was gone. We had to grab the green Pontiac. The bullets hitting the car sounded like hailstones. I really had stolen his wife's car! We both burst out laughing at the memory.

Labor Day, 1936

My first movie at Alcatraz. We get to see one every holiday provided we are first-grade prisoners. Second or third-grade cons are not eligible.

I get a letter from my sister. *Time* magazine has settled out of court over a civil suit which my mother filed against them. They had published an article about me at the time of my arrest and had made some derogatory statements about my mother having served time in jail which were completely false. My parents are both honest immigrants from Lithuania who have problems with the English language although they speak several European tongues.

I wanted the matter handled by my attorney in St. Paul but my parents insisted on using a local lawyer in Chicago. Now it's obvious from the terms of the settlement that the shyster sold my mother out to *Time*. Although she receives money there is no retraction. I'm furious.

Here comes Machine Gun Kelly in a cloud of secrecy and excitement: "Ray, do you know anyone out there who has a plane?"

"I know the owner of an airport in Hot Springs, Arkansas; he's a good friend of mine. Also, I bought a four-seater Stinson once to use in a caper and gave it to the guy who flew it for us," I add, trying to be helpful.

"Hell no!" he hisses. "I mean a real plane, one that will

carry at least ten guys. It can fly around the towers, shower the screws with machine-gun bullets and drop smoke bombs. I'll arrange for a boat to get us over to the flat, sandy beach along Angel Island which is just like an airstrip when the tide is out. The plane can land there and pick us up. I'll finance the whole operation if you can get the plane."

"Sure Kelly, but leave it go now, I have a whole load of socks to distribute into these boxes and it's going to take a long time." As Kelly departs, I think to myself "Oh boy! Is the whole goddamn joint crazy or just me?"

Few people know that Machine Gun Kelly's real name is Barns, that he went to college, or that his father was a wealthy man in Tennessee where he owned and operated a cotton gin south of Memphis.

Another letter from my sister. This time it's about my father and, as I read, I realize he's lucky to be alive.

Shortly after my arrest, I sent him to Texas to pick up my new 1936 Buick Century four-door sedan hidden in a private garage I had rented when I heard the FBI had a description of it and the licence number. Fliers had gone out across the nation describing its owner as "dangerous and heavily armed—approach with extreme caution."

I had warned my father to buy new Illinois plates and to get rid of the old Arkansas plates down in Texas before attempting to drive the car north. Although he assured me he would do so, he neglected to purchase the new plates. Thus when he was involved in a minor traffic accident he was almost scared to death when a ring of fifty detectives with automatic weapons came at him from every direction. The FBI had neglected to cancel their "dodgers". Eventually my father got the car back and immediately purchased Illinois plates.

Filing slowly through the cell house on my way to work, I am yanked from the procession by Suitcase Simpson and led to a desk in the cell house. Behind it sits Warden Johnston. Placing one of the two pieces of paper in his hand on the table top and adjusting his bifocals, he begins: "Karpis, I have something I wish to read to you." He rattles off the legal jargon so fast I understand nothing although I do hear the mention of a $1,000 bill.

"Alright Karpis, sign the receipt on the desk and Mr. Simpson here will sign as a witness." I simply look at him.

"Well what are you waiting for? Go ahead! Sign it!"

Shaking my head "no" I reply, "You read it too fast, I didn't understand a word."

"Okay, okay," he says impatiently, "I'll read it to you again." The second reading is even faster than the first if that is possible. His teeth are clicking up and down like a typewriter.

"Now go ahead and sign the receipt or you will be late for work."

Again shaking my head "no," I reply calmly, "Is that paper in your hands for me?"

"I'll put it in your file for safekeeping after you sign the receipt on the table."

"No, no. If that paper is for me I want it so I can read it over in my own time. I'm not signing any receipt unless I'm given it."

The blue blood vessels on the warden's red nose begin to swell with indignation. "Karpis, all this amounts to is that when Ma Barker and Freddie were killed in their bungalow on Lake Weir and you managed to escape from Miami, you left a $1,000 bill behind in the hotel safe. Now Mr. Bremer is suing you through the Schmidt Brewing Company of St. Paul, Minnesota, a property that the Bremers own, for that money." He pauses. "It's as simple as that."

"If that paper is to be given to me, I want it, if not, I don't know why you're sitting here explaining it to me."

My last remark does it! The old humbug is furious. He jams the paper into my hand, saying, "Take it then, and go to work!" The veins on his mottled old nose have swelled out to the point where I expect them to burst any second. They remind me of a well-smoked meerschaum pipe whose bowl has turned every color in the rainbow.

Scribbling my name on the receipt, I rush to join the laundry line in the yard which has been held up because of me. As I take my place in line I whisper to the con beside me, "I have something for you to read when we get down to the laundry."

The con next to me in the laundry line is the lawyer, Loeb Cossack. Down in the laundry he reads the paper and quickly informs me that the Bremers are bringing suit in Federal Court in Florida to obtain possession of the G note being held by that court, and that the court is giving me ten days to reply. If I do not reply, the money will be given to Bremer.

Nice old man the warden. Going to keep the paper in my file for safekeeping. I have not even been convicted of the Bremer kidnapping and the ransom was paid in small bills, not G notes.

"In the event this fails to reach the court within the specified ten days, I ask that all proceedings be set aside on the grounds that the warden of Alcatraz prevented me from getting the answer back in time." In my cell that evening, I recopy Cossacks's words in my own handwriting and give them to the screw on duty to be delivered to the warden's office in the morning.

The next day at noon a notary arrives from town to witness my signature and the letter is sent to Florida immediately via airmail. My parents go down to Florida some time later to claim the $1,000 bill.

Thanksgiving Morning, 1936

I and several other notorious criminals are jerked from line, stripped and given an ass wave while the gun-cage screw keeps his gunsights focused on us. No explanations offered.

A week later a couple of guys approach me on the yard regarding an escape. They blurt out their rash plan to capture some prominent people visiting the institution and hold them as hostages. It sounds like suicide to me and I tell them so. I'm working on plans of my own.

Mid-December

A few cons ask for permission to purchase and send Christmas cards to their families. Johnston flatly refuses.

Christmas Eve, 1936

No indication in the grey confines of the Alcatraz cell house that it is Christmas. I'm depressed and wonder whether I have turned into one of the lifeless zombies I had scoffed at when I first arrived here.

The saddest time of the day for me, even on the outside, is sundown. It will be another year before I fully adjust to the boring precision which is more brutal and inhuman than the physical tortures. I've been yanked suddenly from a wild lifestyle of drinking and screwing until 2 or 3 A.M., to the dull routine of being confined to my cell every evening at 5:00 P.M. with nothing to do but stare up at a twenty-watt bulb shining down on me until it is shut off at 9:30 P.M. I'm certain Alcatraz is designed to drive us insane.

Sometimes it succeeds. Although the racket of a "bug" tearing apart his cell as he pitches its limited contents out over the gallery is a welcome diversion from the predictable daily schedule, it is also a fearful foreshadowing of my own possible fate.

New Year's Eve, 1936

About 8:00 P.M., six extra screws come on duty, one for each tier in each cellblock, and begin patrolling, trying to catch someone whispering. I unscrew my light bulb and go to bed. Tomorrow will be another year, 1937.

4

January, 1937

A couple of days after New Year's a convict is assigned to the laundry. Keating pulls me aside. "Ray, Blackie Audett has been put to work here. He loves it in the kitchen and he hates laundry work, so he didn't ask to be placed here. If he's here to be punished, he'd be down on the mangle. I suspect his being sent here has something to do with you. Although he's a stupid son of a bitch, he's cunning; watch what you say around him!"

I knew Keating on the outside and have already concluded he is one of the more stable, intelligent, and sensible people in this institution. "Okay Frank. I don't question your word in the least, but do you personally know anything bad about Blackie other than hearsay?"

"You're damn right I do. Just for starters, he was assigned in Leavenworth by Captain Beck to be my watchdog. He kept records on who I spoke to and even tried to listen in on conversations."

The next day Blackie walks up to me. "I understand you were with Ma Baker." Christ! Ma *Baker*! He doesn't even know her right name. "I was supposed to contact you and her in Kansas City in 1933, but got knocked off before I had a chance."

Kansas City, 1933! That was the time and place of the Union Station Massacre engineered by Vern Miller and Pretty Boy Floyd. My fingerprints had been found on beer bottles at Vern's home, so it is no secret I was around the neighborhood at the time. If Blackie or anyone else was to contact me I would have known it; we had a tight operation in those days.

I let Blackie ramble on awkwardly until I know exactly what he has been sent to find out. He turns pale as I end the conversation abruptly. "The word is you're a stool pigeon Blackie, get the hell away from me! Don't try to talk to me again and don't come close to me if I'm talking to anyone else!"

I go straight to Keating. "It's all connected with that murder beef I have in Missouri," I explain.

Laughing, he replies, "Good for you, Ray! But remember there will be other tries at this."

Two days later Audett is transferred back to the kitchen but in less than a week who "drives up" with a work assignment to my department, but Volney Davis. Why here? He has no friends down here.

He tries to be as congenial as possible. During the next few days we have many conversations. I sense Keating doesn't approve of him but, on the other hand, what can I do? Here is a guy I put up money for to get him out from under a life sentence, and who took off some pretty hot scores with us. Then, about three weeks after he arrives, right out of the blue, he asks, "Ray, have you heard any more about you and Freddie Barker killing that sheriff in West Plains, Missouri?"

Instantly, I'm wide awake. "Hell, I wasn't in on that thing, I was at home sick when that happened."

He shoots me a "smart money" grin. "That's a good story, stick to it!"

Then, apparently wanting to reminisce, he continues, "Hell, Ray, have you forgotten I was with you and Freddie a lot and also around Doc and Ma?"

I recall how Freddie had refused to put up a dime to get Volney out of jail even though they had all been kids together in Oklahoma. Doc got two grand off me instead. Freddie told me at the time, "The reason Doc was in jail was because of that son of a bitch!"

Since I came to Alcatraz, Doc has admitted to me that "Freddie was right about Volney! The worst mistake I ever made in my life was asking you to put up the money to get him out."

Volney continues, "Let me see, you got me out in the fall of '32. Remember? You met me at the station in St. Paul and took me to the apartment that you, Freddie, Doc, and Ma were living in out on Marshall Avenue."

He hesitates for a few seconds. I say nothing but just stare at him. "You know when we walked out of the station to your car, I thought those twelve-cylinder Auburns must be the most expensive car there was because, after twelve years in 'Mac,' I hadn't seen a new car for years. I was around you and Freddie and Doc from then until the summer of 1934."

As I raise my eyebrows, he hastily adds, "That is off and on—mostly off because me and Freddie didn't get along at all—anyways, from the way you talked I assumed it was you two guys who killed the sheriff and I have always thought so and now you say you had nothing to do with it."

Just how brazen can a guy get! If Doc's information is correct, and it fits with what the FBI agent in St. Paul told me, Volney is the one responsible for our being charged with the Hamm kidnapping with which they had originally charged the Touhy outfit.

"Look Volney, " I answer, "being wanted for something and having actually did it is a horse of a different color, and to give you an example of what I mean, the Touhy gang wound up being wanted for that Hamm caper and were even tried for it but you know we did it." Then, watching him closely, I add, "You know something? I'm still trying to figure out just how the hell the G finally figured out that it was us guys that took Hamm. I wasn't even indicted until April, 1936, and that was after you guys fell on the Bremer thing."

The conversation falls apart and ends there, as does my relationship with Volney. There's a tension between us now which we both feel.

A few days later Volney doesn't show up for work one afternoon. I think nothing of it until he joins us after smoke period. "Ray, the FBI was over and called me out." He pauses, waits for me to ask why, but I say nothing and he continues, "I couldn't imagine what they would want with me but I went out to see. Do you know what it was? They had an old topcoat of mine that they found in one of my apartments they raided and wanted to know what I wanted done with it. What do you think of that?"

I don't know how to reply. I didn't ask him for an explanation, he volunteered the story of the overcoat picked up by the FBI two years ago. I hesitate too long before pretending to buy his story, but say, "Oh, these things happen all the time with them. For weeks after my arrest, stuff kept coming to the jail in St. Paul for me that they had found in various apartments of mine."

Volney has an angry glint in his eyes as he walks off saying, "I'm getting tired of this laundry, I'm going to get myself a job in the kitchen."

About a week after Volney Davis followed Blackie Audett to the kitchen, Harvey Bailey comes to me on the yard. "Ray, I have a clipping out of a newspaper a screw smuggled it in for you, it's in the book of cigarette papers with this tobacco."

He hands me a package of Dukes papers and walks off with the remark, "I hope nothing comes of it!"

Down in the laundry I quickly scan the newspaper clipping. It states that the Missouri authorities of Howell County are asking the U.S. attorney general to take the necessary steps for me to be handed over to them for the murder of the sheriff at West Plains in December, 1931, and explains how practically every citizen of the county signed a petition that was sent to President Roosevelt demanding that I be handed over.

I call Keating aside and let him read the newspaper clipping before placing it in my mouth and chewing it into a sodden mass which I flush down the toilet.

In the next few days several reports are smuggled in to me. I read the G refused to turn me over to Missouri unless the state gives them an ironclad guarantee I will be convicted and hanged. Hoover makes a statement to the press saying that the FBI knows I'm guilty but being able to prove it in court is another thing. Cummings, the Attorney General, makes a statement saying he is investigating the entire matter and that, if at the conclusion of his investigation the facts warrant it, he will put the legal wheels in motion.

I know that if I am turned over to the hillbillies down in the Ozarks I will be lucky to last until the trial. It is almost a sure shot that I will be lynched less than twenty-four hours after being put in the West Plains' jailhouse.

The sheriff had been a living legend due to his rough and tough ways of tackling criminals. Just a few months before he was killed he captured two different gangs who were terrorizing the area by raping and robbing. In both instances he grabbed the gangs single-handedly. Resentment over his murder ran so high, his wife was appointed to fill his place until the killers were apprehended, tried, and hanged.

As the weeks go by with no word, I become more tense and nervous. I eat very little and lie for hours in my cell before falling into a restless sleep. Each morning I wake with the same question left over from the night before. "Is today the day I leave for Missouri?"

When others speak to me, their fears and imaginings are worse than my own. Only Doc remains calm and confident. "They won't turn you over," he insists, over and over again.

I finally ask him, "Why not?"

"Look Ray, with you dead, in months you'll be forgotten about and so will be the part Hoover was supposed to have played in your arrest. Don't worry about ever being turned over to anyone else while you're his private catch and he's alive to brag about it."

We both laugh over Hoover's role in my arrest.

"Gracie Allen" Shuttleworth is to be transferred to Leavenworth. Now the rumours being flying. The name of every deputy warden in the federal prison system is whispered as his replacement. Since there is no commissary in this prison, cons cannot bet packages of cigarettes in place of money so all bets on who will replace Gracie are made with magazine subscriptions, the standard medium of exchange.

No one wins! When the name of the new deputy is posted not only has no one guessed it, no one will believe it! Johnston has chosen "Meathead".

Meathead is the present first lieutenant, big Ernie Miller. The first day he appears in the dining hall in his new tailor-made civilian suit and highly polished shoes rather than his ill-fitting uniform, he is obviously self-conscious. He stands over six feet tall, blond hair, around thirty years old, not one ounce of fat on his big rugged frame. Meathead is a product of the prison service: his father had been a screw at Leavenworth and it was there that Meathead began his career just a few years ago. He will never have the intelligence or the suave and polished manner of Shuttleworth.

A new rumor rocks the joint. George Thompson hears on his smuggled crystal set that Sanford Bates, the Director of Prisons, has clashed with the attorney general over his policy regarding the treatment of us prisoners at Alcatraz. He threatens to resign.

The rumor is confirmed. Bates resigns as Director of Prisons and his assistant, James V. Bennett of Maryland and Washington, D.C., is promoted in his place. Bennett gives a news conference at which he states that the policy concerning the prisoners at Alcatraz has been established by the attorney general's recommendations and that he will continue to operate the prison in accordance with the established policy.

Our hopes for a more humane system die a political death with Sanford Bates's resignation.

My relationship with Volney Davis has deteriorated to the point where we do not even speak to one another when we happen to pass. Now that he's in the kitchen, he is allowed on the yard every afternoon where he plays handball with such a frenzy the word is that he is planning to beat the joint. The connection between the handball court and escape is simply that he is building up his body so as to be in top physical condition and the most obvious reason is a healthy swim across the bay.

Easter, 1937

Convicts in Alcatraz are not allowed to send Easter or Christmas cards. The reasons given are the amount of administrative work involved in censoring each one in case it contains a hidden message and the problems of ordering cards.

Al Capone asks to speak with Warden Johnston. He has composed a single message which is an Easter greeting appropriate for parents, wife, children, brothers or sisters. He offers to pay for it to be sent by telegram to the relatives of every Alcatraz con.

Warden Johnston refuses his request.

June, 1937

"Karpis, stay in this afternoon!" I am on my way to work when the cell-house screw's words hit me like a low punch to the belly. "Go up to the front end of the cell house!"

Now I'm certain I know what awaits me. This is it! I'm on my way to Missouri, and a necktie party. I can feel myself trembling as I round the corner of the cellblock into the waiting arms of Meathead and two FBI agents who I immediately recognize as Stein, the agent in charge of the St. Paul field office, and a hog-jowled black Irishman by the name of Kelly.

"Karpis, these men tell me you all three know each other. They wanta talk to you 'bout something." With those words Meathead starts for the door leading into the administration building, a door carefully protected with various devices including a combination of mirrors designed so the screw on the other side of the door can see the entire width of the cell house in both directions. I stop Meathead in his tracks.

"I never sent for these guys, I don't intend to talk to them, and I want to be sent back to my cell right away!"

"Look Karpis," Meathead is beginning to bristle up, "at least talk to them and find out what they want. Hell, for all you know they might want to help you."

"Them bastards helping anyone will be the day!" I retort, louder than I meant to due to my anxiety.

Meathead starts to redden. "Watch your language, Karpis! Will you talk to these men or not?" Mistaking my hesitation for wavering he continues, "After all, they came all the way from St. Paul to see you, no one ever came that far to see me."

He punctuates his last sentence with a chuckle but the impatient angry glare in his eyes doesn't match his tone. Meathead's temper tantrums are legendary around Alcatraz. I decide to avoid one at this moment since he has always treated me decently.

"Mr. Miller, I'll tell you what. If you will stay right here with us during the entire conversation, I'll go ahead and talk with them—otherwise, I won't."

Meathead is flattered; he looks at the two agents to see how they are taking it, not very gracefully. Stein nods a reluctant "yes" and Meathead is bursting with self-importance.

"Okay, just what the hell do you guys want?"

Ignoring my rudeness, Stein puts on his smooth manner. "How are you getting along out here and how are you feeling?"

"You sure as hell didn't come all the way out here to find out how I'm feeling or how I'm getting along, so just get to the point!"

Stein's voice loses some of its smooth edge as he proceeds. "I'm sure you know Joe Adams is under indictment down in Miami on a charge of conspiring to harbor and aiding and abetting a fugitive—namely you." I remain silent, so he continues. "The Director, Mr. Hoover, wants a conviction on this very badly but we need a witness who will testify truthfully that Adams knows who you are. We went to Milan and spoke to Delores." (She was my girlfriend, doing a rap on harboring charges.)

"As you know, the court was very harsh with her when it gave out a five-year sentence but she'll be coming up for parole in a few months and, if she cooperates with us and says she heard Adams call you by name, we'll get her a parole."

"Well, what did she tell you?"

He hesitates and looks at Kelly before replying. "Now don't blow your top until you hear me out completely. Agreed?" I nod my head.

"At first she wanted no part of us but finally agreed to testify but only if she receives a letter from you telling her to go ahead."

"But if I won't send her that letter, what then?"

"She'll do a full forty-five months and, I don't know whether you know it, but right now Washington is deciding whether or not to let the state of Missouri get a crack at you. Mr. Hoover authorized us to tell you that unless you help us, he is going to do all in his power to see you hang down there or, if not, he'll see to it that you stay here in Alcatraz until you rot!"

By now his voice has turned tough. Meathead looks startled at the blatant blackmail. The agents stand calm and cool. I can feel myself shaking from head to foot. Certain he has me in the bag, Stein speaks in his harshest voice, "Alright Karpis! What shall I tell Hoover?"

I'm on the verge of flying apart. My lips are trembling uncontrollably, my teeth are chattering as if I'm about to go into shock. "Go back and tell that half-nigger, son of a bitch that I said as far as the Missouri thing goes, I can't say, but as for him seeing me rot on this rock, I intend to see the day that I piss on his grave!"

Turning to Meathead I add, "I want you to put a notice in my jacket out in the record office that I don't ever want any of these bastards to come here to see me again. So far as I'm concerned everyone connected with the department of justice are no good sons of bitches!"

I fully expect Meathead to retaliate with a tantrum of his own but he simply turns to the agents. "Are you fellows finished?"

Stein looks at me a moment then concludes the interview. "Alright Karpis, I'm going to tell Hoover *exactly* what you said, word for word. You know he will never forgive or forget it!"

"An officer will be up from the industries to take you to work soon," announces the cell-house screw as I walk past him onto the yard following my interview with the FBI agents. I'm still upset from the ordeal as I step through the electronic stool pigeon and encounter a human stool pigeon on the other side. Blackie Audette is playing bridge up near the head of the steps with three other cons from the kitchen who are on the yard for their afternoon recreation.

"What a soft touch that kitchen detail is," I think to myself. "A shower every day, the yard every afternoon, all the food you can eat. If I wasn't more interested in finding the weakest point in the security around here, I'd get myself a job in the kitchen."

I pass Blackie and continue to the bottom of the steps where Volney Davis is on the handball court giving it everything he has. Instantly I recall the rumor about him planning to beat the joint. "He sure as hell is getting in shape for a long swim," are my thoughts as I pass the athletic Davis and make my way to the other end of the yard to say hello to some fellows I know from the kitchen.

"What did the G want with you, Ray?" is the first question. By now I know there is no way for agents to speak to anyone over here without the cons knowing it.

"Oh, those bastards—" but I'm interrupted before I get started.

"Ray, I think Volney wants to see you. He's pointing to you and nodding his head." My back is toward the handball court at the other end of the yard. Following the speaker's gaze over my shoulder, I turn around to see Volney in the center of the ball diamond maybe thirty yards away. He motions that he wants to see me which is strange because we haven't spoken for weeks. I approach him.

"Yeah Volney, what is it?" I see at a glance that he is tense.

"I want to ask you something."

"Go ahead!"

"What's the matter? Don't you want to talk to me or have anything to do with me?" I look at him but, before I can reply, he continues, "If you don't want to talk, I don't care 'cause I never did like you anyhow and now I like you even less and if you don't like what I'm saying just open your mouth and I'll beat the piss out of you right here and now!"

In the second following the remark, I understand why Volney has been exercising on the handball court. Here is a guy in perfect condition, hard muscles, excellent coordination and, to top it off, he fought in the ring at McAllister many times. The moment calls for discretion, but there is really only one thing to do. Even as I swing, I know the end is a foregone conclusion.

My knuckles graze the bridge of his nose tearing the skin slightly as he jumps back and the fight is on. In less than a minute he floors me with a couple of right hooks and a left to the head. I'm trying to recall where I am and what's happening as I push myself up from the yard where I've landed. A well-aimed boot bashes against my rib cage leaving me breathless and confused. Somewhere in the blurred background I hear an indistinct cry.

"You bastard, don't you be kicking that guy, he's no cat!" I recognize the voice as "Boxhead" Brown's (AZ-131), one of my friends who I was speaking to on the yard. "Fighting is one thing but kicking is another." Boxhead's voice is clearer now and seems to be coming from somewhere just above me.

"Goddamn it! I gave him first punch!" Volney's angry reply pulsates in my head.

"So what! Look at the difference in your size and condition." I'm turning my head to focus on the two men standing over my body when a third form joins them. I recognize the blue pant leg of the cell-house screw. "Okay! Break it up!"

Less than a minute later, we are standing in front of the cellhouse desk used for interviews and court call. Meathead arrives and looks me over. "Okay Karpis, come on over here! Are you alright?"

I nod.

"Are you sure? You don't look in too good a shape to me. You were kicked in the ribs, weren't you?"

"I don't know."

"Goddamnit! This isn't a gangster movie so quit acting like it. Yes or no? Are you alright or should I send you up to see the doctor?"

"No, I'm alright."

"You sure as hell don't look like it to me but, if you insist, it ain't no skin off my ass. Now what were you two fighting about?"

By now my head is aching, my jaw is sore and my side is smarting. "Look," I tell Meathead, "I have nothing to say about it. Whatever Davis tells you is alright with me."

Meathead is trying to control his temper: it's almost a full minute before he gives an order to the screw. "Take Karpis over to A block and put him in the hole." As I'm being led away, I hear Meathead's voice, "Alright Davis, come over here!"

I have hardly got my eyes accustomed to the gloom of the hole when I hear them placing Davis in the next cell.

It really isn't bad as far as holes go. I'm on the top tier of A block with a solid door on the cell except that there is an eighteen-inch hole cut across the bottom of the door which is covered with heavy mesh wire screen. Every night I am handed two blankets which are picked up in the morning when I receive a piece of bread. I get three slices a day. On the fourth day, I hear Davis in the next cell ask for a cop-out slip. After Davis has filled it out, the screw opens my door.

"Karpis do you want one of them?"

"Them what?"

"An interview slip. You fill one out, asking the deputy to let you out of the hole, and promising not to get in any more trouble."

"No thank you."

The next noon, Davis is called out and sent back to his regular cell. A few minutes later I am turned out of the hole in spite of the fact I didn't fill in a cop-out. Meathead warns me, "Karpis, I'm letting you out but if anything happens to Davis I'm holding you responsible regardless of who does it!"

I have hardly rolled and lit a cigarette back in my cell when Bates arrives from the library. "What was the fight all about?" he asks.

"Look Bates, if you don't mind I don't want to discuss it right now. Okay?"

"Alright! Alright!" he replies, but I can see it is just one hell of a long ways from being alright with Bates. He is offended at my refusal to discuss it with him and his face shows it as he remarks before leaving, "I wasn't being nosey, I just wanted to know."

Puffing thoughtfully in the solitude of the empty cell house, I realize the whole place will be waiting and watching to see what I do about Davis. If I kill him, it won't be because I allow the prison population to pressure me into the decision. That evening at dinner all eyes in the mess hall are fixed on me. There is pie for dessert and every guy at my table offers me his by pointing at it and then at me. I shake my head "no," but I appreciate the gesture.

Monday Morning, Laundry

Five minutes after I begin work, George Thompson presses a newsclipping into my hand. It's the headline from the front page of the *San Francisco Examiner*.

KARPIS KNOCKED DOWN AND STOMPED BY DAVIS

Sunday Morning

I'm told to stay in my cell rather than going out on the yard. As soon as the cell house has cleared my door opens and I'm taken over to A block again. This time, however, I am given a chair, not a hole cell and the screw says, "Go ahead and smoke if you want to."

I'm trying to figure this one out when I hear footsteps approaching. It's Father Clark, the Catholic chaplain. He's a rather self-centered, narrow-minded prig who is always trying to persuade me to join his services because I had been baptized a Catholic. He offers me a handshake. "Hi Ray. I was hoping to see you up at church this morning," he laughs. "Seriously I want to talk to you about this trouble with Davis."

"Sure, go ahead."

"You've been watched very closely since you were released from the hole and the officials know some very dangerous psychotics and even paranoids have been seen speaking with you. They're afraid this might be the start of a lot of trouble."

"Have you spoken to Davis about this?"

"My goodness, no. Why do you ask?"

"Because in a thing like this just one of the participants can't talk for both. You don't know what happened out on the yard except that we had a fight."

"You are mistaken about that," he volunteers. "I don't know whether you are aware of this or not but you are being watched constantly all the time you are not in your cell. Those orders are from Washington.

"The report on the fight states you came out of the cell house and started toward the other end of the yard immediately. Blackie Audette shouted down to Volney Davis, who was on the handball court, and nodded in your direction. Davis quit the game and followed you across the yard to the middle of the baseball diamond where he pointed at you until someone in the group you were talking to said something to you. You turned around and, when Davis motioned to you, you went over to see him. After a few words you made a pass at him and the rest followed."

"That only proves I started the fight. What do you want from me?"

"I'm sure that you know Lieutenant Madigan and I are close friends. As a matter of fact, I almost always have my Sunday meal at his house here on the island."

"I've heard of him but he works out front and I wouldn't know him if I saw him."

"Well Paul and I would like you to agree not to retaliate for the next two weeks—give yourself time to calm down and think it over."

I know Father Clark has confided information to me which would get him in trouble if the authorities knew, so, I agree to his proposal on the condition Davis doesn't start more trouble.

Rarely a night goes by that I don't worry about the murder charge in Missouri, where the sheriff was shot. I expect at any moment to be taken from my cell and shipped back there to be lynched. One day as an ignorant screw is needling me over the fact that I'm a captive in Alcatraz, I reply, to his chagrin, "This isn't a prison to me, it's a sanctuary—if I weren't sitting here in safety, I would have been executed long ago by one of several states."

The "Count" (AZ-300) comes to see me only days after my promise to Father Clark. On the outside he is famous as Count Van Lustig who invented a money machine. He sold the gadget to many legitimate businessmen, several "honest" bankers, and even a few sheriffs in Texas. Blank paper was placed in one end and good $100 bills rolled out the other end. The bills, when taken to a bank for verification, were always authenticated, but once the victim had paid $25,000 to $50,000 for the illegal machine, he spent days or even weeks trying to figure out why it wouldn't work.

The Count is a feeble old man, unable to cope with the prison environment. He can't con ignorant convicts as he could influential socialites and businessmen, and asks my advice about a problem he has.

An inmate who works with him downstairs in the laundry is giving him a "hard way to go" for no reason that the old Count can think of. It has obviously upset him. The convict in question is a former Miami policeman named Allie Anderson (AZ-340). I tell the Count there is nothing I can do, but a friend of Anderson's cells next to me. While walking down the steps to the yard, I explain to him that the Count is an old man, already on the verge of a nervous breakdown who doesn't need trouble from a fellow con to add to his burdens.

The next morning before I have even changed into my work clothes, the ex-cop comes upstairs and right back to my department. I'm talking to George Thompson when he calls to me from a few feet away. "Hey, Karpis, can I see you for a moment?"

"Sure, what's going on?" I ask.

"I understand that you don't like the way I've been talking to the Count, is that right?" The challenge in his voice can't be mistaken so I take a close look at him for the first time. One ear has been badly chewed up by someone or something. He stands six feet and weighs close to 200 pounds. My guess is he's in his twenties.

"Actually, it isn't a matter of what I like, it's none of my business, but the Count is an old man who does no one any harm, he's meek and inoffensive. You should leave him alone."

His reply is prompt. "Maybe I made a mistake about him so I'll forget it."

As he turns to go I also turn back to resume my conversation with Thompson. Too late, I hear him spin around and feel his looping haymaker on the side of my neck as it sends me sprawling on the floor. In an instant he's all over me, both hands tight at my throat.

If Anderson thinks he can score a quick victory like Davis, a well-trained and competent boxer, he is mistaken. I know what to do. Gasping and squirming in his choking grip, I locate his nose with my fingers and jab a thumb up one of his nostrils as hard as I can. He loses his grip as he jerks away from me and we both recover our feet.

A blur goes past me, taking a swing at Anderson which if it had connected would have ended the fight right there.

Instead, the guy coming to my aid loses his balance and falls over the clothes hamper spilling laundry and himself across the floor.

The cop rushes me again and, being seventy pounds heavier, takes us both to the floor a second time. A shout from the foreman alerts the screw on duty who immediately tries to pull us apart, locked in a senseless struggle.

Back to the cell house, the interview desk, and Meathead.

"Okay Karpis, Come over here!" I step forward. "What was *this* fight about?"

"I'll tell you what, just anything that he tells you will be okay with me."

Meathead swells up like a poisoned pup. "Goddamn you! I'm asking you, not him! What was it all about?"

"I have nothing to say."

Stretching his coarse voice to the limit Meathead shouts to the cell-house screw. "Put this son of a bitch in the hole, D block in the end cell! You'll stay in there the limit, eighteen days. If that ain't enough I'll take you out for a day and put you back for another eighteen!"

D block isolation unit is exactly the same as A block, three tiers of old army cells not yet remodeled as are B and C blocks, and houses the most dangerous criminals in America. Whereas the hole cells in A block are on the third tier, there are only three hole cells in D block and they are cells within cells on the bottom tier. I am ushered through a door, which is part of a wood-framed extension, before being shoved through the actual hole cell door into darkness.

My eyes have not even adjusted to the black interior of the hole when a voice speaks to me. "What happened Ray?"

The voice is coming from one of the isolation cells somewhere above me. I recognize it as "Soldier Tommy's" (AZ-149). He and another kid, Jimmy Walsh (AZ-43), known as the "Parrot" due to his ability to carry on two or three arguments with different guys on different subjects at the same time, while reading a book, have been in D block isolation for some time now, and are not likely to leave.

The Parrot has convinced the doctor he should be in the hospital or in isolation due to the condition of his nerves. Soldier Tommy has convinced the screws he should be here for punishment because he refuses to work on the jobs they assign to him. Both are blatant homosexuals and lovers. Ironically, the isolation unit is the least secure and least guarded of any area in the prison. It is a simple task to beat the old locks on the regular cells here and the count only takes place a couple of times a night. Soldier Tommy and the Parrot carry on a torrid affair every evening.

I don't have time to reply to Soldier Tommy's question since the screw returns to the cellblock to throw the ex-cop in one of the two remaining hole cells. Meathead specified the end cell for me because it is colder, damper, and more drafty than the others.

On the eighth day, Meathead comes to the cellblock to speak with the ex-cop. Anderson fills in a cop-out and by noon the next day, the cop *is* out. Several days later Meathead appears at my cell door. "Well, how are you getting along?"

"Oh, alright, I guess." He slams the door shut and stomps away.

Two days later Meathead is again at my cell door. "Do you want out of there and back in your old cell and job?"

"Sure I do."

"Then ask the officer for an interview slip and fill it out."

"I tell you what, suppose we forget the cop-out business and instead you keep me here until you feel I've been punished enough."

"Karpis, everyone puts in a cop-out to be released from the hole," he explains in an exasperated tone, ignoring the fact that I hadn't made one out the last time I was in the hole.

As cold and hungry as I am, I realize that I am in a position to antagonize Meathead and since I have no other means of retaliation, I insist. "No, I'm not beggin' you to let me out. If you're waiting on a cop-out from me, it ain't going to happen!"

Meathead stands looking at me for a full minute before exclaiming, "Well shit! I'm going to tell the cell-house officer to let you out around three o'clock today. Tell him to give you a razor blade because I want you clean and shaved before going into dinner." Meathead is hardly out of the cell block when Soldier Tommy and the Parrot both break into wild cowboy whoops.

"It's about time someone stood up to that son of a bitch!"

"Way to go Ray!"

"You sure told the old bastard!"

I disappoint them. "Listen you guys, truthfully, I am thankful to Meathead for not keeping me in the hole on bread and water the eighteen-day limit and then leaving me over here in isolation with only one meal a day for a few years."

They object strongly. "Fuck no, you've already been over here longer than Anderson by several days! You don't owe Meathead no thanks."

Realizing I'm dealing with irrational people, I end the conversation with, "You may be right but we all have to do our time as we see fit and not interfere with anyone else's business. Okay?"

An unexpected hero comes to my rescue putting an end to my nightmares and fears. J. Edgar Hoover announces he will not turn me over to officials in Missouri to stand trial for murdering their sheriff due to lack of evidence. I think the matter is closed but, if I had the power to look fourteen years into the future, I would not feel so relieved. Nevertheless, the immediate danger dissipates.

A few weeks after I'm out of the hole, my partner Freddie Hunter (AZ-402), who was caught with me in New Orleans, drives up with a transfer. He has a twenty-five-year sentence over a train holdup we pulled in Ohio, on November 7, 1935. I had bought an airplane for that caper to use in the escape.

The new Director of Prisons visits Alcatraz—James V. Bennett stands at the steam table in the dining hall during a couple of meals. He's a handsome, well-dressed, immaculately groomed individual in his early forties.

When it is announced he will conduct interviews with the cons the response is enthusiastic. Perhaps eighty-five percent of the population puts in requests to see him. I have no reason to speak to him but the attitude of those who do talk to him is that he has agreed to grant us more privileges such as newspapers, radio, and commissary. However, during a press interview in San Francisco, following his visit to Alcatraz, Bennett makes a statement to the press: "The convicts in Alcatraz are nothing but a bunch of cry babies who already have more privileges than they deserve. Alcatraz will remain a place of maximum security and minimum privileges."

Bennett's remarks precipitate a strike. Many of the cons belong to communist or socialist organizations on the outside and they influence a large portion of the prison population who are troublesome by nature. The strike is organized and effective.

A number of cons simply want to do their time and get out. They stand to lose "good time" if they participate in the strike. "Good time" is an effective weapon used by the officials whereby one-third of a con's sentence is taken off when he arrives in prison but infractions of the rules or misbehaviour cause it to be added back on.

A third group of us is not interested in "good time" but we are more interested in escape than confrontation. We join the strike to avoid suspicion; if we refuse to strike the officials will ask themselves why and it will make our escape plans more difficult.

It is obvious now that the first escape from Alcatraz will be out the back windows of the three-storey factory building which sits down close to the water on the far end of the island. The mat factory is on the first floor of the building and among the Okies who work there are the most dangerous and desperate in the history of the United States: Doc Barker, one of Ma Barker's boys; John Chase (AZ-238), partner of Baby Face Nelson; Charlie Berta (AZ-132), involved in the 1931 October crash out of Leavenworth; Freddie Hunter, my fall partner; and Ralph Roe, who was trapped in a bungalow in Shawnee, Oklahoma, with the notorious Wilbur Underhill who was torn apart by dozens of FBI bullets sprayed through the windows.

Underhill, in spite of his numerous bullet wounds, staggered through the front door of the house, guns blazing, and disappeared down the dark street followed only by the trail of tear gas gushing from the large shell embedded in his back. The tear gas shell had been treated with a solution which caused it to stick to him like glue, but no FBI agent wanted to follow the obvious trail of gas into the guns of the madman Underhill. He was found unconscious the next morning on a bed in a back room of a furniture store which he had broken into during the night. A day or two later he was dead from his many wounds.

Ted Cole holds the distinction of being the first person in Oklahoma to receive the death penalty for highway robbery, the law having just been passed a few days before Ted held up the Coca-Cola bottling works in Tulsa. Because of his youth and the many letters received by the governor, his sentence was commuted to life. He escaped almost immediately from McAllister by hiding in a barrel of swill going from the penitentiary kitchen to the hog farm outside. Eventually he was scooped up by the FBI and sent to Alcatraz.

The mat factory is Alcatraz's weakest link. It has ready access to the bay which washes upon the rocks directly behind the building. The windows have no tool-proof bars.

When the strike comes off everyone in the factory building will have to join it or the officials will take a second look at their security.

The strike starts on schedule. On day one eight convicts quit work. However, on day two, no one quits. Meathead is jubilant. He tells the eight inmates in solitary, "Come on out and go back to work. There ain't enough of you guys to even form a softball team."

On day three, fifteen prisoners quit work. Meathead doesn't want the first eight to know they've been joined by others so he sends the second group to isolation in A block, not D block. On day four twenty-five convicts quit work.

Every day adds new numbers to the revolution until over 160 are locked up. Morale among the cons is high. No one can sleep anywhere on the island at night—the rule of silence is shattered beyond repair.

Joe Urbaytis (AZ-213) is one of the first eight who went on the strike. His sister travels all the way from Toledo to visit. The officials try to use the situation to their advantage.

"You can't have visitors in isolation. If you want to talk to your sister quit the strike!"

Joe's decision is uncomplicated. "If I did that and she found out, my sister would never talk to me again!"

During the strike Soldier Tommy is escorted by several screws to A block isolation. A screw named Dennison orders Soldier Tommy up the spiral staircase leading to the hole cells on the third tier—"Get up those stairs you punk!"

In one quick motion, Soldier Tommy turns and clobbers Dennison. A second screw, Kranz, rushes at Soldier Tommy but he too is flattened by the experienced fists of the young con who was once an amateur boxer in Leavenworth. A third screw is downed before Suitcase Simpson pulls out his "sap" and beats Soldier Tommy into submission.

"Whitey" Phillips (AZ-259), a bank robber and kidnapper, is attempting to maneuver his way out of prison through a legal writ. One day he returns to his cell, in the midst of the strike to discover all his legal papers confiscated. He is told that they were removed on orders of Warden Johnston. Being locked in a cage and treated like an animal is a frustrating experience at any time but when your legitimate efforts to obtain a legal release are hampered by such a highhanded action, even the coolest personality becomes violent.

It is the custom of Warden Johnston to be in personal attendance at the noon meals in the mess hall every Wednesday and Saturday. He and the deputy warden stand behind the steam tables as the cons file in and, after the meal, as the tables empty from the kitchen end of the dining hall, Johnston moves up the center corridor eyeing the cons as they pass by him on the way back to the cell house. Whitey

Phillips shows no sign of emotion as he clears the table and meets the smug eyes of Johnston but, without warning, the kid turns suddenly and smashes his fist into the surprised look on the warden's face. Johnston's false teeth crumble under the blow and he is thrown backwards onto the floor of the mess hall out cold!

Instantly, I hear the crash of glass behind me as the guard on the catwalk gun cage outside the mess-hall windows shatters the pane with his machine gun. My eye catches the motion of the riot gun held by the screw on the cell-house catwalk above the mess-hall door as he "throws down" on the confused scene below. If he attempts to use the riot gun, he'll hit the warden along with many guards and innocent cons in the crowded isles.

The dining hall is only seconds away from a blood bath when the day is saved by a big, heavy, 225-pound screw in charge of our section of tables. The screw, Joe Steere, lunges into the air and hits young Whitey with a flying tackle that would have earned him a job on any professional football team in the country.

At almost the same moment, Lieutenant Culver rushes in from the cell-house door with his "gas-gun billy club" high in the air. "Hold that fire! Hold that fire! Don't shoot!" He is calling to the guard outside the window whose hands are clamped tightly around his weapon. I notice then the frantic look in the eyes of the screw outside the window. It is the same son of a bitch who blasted Dutch Bowers off the fence.

Lieutenant Culver quickly places three taps on the head of Whitey with his billy club which knocks Whitey into the same condition he had rendered the warden. There is nothing wild or uncontrolled about the blows. Culver, who served time with the Marine Corps, is cool and calm. Phillips is dragged quickly from the mess hall to the hospital upstairs where he is handcuffed, still unconscious, to the bed. The warden is rushed to a mainland hospital, his condition critical.

As a result of his fast action, Joe Steere becomes the private bodyguard of Johnston whenever the warden finds it necessary to be in the dining room. Whitey Phillips is thrown in the hole and never seen again in general population as long as Johnston remains the warden of Alcatraz.

"The Dungeon" lies deep beneath the cell house of Alcatraz and is entered from either D or A blocks. It is unofficially used for prisoners not intimidated by the hole, and during the strike there are many of us.

I'm escorted down the steep steps leaving daylight, humanity, and civilization above. Flashlights jerk roughly across ancient slabs of stone cut by primitive Spanish instruments in another century.

Somewhere in the depths of the rocky island, the granite expression on the screw's face is momentarily illuminated in the beam from his flashlight as he clumsily chains and padlocks the door shut. A moment later, I'm alone in the darkness. Water is running off the walls, continuously, keeping the dungeon cell damp. There is no toilet. At noon I receive two slices of bread which is the only meal of the day. One of my greatest fears during the three days in the barren tunnels is that I'll fall asleep and wake up, my body covered with large rats whose green eyes sparkle from jagged recesses.

I'm removed from the opposite end of the dungeon so those who saw me descend in the other cellblock will believe I'm still down there and think twice before joining me. It takes weeks for the officials to beat and starve the strikers into submission but even as they try to put their cell house back in order, they know it will never be the same again. There will be other revolts, rougher and more ruthless.

When the reports of the incidents during the strike of 1937 reach Washington, they indicate that Soldier Tommy, who weighs only 150 pounds, flattened three screws who were all larger than he was. They also note that Warden Johnston was put in the hospital by Whitey Phillips. The conclusion is reached that the guards of Alcatraz need some lessons in self-defence.

A 240-pound Polack, a former boxer and wrestler, is

sent down from McNeil Island to give the Alcatraz guards training in self-defence. He begins with fists. Lining up the Alcatraz screws, who wear boxing gloves, he comes down the line challenging each of them to take a swing at him as he successfully repulses every blow.

Then he stops in front of a red-haired Irishman from Minnesota. "Go ahead, try to hit me!"

"Are you sure you want me to do this?"

"Yeah, try it. Punch me!"

The Irishman feints him out of position and knocks him colder than a well-digger's ass in Montana. It's Father Clark's friend, Lieutenant Madigan, who becomes the hero of the screws who resented the outsider being sent to teach them their business, and also the cons, who are delighted that their screws are tougher than McNeil Island's best.

About a week after the strike, Harvey Bailey approaches me on the yard to say Jim Clark (AZ-242) wants me to ask for a work change so I can join him and Bailey in the clothing factory. Clark doesn't want to be seen talking to me on the yard as it might alert the suspicions of the guards. Since Bailey and I robbed together on the outside it is natural for us to be speaking on the inside. They have an escape plan and want me to join them.

Bailey explains the plan to me. It's a practical one. The clothing factory is on the second floor of the factory building above the mat shop where Doc Barker, Ralph Roe, and Ted Cole plan their own escape. I realize immediately that whoever makes his break first, the other group will have to abandon its plans since the entire area will be resecured once it is made obvious to the officials just how weak it is. Jim Clark's plan involves my coworker George Thompson, who is "getting short" and will be released early in 1938. He's a San Francisco product and agrees to show up with a speedboat at the tip of the island.

When I inform Doc that I've asked for a work change to the clothing factory above him he's not happy to hear it because he realizes that he, Ted, and Ralph now have competition. We agree to keep each other informed, but, since our plan hinges on the release of George Thompson, they will most likely be ready first.

Clothing Factory, 1937

Harvey Bailey won himself the nickname of "Shotgun Tom" when he cleared the streets outside during a bank job with a twelve-gauge automatic shotgun. He was the "outside man" and could be relied on to keep the exit clear for his companions inside the bank.

Shortly after I've joined him and Jim Clark in the clothing factory I'm listening to him complain about being in Alcatraz on a "bum beef" because he was on the farm used by Machine Gun Kelly during the Urschel kidnapping when the FBI raided it. He's right, he had nothing to do with the kidnapping but I jog his memory.

"Do you remember when we robbed the Fort Scott Bank? Three other guys were picked up and charged with the holdup. I asked you after the robbery what we could do about them and you said, 'They shouldn't have been there on that road at the wrong time.' Well you shouldn't have been there on that farm at the wrong time!"

Doc reports to me that the boys down in the mat shop have realized that in order to give themselves an hour's head start, only two of them can actually jump into the bay.

We are counted in our cells in the morning. We are counted at breakfast. We are counted after breakfast. When we're back in our cells, we're recounted on the way out of the cell house onto the yard. We're counted going out the gate and down the cliff face to the industries. We're counted when we arrive at our work stations and, when all the counts are called in and checked out, we are counted every half hour by the screws in charge of each industry who then phone in the count throughout the day.

The guys in the mat shop have made a practice of having two cons out of sight in the back rooms when the first count of the day is taken. The screw on duty has gotten used to the idea over the weeks and no longer goes back to check them out. This will give two of them an hour's head start, but only two.

Ralph Roe and Ted Cole will be the ones to make the plunge. I know how much Doc wants to get off the island and how disappointed he must be. Once Ralph and Ted reach the mainland they plan to steal a car and head for Texas and then South America via Mexico.

Suddenly, the Sacramento River which empties into San Pablo Bay just below Vallejo, floods as its tributaries overflow due to heavy fall rains. It's the worst in years. As the tide goes out past Alcatraz Island, it is stained a muddy brown and floating past us are barns, parts of houses, cadavers of horses and cows. Even a few dead people drift with the debris heading between the two segments of the uncompleted Golden Gate Bridge, reaching toward each other from opposite shores, to be lost in the ocean stretched across the horizon. Ralph and Ted decide to hitch a ride with the swift outgoing tides on the first foggy afternoon.

December 16, 1937

As we file out of the cell house onto the yard before proceeding to work this noon, it is obviously going to be a fairly foggy afternoon. The white camouflage hugs the shoreline around our isolated island. So long as the tower guards can view us on the road to the industries, the officials feel secure after we are inside the factories and counted.

As I enter the clothing factory I know this is the day. Once the screw has called in the first count of the afternoon, I walk over to the toilet and washroom area where I can look into the misty water and down behind the building where no tower guard can see. If the guard in the tower on top of our building was to walk to this end of the building and step out on a catwalk extending ten feet beyond the building, he could look down at the window which Ralph and Ted are prying open at this moment. Weeks of observation have proven he is not likely to do so, especially following the "count all clear" signal from the main cell house.

Joe Steere, the screw who tackled Whitey Phillips in the dining hall, is on duty downstairs in the mat shop. He calls in the first count of the afternoon. Jim Clark watches at the front window as Joe Steere comes out to the telephone to make his first call. Now Jim joins me at the back window. The screw on our floor is busy at his desk arranging the count sheet for the afternoon.

As we watch, Ralph and Ted pop out of the window from the floor beneath us. Ralph has a wrench in his hand to tear off the padlock on the fence gate that runs behind the building separating it from the rock and water below. Both are in work clothes and bare feet. Each has a shiv, hand made from files, to aid them in hijacking transportation once they reach the mainland. They carry square five-gallon gas cans with handles strapped on them and the tops welded shut.

Ralph Roe tries to wrestle the padlock off the fence gate with the wrench but he's all nerves and is making no progress. Ted Cole takes the wrench from him and calmly twists the lock open. Out in the fog-screened water the buoy just beyond "little Alcatraz," a tiny island, lies flat on the water in the fast flowing current.

The two make their way to the water's edge; access is difficult because rubber tires circle the shores of the Rock. Underneath the water, all around the island, are rolls of barbed wire to prevent escapes. Ralph and Ted move cautiously past the barbed wire but as they reach open water they are picked up by the current and taken off rapidly in the direction of the Golden Gate Bridge, now safely invisible in the low-hanging fog.

As Jim Clark and I turn away from the window to an anxious Harvey Bailey, I whisper, "They're gone."

Half an hour later Joe Steere comes out to the telephone in front of the building and sends in his count as usual, but an hour later he stands in front of the same telephone, looking perplexed. He comes up to our shop on the second floor, looks around, continues upstairs to the model shop above us. In less than a minute he descends slowly, takes off his cap, wipes his forehead with a handkerchief and calls in his "count". In two minutes the sirens are cutting through the fog and a coastguard boat is circling the island just off the mat factory. The prison launch joins the coastguard vessel.

Rifle bullets and hand grenades rip apart the debris of tires pressed close against the shoreline, in the hope that the pair is still hiding beneath them.

As the rest of us are paraded back to the cell house to be locked up in our cells, I see Warden Johnston on the wall surrounding the exercise yard, binoculars clutched in his hands, peering desperately into the low-hanging fog.

It's a happy bunch of cons who goes into supper. The escape-proof prison has been beaten. Elsewhere, Walter Winchell reports to America that "Attorney General Homer Cummings swallowed his false teeth when he heard the news."

For two days following the disappearance of Ralph and Ted the screws "shake down" the island. The FBI enters the picture. The G-men interview any cons who might have been in the vicinity including myself. The next morning we are kept in our cells but suddenly my door jolts open. I'm escorted to the warden's office where two agents sit with Warden Johnston at the interview desk.

"Karpis, I've already told these two gentlemen that this will be a waste of time but I'll ask anyways. Do you want to discuss this thing with us?"

"Hell, no!"

"That's what I already knew. Take him back to his cell."

The FBI agents have arrived with enough equipment to discover almost anything on the floor of the bay and even the ocean beyond. Day after day they persistently perch on the roof tops of Alcatraz buildings with telescopes on tripods, cameras, binoculars, time watches, and coastguard charts, indicating the speed of the current off the island's tip, in an attempt to trace the escape route.

Then a call comes in. Armed guards pile into the prison launch and rush "up bay". A hunting lodge has been broken into and two shotguns along with some clothing are stolen.

Next, two guys hold up a filling station with a hot car and two shotguns. Ted Cole is identified by the owner.

Convinced the two are no longer on the island, they allow us to return to work.

Roswell, New Mexico

The stolen car is abandoned by two guys during the robbery of a filling station. One thousand silver dollars are stolen along with a truck.

Photos of Ralph and Ted are sent to Mexico as well as Canada. Every year after 1937, Warden Johnston is reported to receive a postcard from South America signed "Ralph and Ted".

On the afternoon of the escape Doc had been called for his once-every-three-weeks haircut. Many fools are critical of Ralph and Ted for leaving their friend Doc behind. They don't realize the nature of the escape demanded that only two could leave. Doc is lucky; if he had not been up in the cell house getting his hair cut, the same fools would be criticizing him for not going with his friends.

The first weekend following the escape, Freddie Hunter joins me in the yard, a broad smile across his face.

"Don't kid yourself," I tell him. "They didn't make it!"

"Wh-Wh-What d-d-do you you m-m-mean?" Freddie always speaks with a pronounced stutter, except during the crisis of a holdup at which time he comes across loud and clear without any indication of an impediment in his voice.

"They're dead! Jim Clark and I saw them go down!" As Jim and I had stood at the window watching, Ralph and Ted picked up speed. They had just passed the buoy straining on its side from the strong current when, less than 500 yards from shore, Ralph disappeared as if someone grabbed him from under the water. The five-gallon can he had been clutching jumped high out of the water and sailed off on the swirling surface of dark water.

Jim Clark and I looked at one another in shocked silence and back again to the bay just in time to see the strong undertow pull Ted into its cold arms, as he too disappeared beneath the surface. His homemade water wings spurted forward released of his weight. The shroud of white fog pulled itself respectfully over the spot where we last saw the faces of Ralph and Ted.

Clark and I agreed instantly to keep the secret of the murderous waters from all but a few trusted friends.

Security around the factory building tightens, as we expected, following the breakout by Ralph and Ted. An extra gun screw is assigned to stand out on the catwalk behind the building where he can watch the back windows. Tool-proof bars are placed over all windows. Jim Clark and I abandon our plans.

"Karpis, are you going to be in on this strike coming off at New Year's?" Lieutenant Culver inquires one day just before New Year's.

"You're goddamn right I am!"

The next night a bulletin is distributed to all the cells. As of the first of the year, "good time" is increased from two days a month to four days, we can order twenty magazines a year instead of $20 worth, we can have all the fiction books we want in a week. Petty gains but, like a water wheel, we are methodically wearing down the system at Alcatraz. There had been no strike planned, only rumours deliberately spread by cons. Fearful of a second strike in the same year, the officials fall for the "okey dokey" and grant us a few more privileges.

5

Alcatraz, 1938

When it becomes obvious that the added security around the factory building will prevent any attempt to escape from there, I get a work change to the library, up on the hill in the main cell house. Bates, Machine Gun Kelly's partner, works there and has been hinting around that there's an easy way to escape.

Anyone who does time, or works around a prison, has something wrong with their mental make-up. The more obvious cases are separated by the Alcatraz officials and placed in A block isolation next to the library where I work with Bates and a couple of other convicts under the supervision of the Protestant chaplain.

"Quack-Quack" (AZ-414) is heard by the hour making his duck imitations throughout the cellblock. He and the other undisciplined "bugs" in A block ignore the rule of silence and are constantly being beaten by the "bulls" as a result. Meathead's nerves are so rattled, he shoves his way into the cell and slaps Sink (Quack-Quack) senseless.

The Protestant chaplain returns to the library, his eyes in tears and asks, "What happened in here?"

"That fat son of a bitch Suitcase Simpson broke open the tear gas shell on the end of his billy club over the head of Vito!" a con replies.

The clubs carried by guards are eight inches long, one inch in diameter and contain a tear gas shell on the end. The clouds of gas from the tip of the one club have saturated the entire cellblock. Vito Giacalone (AZ-376) is an Italian of the "old school" in the days of the "Black Hand". He speaks broken English to the other cons, but strictly swears in Italian and spits through the bars of his cell on any screw who passes. After several brutal beatings from the guards, such as the one today, they place him in the "bug" cage up in the hospital and ship him out to Springfield, the medical center for the federal prison system.

Because the officials are paranoid that some cons might feign madness to escape the rigors of the Rock, the convicts who are sincerely insane are forced through the most vicious physical abuse before being certified as authentic mental cases. Anyone would have to be crazy to undergo the tortures in the "bug" cage voluntarily, even for the sake of a transfer.

A former guard in Alcatraz, who quit in disgust following the atrocities he observed during the 1937 strike, reveals the conditions in Alcatraz to the American public.

Mercury magazine prints his story entitled "The Torture Chamber of America" in which he refers to Warden Johnston as "Torquemada". Among other examples, the article cites the conditions of Vance (AZ-412), who retreats in fear at the sound of an airplane flying over the cell house, his towel wrapped around his head for protection as he cowers in the corner of his cell.

Vance can be described at best as feebleminded. Back in Oklahoma he attempted to counterfeit fifty-cent pieces out of lead. They were such poor imitations, he was caught the first time he tried to spend one. About forty other coins were discovered in his possession. Unfortunately, the district judge who tried him was an eccentric, senile old bastard known for "giving the limit". Vance received a twenty-year sentence, one year for every dollar of counterfeit money. Eventually he, along with Quack-Quack, is worked over by the "goon squad" and sent to Springfield.

There are others among the 250 elite secured secretly on Alcatraz island under the guise of being the "most dangerous public enemies in America" who leave me scratching my head. The Parrot should have been put in a "bug" house following his ridiculous escapade. He and a couple of other kids tried to hold up a large gambling ship anchored outside the three-mile limit which was run by racket interests. Water ferries shuttled customers between Los Angeles and the vessel. With the number of professional gunmen and armaments on board, they would have needed an army and a navy to rob it.

Joe Vigouroux (AZ-507) sits in his isolation cell singing the same tune over and over. "I came from Alabama with a banjo on my knee . . ."

He wasn't put in isolation until he came screaming out of his cell one day, his eyes wide and wild behind glasses with one-half-inch lenses. He took a clothing hook, dismantled from the shelf in the back of his cell, and slashed it several times across the neck of an Irishman, John McGlone, before he got a grip on the madman and held him until the screws arrived. McGlone, one of the New York outfit, was not attacked for any logical reason, it could just as easily have been anyone else.

It's not because Stuart (AZ-396) is a danger to the American public that he is on Alcatraz, it's because he's a danger to himself. Of all the "jail-house lawyers" I met, he is probably the most ludicrous.

When the judge was preparing to sentence him for passing "hot" postal money orders, he noted that Stuart had been caught with thirteen of them. "There is no point in giving you a lot of time," observed the judge in a presentencing lecture. "I'll run the thirteen counts concurrently rather than consecutively. Be thankful I'm giving you a break!"

The judge was about to give him two years for each money order and was pointing out that it would only be a total of two years rather than twenty-six years when Stuart got on his legal soapbox. "You ain't givin me no break! You can't sentence me consecutively even if you want to. That's the law!"

"Oh, so that's the law, is it?" observed the judge, upset

by being told his own business by a criminal, and proceeded to read off each sentence as he ran them consecutively.

When Stuart found himself in Leavenworth with twenty-six years to serve he still couldn't keep quiet. He whined and complained until they sent him to Alcatraz because he was a nuisance.

In Alcatraz he began to prepare legal papers claiming that all federal prisoners by law had to be treated equally and thus Alcatraz was "illegal" because it deprived its occupants of access to radios, pay in the industries, commissary, and newspapers. He was right, but the authorities went out of their way to frustrate him by losing his papers, changing his cell, and soon he developed a duodenal ulcer which perforated.

Stuart dies in the Alcatraz hospital three or four years after he arrives with approximately twenty years left to serve. If he had kept his mouth shut in court, he would have been free eighteen months after his sentencing.

The first thirty-five convicts in Alcatraz were army prisoners left over from the days when the military used the island. However, throughout the existence of Alcatraz, prisoners arrive who began their sentence in the army before being placed in the federal system and it is not unusual for them to have long sentences over minor offences such as "insulting an officer".

A couple of the young kids who arrive were "assaulted by officers," having been caught committing the act of sodomy with their superiors. The strangest case, however, is Walter Wiggins (AZ-183), who is pointed out to me on the yard one day.

"Ray, I'll bet you can't guess what Wiggins is in here for. I'll give you a hint, he's an army prisoner."

"Probably for spitting on an officer or refusing to obey an order," I suggest as these are common crimes among army prisoners.

"No, he was caught cold turkey fuckin' a mule," laughs my informant. It turns out his information is accurate.

It's when Conway (AZ-293) is released from Alcatraz that Jack Alexander, a feature writer for the *Saturday Evening Post*, contacts him and persuades him to give an exclusive story on the mysterious superprison sitting in San Francisco Bay.

In the story Conway describes the case of Hard-Rock whose real name is Rollie Rector (AZ-262). He and Whoop-em-up had greeted me in the shower room when I first arrived. He's a young kid from Texas who had been in trouble a few times as a teenager before he was caught with a stolen car. Recalling the threats of the screws in the Texas prison, that they would kill him if he ever returned again, he decided to plead guilty to a bank robbery which would place him under federal jurisdiction and in a federal prison. Cons and officials both know Hard-Rock is innocent but the FBI is happy to have the case solved in its books.

The magazine follows up on the story with an editorial which forces the government to commute Hard-Rock's sentence to "time served" and release him within thirty days.

Filing down the gallery toward the dining hall this morning, I almost bump into the con in front of me. The entire line is slowing down as it passes an unusual obstacle on the walkway outside the cells.

The obstacle is Al Capone, causing a bottleneck of traffic as everyone stares as they pass him. Capone is in a daze, I can see he has no idea where he is; the guard on duty is watching him closely. He's dressed for the yard, not the mess hall. His work gloves have been shoved in his back pocket at the last moment and protrude from beneath his coat.

Continuing into the mess hall and sitting down with my meal, I see the end of the line coming through the cell-house door. In the last position, alone and disoriented, Capone shuffles down the middle isle toward the steam table. Under the strict regulations here no one is ever permitted to be out of his regular position in line.

About halfway down the isle, Capone staggers, turns looking for help where none exists, and vomits on the dining-hall floor. Two screws escort him upstairs to the hospital. He never returns to population.

Capone spends the balance of his sentence in Alcatraz in one of the "bug" cages on the hospital ward. The syphilis he was suffering from when he arrived at Alcatraz has finally reached his brain. Paresis has set in. The "silver bullet," a painful inoculation, was the only medication available when Capone arrived at Alcatraz. When tests indicated he was infected, the authorities gave Capone his choice of whether he would receive it, and he decided not to.

May 23, 1938

Screw Cline stands six feet, four inches tall, and brags openly of the "wetbacks" he had killed on the Texas border patrol. Everytime a fight breaks out on the yard he charges into the midst of the squabbling cons laying them out left and right with his "billy". His brutal actions inevitably initiate a chorus of boos from onlooking cons; he is hated for his sadistic streak.

In the model shop, on the third floor of the same building from which Ralph and Ted disappeared, Cline is struck from behind by a carpenter's claw hammer. The blow smashes a hole in his skull.

The death of Cline is the first stage in a doomed dash for freedom. Three cons cut through the bars on the model-shop window, climb cautiously past a barbed wire barrier protruding around the top of the building between the upper windows and the roof, and reach the rooftop undetected. It's a bright, sunny day and they are in full sight of two manned gun towers, yet no one sees them.

Crouching on the sunlit roof top of the factory building, they hesitate only a moment before rushing the glass enclosed guard tower at the other end of the roof. The armed guard in the hut usually sits with the door open. The three surprised inmates skid to a stop outside. The door is closed—not only closed but locked. The shocked expression on the face of the screw inside explains it all; he's not the regular guard, he's a relief screw who has locked the tower door.

The guard responds by blasting them apart, killing one instantly and wounding another who staggers to the end of the building and falls onto the barbed wire around the perimeter. As the con hangs in the entanglement of wire, three storeys above the ground, the screw opens the door of the gun cage, steps softly out onto the freshly shattered glass, and calmly aims his .30-.06 rifle at the helpless figure sprawled in front of him. The body of the screw eclipses the sun, throwing a dark shadow across the wounded man hanging in the wire like a puppet on a string. He fires point blank, the slug rips violently into flesh almost tearing the man off the barbed wire.

The dead con sprawled in broken glass on the roof top is Tom Limerick (AZ-263), a well-known Nebraska bank robber. The wounded con caught in the still vibrating barbed wire is Rufus Franklin (AZ-335), another bank robber. Hiding behind the elevator shaft at the far end of the roof top, eager to give himself up, is Jimmy Lucas, the little punk who had stabbed Capone down in the shower room.

November, 1938

Lucas and Franklin, who recovered from his wounds, are on trial in San Francisco for the murder of Cline. The phone in the cell house rings. Madigan is acting captain, he answers it, turns redder than his hair, slams it down, growls at the other guard. "They got life! That's all, just life!"

Following the death of Cline, discipline becomes looser in Alcatraz, not tighter. The screws know the reputation Cline had among the cons; they think twice before obtaining a similar one that might get them killed one day.

The postal inspectors arrive at Alcatraz to interview John Paul Chase who was with Baby Face Nelson when he was trapped and killed. Nelson took two FBI agents with him.

After two juries have disagreed, they are trying for the

third time to work up a case against Graham and McKay, my old friends from Reno. Baby Face worked for them and the postal inspectors hope Nelson told something to Chase before he died.

John Chase is no big time criminal but received a long prison sentence in Alcatraz because of his association with Baby Face. Chase and Nelson met back in 1931, when they were both getting $100 a night for rum-running between Canada and the U.S.A. Chase was unloading the booze along with other workers while Baby Face, armed with a machine gun, protected them from unexpected and unwanted intruders. Years later, after the "Little Bohemia" shoot-out where Baby Face shot down an FBI agent during his escape, he returned to the west coast and looked up Chase. He needed someone who would not be recognized to run errands for him, to help him rent rooms, and buy food. Chase agreed to help.

One day as they twisted their way up a little mountain road between Virginia City and Carson City, Nelson pointed out the car window in the direction of some deserted mine shafts. "Me and another guy dropped a banker down one of them old shafts. We brought him out here with barbed wire around his wrists after grabbing him outside a movie house in Reno. He was going to testify against Graham and McKay for the government, so I put a gun against his skull and blew his brains out!"

Doc Barker brings me the news that Chase was interviewed by the postal inspectors and some assistant U.S. district attorney for four or five hours in the visitors' area. "They were looking for evidence to use against Graham and McKay in New York when their new trial comes up," Doc explains, "but Chase says he didn't tell them anything."

Doc works with Chase in the mat shop and is upset with my reply. "Bullshit! No one who has nothing to say talks for four or five hours. Those agents and lawyers wouldn't waste so much of their time if Chase was saying nothing."

Doc Barker has never been too bright and always trusts people whom he should suspect. He stomps away from me in anger.

I stand meditating for a few minutes. The case of the missing banker is well known to Doc and I because we had been asked to kill him before Baby Face and another friend took the job.

The story begins years ago when Graham and McKay were running a lucrative con game with legitimate businessmen. They would convince some wealthy businessmen that a certain horse race was "fixed" and the outcome was a "sure thing". When the businessmen put up $200,000 or so, to bet on the horse, they would pocket the money rather than bet it and when the horse lost the race the businessman could not ask for his money back.

One of their victims, a New York businessman, was taken for $250,000 and swore he would spend a million if necessary to convict Graham and McKay of fraud. During their investigation the postal inspectors discovered that the New York businessman sent the payment through the mail in the form of bonds to an assistant cashier in the Riverside Bank in Reno, who accepted it on instructions from Graham and McKay. They laid a charge of "using the mails to defraud" and the young banker was caught in the middle. He was told by the postal inspectors that he would be sent to the penitentiary if he did not cooperate and testify that he had been acting on instructions from Graham and McKay when he converted the bonds to cash. He agreed to give evidence at the trial.

One night in March of 1934, before the trial, he told his wife he was going to see a movie. The next day his car was found on the street outside the theater but he was never seen again. The lawyers for Graham and McKay claimed he took the money himself and went to South America thus proving the innocence of their clients. The jury could not reach a verdict.

Before the banker's disappearance, Doc Barker visited Reno to cash in $10,000 of the $200,000 we netted in the Bremer kidnapping. Graham and McKay changed the "hot" money for Doc and asked him if we could help them out with a problem they had. The plan was that Doc, his brother Freddie and I would hold up the bank in Reno. Some people in San Francisco would ensure that $150,000 to $200,000 would be in the bank vault for us.

We would shoot the banker during the holdup making it look like an isolated incident not connected with Graham and McKay. Doc agreed to relate the plan to Freddie and me.

When Doc, Freddie and I discussed the proposition back in Chicago my reply was fast and sure. "I ain't going to shoot that guy! If one of you wants to, then go ahead. If he was involved with Graham and McKay in robbing and was ratting out on them to save his own skin, I'd shoot him in a second but he was only an employee taking orders, he wasn't mixed up with them."

Freddy was pretty trigger-happy and willing to go along with any scheme but in this instance he agreed with me, and Doc returned to Reno to see Graham and McKay.

"You remember that proposition that you made me when I was out here—" Doc began to ask Graham.

"It's all taken care of, Baby Face Nelson is going to handle it for us."

Within a week I read about the mysterious disappearance of the Reno banker in the local newspapers.

As I stand in the grey confinement of Alcatraz remembering the colorful days of the past, I wonder if Baby Face did confide in Chase. I can't think of anything else that would have kept the agents talking for four or five hours with Chase.

There is a screw who I do a little "business" with. I speak to him. "I'm expecting something to break soon. It will be sensational and will take place in the Nevada area. Could you smuggle me in a newspaper when it happens?"

Four days later he hands me a headline from a San Francisco paper:

BANKER'S BODY FOUND IN MINE SHAFT

It's too much of a coincidence that a body which disappeared four years before should be found in a deserted mine shaft a few days after the postal inspectors have a long talk

Karpis, handcuffed, is escorted by FBI agents at the time of his arrest in 1936.

Alcatraz Island

"Broadway" — the main corridor between cellblocks C and D.

An Alcatraz cell

The Alcatraz dining hall

Convicts on the Alcatraz exercise yard

The steps overlooking the yard

Convicts and guards on the yard

Alcatraz guard on the wall surrounding the yard

Convicts waiting for their cell doors to open

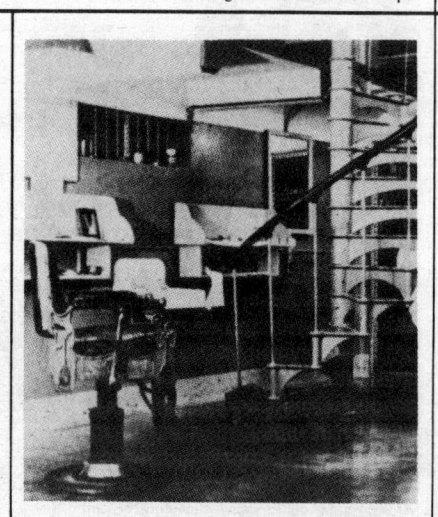

The barbershop in A block where Curley Thomas (AZ-687) killed Barsock (AZ-884).

Convicts pass through electronic "stool pigeons" on their way back to the yard from the industry buildings.

View of the walls around the yard and the cell house from the industry buildings

Guard tower on top of industry buildings

Convicts at work in the industries

with John Chase. My suspicions are shared even by Doc when Chase is shipped to New York City and sits in the courtroom during the trial of Graham and McKay. He never actually takes the witness stand but his presence is damaging and the assistant district attorney makes full use of it. Obviously, the dead banker did not steal the money—Graham and McKay are found guilty.

Bobby Charrington (AZ-199), and Sparks (AZ-200), strut around Alcatraz posing as part of the Dillinger Gang. I have to laugh to myself. The only connection they have with Dillinger is that Spark's Indian wife, Evelyn Frechetti, was Dillinger's girlfriend and Patricia Charrington, Bobby's wife, was with Homer Van Meter when they, along with Baby Face Nelson and others, were trapped at "Little Bohemia".

Dillinger, Hamilton, and Van Meter left the girls behind and crashed through a roadblock in a spectacular escape. Hamilton took a slug in his back as the car was riddled with bullets. The syndicate in Chicago put out orders no one was to help them but I decided to ignore the racket guys and hid Dillinger, along with the dying Hamilton, in one of my apartments. Baby Face lammed for the west coast where he used to be a rumrunner in San Francisco.

I first ran into Nelson when I was the guest of Graham and McKay in Reno. He was just a kid who ran messages for me and worked at odd jobs for Graham and McKay. I was impressed with his knowledge of automobiles and would frequently have dinner with him, his wife, and their two children. Nelson was a stern but understanding father and had been a churchgoing member of the community in California until his moonlighting activities caught up with him. When he asked if he could join our outfit, I gave him an address where he could reach me back east.

After he arrived in St. Paul, I introduced him to Peifer and Sawyer and before long he was running with Dillinger and the others. When bank robbing became a full-time occupation for him he quit his part-time job of selling cars, which Peifer and Sawyer had found for him, much to the dismay of his employer who claimed, "He was the best salesman we ever had here!"

December, 1938

One day Doc Barker approaches me on the yard. "Ray, we're breaking out of this lunatic asylum. Do you wanta come with us?"

"Yes Doc, I'm interested but first I want to know the details of who's involved and what your plan is before I say yes or no."

"Well, there could be others that wanta get in on it but as of right now it's me, Henry Young, Dale Stamphill and Rufe McCain. We're goin' to get ourselves thrown into D block. Hell, Ray, you know very well that Soldier Tommy and the Parrot pick the locks on those cell doors over there every night. There's no regular screw, the cell-house screw only goes over a few times a night to check the count, not every hour like B and C blocks. Once we're there, we have all the time we need to break our way out."

I look thoughtfully at Doc as we pace up and down the yard together. He's right. The isolation cells in D block are the least secure of any in the prison. In D block as in A block the cells are the old ones used by the army. A child can pick the locks.

The others involved in the plot are reliable. Rufe McCain (AZ-267), Dale Stamphill (AZ-435), and Henry Young (AZ-244) are all known as homosexuals and perverts but it is usually the rash and reckless kids who get involved in escape plots. Doc has chosen his companions for their daring and toughness. Each will hold up his end of the plot.

Unlike the counts every hour of the night in B and C blocks, there is one count at midnight and no other until 3:30 A.M. in D block.

"But the bars on the outside windows are tool-proof; once you are free to run around inside D block how do you figure on getting outside the building?" I ask.

"We'll smuggle in a hacksaw blade from the industries

to cut through the soft metal on the outside of one of the window's bars. When we hit the hard core in the center of the bar, we'll use a homemade bar-spreader to snap it. Once the bar is snapped we'll cover over the broken ends with aluminum paint so no one will notice it. Then it will be just a matter of waiting for the first foggy night when the road tower guard can't see the windows on the outside of D block, and we'll slip out after the midnight count. We'll have three-and-a-half hours before they know we've gone."

I admit the plan sounds plausible, but I'm still uneasy. "How will we get off the island and over to the mainland?"

"We'll sneak down to the shore, jump into the water with some homemade water wings and swim for it."

I ask Doc to let me think it over before I give him a definite answer. That night in my cell I realize what is wrong with the plan. They have given a lot of thought to getting out of the building but they're too vague and hazy about getting off the island. I decide to speak to Doc tomorrow.

"Look Doc, I'm not going to jump into that water. Back in Arkansas I used to swim a mile a day, but even then it took me an hour to cover a mile and the currents around Alcatraz are heading for the ocean at five or six miles an hour. Let me think about it a little more before I say absolutely no."

I think of little else for weeks and finally work out an alternate plan. I tell Doc, "I'll go along with your plan to get out of the building, but then I suggest we do this. There's a screw who patrols the outside of the building every hour of the night. He goes down to check on the road tower screw. I've heard him on the catwalk that runs along the outside of the building. Once we're outside, we'll wait for him and take him by surprise in the dark and the fog. Armed with his forty-five and dressed in his hat and coat one of us can walk down the catwalk to the road tower and capture the screw on duty there. We'll have a machine gun, a rifle, a shotgun, and another .45 pistol which the screws in the towers always carry. It'll be easy then to work our way around to the warden's house and capture him and his wife. We can force Johnston to call the doctor up to his house in the middle of the night on the excuse that his wife is sick. Next we force the doctor at gunpoint to call the dock tower where they keep the key to the prison launch and say, 'The warden's wife has an acute appendix! Have the boat ready and running!'

"Also, he can order the panel truck used as a bus on the island to come to the warden's house and once we capture the driver we'll drive down to the dock where the launch'll be waiting for us. With the warden, his wife, and the doctor along as hostages, the boat operator will take us wherever we want to go.

"I'll try that," I conclude, "but I saw what happened to Ralph Roe and Ted Cole—I'm not jumping into that water."

Now it is Doc's turn to say, "Let me think about it." His answer the next day is, "No, it's too complicated!"

"What's so complicated," I challenge him. "Just tell me one thing that won't work."

"Maybe the screw in the road tower calls in on the phone every hour," he suggests. "If he misses his call they'll be shittin' and gettin' out there to see what's wrong."

"If he does call in why does the other screw go down to check on him?" I retort. "But we can find out easily enough by watching him on a clear night. Even if the two screws are missed after an hour, by the time they go to check on them, we'll be in the boat and gone."

A few weeks later Doc again meets me on the yard. "Ray, I spoke with Rufe McCain but I haven't sounded out Dale Stamphill yet."

"Suit yourself Doc, but I'm not going to be in on it unless it's my way!"

Doc decides to suit himself.

It's shortly after our conversation that Doc picks a fight with a well-known stool pigeon, Blackwood (AZ-180), in the exercise yard. The guards are on top of him before he does much harm to the bewildered con. Meathead is on a month's vacation and Gracie Allen, the former deputy warden, has been transferred back to take over his duties. Shuttleworth doesn't like Doc—he throws him in the hole for nineteen days and orders him to remain in isolation where he receives only one meal a day and loses his yard privileges. Doc is delighted.

By the time Meathead returns to his duties as deputy, Doc has been joined by the others. Dale Stamphill and one of his lovers cook up a phony fight where they pretend to have a disagreement. Fights among the "nic nacs" are so common no one is suspicious. He goes to the hole.

Henry Young is insolent to a guard and thrown into D block. Rufe McCain is deliberately caught with some contraband articles and joins the others. Ty Martin (AZ-370), a big, broad-shouldered negro is already in isolation when the others arrive. He is a strong ex-fighter out of Chicago who is in Alcatraz for bank robbery, a rare occupation for negroes in 1938. The others enlist him in the plot.

The next step is to smuggle in a hacksaw. As the inmates come up from the industries or into the cell house from the yard they parade through the electronic gates which detect any metal objects. The electronic stool pigeon never prevents a knife or small object from being smuggled inside because the cons discovered early in the game that the wires stop a few inches from the ground. Thus the hacksaw blade is placed inside someone's shoe and he shuffles through the gate being careful not to raise the bottom of his shoe to the height where the metal will come level with the wiring. In the early days of Alcatraz, D block is not walled off from the rest of the prison as it will be later. Thus, once the saw blade is inside the cell house there is no problem passing it over to someone in D block.

The homemade bar-spreader is too large and awkward to bring up from the industries building in a shoe. "Slim" Bartlett (AZ-239), who used to be an engraver and a machinist on the outside, comes to the rescue. He asks permission to build a metal guitar for himself where he is working in the industries. The parts for the bar-spreader are built into it and when it is completed he asks permission to bring it to his cell. The metal guitar will obviously set off the electronic stool pigeon so Slim merely hands it to the screw on duty as he walks through the device and picks it up from him on the other side.

Now Doc and his boys are in D block, armed with a hacksaw and a bar-spreader.

Alcatraz
January, 1939

Doc and his companions in D block cut through the outside layer of the bar they plan to break. The hacksaw has served its purpose, so they take the shelf from an empty cell, cut a slit in the back of it large enough to hold the blade, fill the opening with paper, paint over it and replace the shelf in the cell.

One night in early January there is a great commotion in B and C blocks as a few dozen cons raise a racket to attract the attention of the guards on the evening shift. In the midst of the yelling and hooting, a loud crack echoes in the cell house which sounds like a rifle shot. The cell-house guard and the gun-cage guard hear it, but, with the other noise being created, they cannot tell where it came from or what it was. They remain mystified and curious for a few minutes but soon relax and, as the cons quiet down, they probably forget all about it by the time the midnight shift comes on. Over in D block the tool-proof bar on one of the windows has been snapped with the bar-spreader. Now there is an opening leading to freedom.

Friday, January 13, 1939

Finally comes the ideal foggy night. The midnight count is taken in D block and five men go into action. There is one suspense-filled moment when Ty Martin's large shoulders stick between the bars. He wriggles and squirms to work his way down through the narrow opening allowed by the broken bar. His huge frame hangs suspended high in the window blocking the escape route for those waiting to follow him. Without hesitation Dale Stamphill climbs above Ty on the bars of the window, places his foot on Ty's head and rams him through the opening. Within five minutes five grey shadows drop into the protection of the fog outside.

Back in the main cell house the guard makes his regular head count each hour not realizing that about sixty of our sleeping forms are wide awake and listening to hear how long it will be before the five men are missed.

The screw who goes in to make the 3:30 A.M. count in D block comes running out. He rushes up the spiral staircase checking all the empty cells in D block and then sounds the alarm. The cell-house lights come on and the siren begins to scream out its angry lament. As the screws race through the cell house taking an emergency count, the guards rush from their beds to action stations all over the island in fear that the escapees might reach the area where the married couples live with their children. The broken bar in D block is spotted and the search is on.

Foot patrols crisscross the island, the coast guard is notified and Meathead leads a crew in the prison launch as it circles Alcatraz. No one inside the cell house adheres to the rule of silence as cons shout news bulletins back and forth to each other and heckle the already confused screws.

"They must be on the mainland by now, they left over three hours ago!"

"I heard machine guns firing out there!"

"Them are sure good tool-proof bars this prison has!"

When I hear the panel truck climbing the hill and coming to a stop outside the basement door, I know something is wrong. Shortly after that the cons celling on Broadway begin shouting, "Hey, they're carrying men up to the hospital on stretchers!"

"How many did you count?"

"Three bodies!"

I know now that the machine-gun fire we heard took its toll. Shortly afterwards Ty Martin and Rufe McCain are dragged back to D block and thrown into the hole. Three bodies upstairs in the hospital and two over in isolation in the hole; the excitement is over for the night.

Months later, I have the opportunity to speak with Dale Stamphill and get the story firsthand. As the five reached the water's edge in the dense fog, they were stopped by the huge waves crashing against the sides of the rocky shoreline. "From 300 or 400 feet above, the ocean looks pretty inviting," he explains, "but when you're standing on the beach with those cold angry waves splashing in your face, you give it a second thought. We began scrambling around, looking desperately for pieces of driftwood to build a raft."

I know as Dale describes the scene to me that even if they had succeeded in getting enough wood and tying it together securely it would never have held all five of them and—if it floated—they would have no means of steering it through the strong currents around the island.

"Doc and me was trying to put the raft together on the beach while the other three was lookin' for more boards," Dale continues. "What with the waves and the wind and them fog horns howling, there was just no way we could hear the goddamn siren go off. First thing we know, there was that searchlight from the boat blinding us. We tried to duck out of the beams but when we started to run our legs was shot out from under us. We was hit about a dozen times each.

"Meathead was in the bow of the boat as it nosed onto the beach in front of us. We couldn't even crawl without a fuckin' lot of pain. I remember Meathead pointin' at Doc and shoutin' above the confusion, 'If that son of a bitch even moves an inch, shoot him in the head!'

"Doc was hurtin' bad and twistin' his body tryin' to straighten so as to ease the pain some. That was all those motherfuckers needed for an excuse. They shot him in the back of the head as he tossed around in the cold sand. Doc was still alive when they drove us up to the hospital but when they put the blood transfusions into his arms he roared like a bull elephant and tore them out. He just wanted to die!"

I understand how frustrated and disappointed Doc must have felt. Like his mother and two brothers he died a violent death leaving his brother, Lloyd, doing twenty-five years in Leavenworth, the sole survivor of the Barker brood.

The third body taken up the hospital steps was Henry Young. While he was running from his pursuers in the dark fog, he ran right off one of the high cliff sides around the edge of the island.

The next morning we eat breakfast and go to work as usual. The screws are clearly jubilant after their night's work. Or I should say everyone goes to work but me. When they let out the guys who work in the library, my cell door remains locked. Shortly afterwards the Protestant chaplain, who is my boss in the library, comes up to my cell. His name is Wayne Hunter.

"They want me to talk to you alone, Karpis. The officials want to know how you feel about Doc being shot. You must have some feelings about it. Are you angry or mad?"

"Hell, no!" I reply honestly. "But if *I* had been shot I would have been angry."

"Doc and his friends had no guns as you know," he continues to probe. "Maybe you feel they were deliberately shot?"

"Of course they were deliberately shot. So what? What of it? Anytime I stick my head out of these windows or anywhere it ain't supposed to be, I expect to be shot by you people."

The minister's face flushes red for a moment but he doesn't comment. I find out later that I accidently hit a guilty nerve when I used the phrase "you people". The concerned little padre had been running around the island that dark night with a forty-five in his hand and ungodly murder in his eyes.

"I didn't tell Doc to go out there—and I don't know nothin' about it."

"You probably knew all about it," he smiles knowingly.

"No I didn't," I lie, "and I don't care because I'm not involved in it. If I did care, I still wouldn't tell you." I add more truthfully, "But I don't care. I'm just glad it wasn't me!"

Poor Doc knew he would never get another chance at escape from Alcatraz. With Ma and Freddie dead he has been unhappy, he is better off dead.

An hour later my cell door opens and I go to work in the library as usual.

GERMANY INVADES POLAND
ENGLAND AND FRANCE DECLARE WAR

Machine Gun Kelly cells on the same gallery as his partner Bates. Today he confronts Bates. "I can't lick a postage stamp but if you don't get the hell off of this gallery, we're going to tangle."

Bates moves.

The guys on the mangle in the laundry are a rugged breed and prejudiced. It is understood no negroes work there, so when one shows up he is told, "Don't come back here or you're a dead nigger!"

The negro never returns but, a short while later, another one arrives. He's nervous from the moment he enters the building. The black is always in trouble with the officials and has probably been sent down to the mangle as a cruel practical joke. He has just taken off his coat when four cons surround him. One knocks him down with a single punch and the poor victim drags himself under the mangle where he stays in hiding, his eyes peering out, like a frightened raccoon surrounded by a pack of dogs, until the foreman comes to his rescue. He leaves immediately under escort.

A well-known stoolie arrives. He's worked over so badly you could swear he's been forced through the mangle. He too is escorted from the laundry, his features indistinguishable behind the layers of blood.

Two notorious New York robbers come to work in the laundry. Oley (AZ-455), and "Angel Face" Geary (AZ-456), cleared $450,000 in the Rubel Ice Company robbery when they hit an armoured truck. They broke jail in Albany but were recaptured and sent to Alcatraz.

They describe to me their bootlegging business in Albany during prohibition when their best individual customer, other than local speakeasies and private clubs, was President Roosevelt who at the time was the governor of New York State. They would deliver the booze directly to the back door of the governor's mansion in Albany.

Two members of Doc Barker's escape crew have a falling out. Rufe McCain had neglected to inform the others that he couldn't swim until they were on the beach. Henry Young, looking for a scapegoat, blames him for the failure of the escape. They argue violently.

"Lefty" Egan (AZ-266) is a gossip but a useful and likeable one. He and his fall partner must have made a strange pair of kidnappers. Lefty has a badly withered arm while Harold Harpin (AZ-294) has only one leg. Lefty cells next to me and whispers in confidence one night, "Henry Young made two shivs for himself up in the model factory."

Since his release from isolation following the escape attempt with Doc Barker, Young is on the third floor in the model factory and below him in the tailor shop is Rufe McCain whom he blames for the failure of the escape. I see to it that Rufe is informed of Young's weapons.

Alcatraz, Hospital Wing, Bug Cage

In the detective magazines and newspapers, Carl Janaway (AZ-393), a bank robber, is referred to as the "Terror of the Ozarks." Well, maybe he was, but he certainly doesn't terrorize Alcatraz.

He stands five-feet three-inches tall and weighs about 100 pounds. When he was finally shot, he was trying to escape in a car which rolled over, trapping him inside. The doctors place a board across his damaged back which extends beyond each shoulder. He looks like a comical version of the hunchback of Notre Dame.

Janaway isn't to last too long in Alcatraz's cell house. He "flipped" shortly after his arrival and was placed in the hospital wing in one of the three "bug" cages. The three "bug" cages have been constructed in a long room separated from the main ward. They are made of hog wire and sit side by side.

As I climb the steps to the hospital wing to visit Red Kuykendall (AZ-434), I pass by the open door of the room housing the "bug" cages. Janaway is in the cage closest to the door. Al Capone is in the next cage and the third one is empty. When I stop outside in the hallway while a guard opens a lock on the door to the main ward, I hear the voices of Capone and Janaway in the midst of an insane argument.

"When we both get out of here, I'm going to give you millions of dollars Janaway. I'm going to make you a millionaire."

"Fuck you, Mr. Millionaire!"

"Bug House Janaway, the millionaire."

"Don't call me that! Don't call me that! You goddamn dago!"

"Bug House Janaway! Bug House Janaway!"

It's like listening to two six-year-olds arguing in a sandbox, but then the name calling ends abruptly as the "Terror of the Ozarks" picks up the bed pan in his cage. Grabbing a handful of its contents, he aims and fires in the direction of Capone. The missile hits the hog wire separating the two cages, splattering throughout Capone's cell and freckling the body of Scarface like a volley of lead from a machine gun.

Capone bellows in rage and quickly retaliates by dashing for his own bed pan and sending a handful of ammunition ricocheting through the hog wire. It leaves a stained trail across Janaway's cage and studs his shoulders and neck. The thin marks form a line on Janaway's fair skin giving the impression he is oozing brown blood. The war is on!

Both contestants now pull large juicy handfuls from their respective armories and fling them with the glee and joy of youngsters involved in a snowball fight. Everything within range slowly changes color as sickly green-brown lumps land indiscriminately, decorating the room.

Janaway and Capone, laughing and cursing, continue their mad warfare while alarmed orderlies crouch in the doorway, afraid to enter the line of fire. The two opponents slip and slide on the well-fertilized floor before the encounter ends in a draw, as they both run out of ammunition.

I don't envy the orderlies who have the job of placing the two desperadoes in a bath and scrubbing down the cells.

Until I witnessed the battle in the "bug" cage, I hadn't realized the extent to which Capone's brain has been infected by syphilis. One of the hospital orderlies tells me that Janaway and Capone spend hours and hours, day after day, arguing over petty differences and teasing one another.

The "Terror of the Bug Cage" is transferred shortly afterwards to Springfield. Capone is kept in his "bug" cage in Alcatraz until 1939, when he is transferred to Terminal Island. When his time is completed he is released and dies in Miami, Florida, January 25, 1947, completely insane.

There is a vacant look in Henry Young's eyes as he ceremonially ties a handkerchief around his long bushy hair, pirate style, and proudly inspects his two homemade shivs. No one knows what thoughts flicker through his decorated head as he descends to the tailor shop below. Perhaps he is reliving moments from his days as a cowboy working the rodeos. Perhaps he's working his warped emotions into a frenzy over his unsuccessful bid for escape.

Rufe McCain stands next to the water fountain on the floor below talking casually with a fellow inmate. His back faces the staircase which Henry descends. The con speaking with Rufe gasps out a warning: "Young is coming with a couple of shivs!"

Rufe turns calmly to meet Young, his mouth half open in greeting. The words are never uttered.

One slash rips across Rufe's stomach—one only—it slices his liver in two and his guts burst from the crevice in full view of the insane stare radiating from Henry Young's eye sockets.

The same intestines meet the amazed expression on the face of the doctor in the hospital at Alcatraz. Rufe's naked body lies on the emergency room table.

"I don't know what I can do about this!" complains Dr. Green as he covers the wound with cotton. "I can't do anything but call over to town for help."

Rufe McCain dies.

I'm angry and sick. The senselessness of the killing alarms me, it's an unnecessary waste.

Henry Young's trial is a shambles. The prison is tried, not Young. Cons parade over to town to testify, falsely, that Rufe McCain was an aggressive homosexual, threatening to kill Young if he didn't cooperate. Young is given a two-year sentence for "involuntary manslaughter".

An escape route through the hospital skylight is feasible. I interest my fall partner Freddie Hunter in it. He suffers from T.B. and arthritis so he has no problem getting admitted to the hospital to plot with Red Kuykendall. Whoever goes on the break will check into the hospital. Then in the middle of the night we will take a hacksaw to the bars on the hospital doors and capture the guard and MTA* on night duty. The pair will be unarmed and easily intimidated by a shiv or a crank-handle from a hospital bed.

I smuggle a hacksaw up to Red while visiting Freddie Hunter. He entrusts it to Pete Norman who unscrews the fixture over a light switch and shoves the file out of sight before replacing the plate. The next step is to make water wings or rafts out of rubber sheets which I could do in the library but one day as I'm on my way to work I see something that brings an abrupt end to the scheme.

Outside the blacksmith shop I find an unusual object—a frame of bars, built like the peak of a roof the same size as the skylight in the hospital. When I inquire, I learn that it is to be constructed over the skylight. Obviously someone knows about our plans. I visit Red in the hospital and tell him to get the hacksaw back to me. Within a few days the authorities announce they discovered a hacksaw up in the hospital. Everything points to a "stoolie".

*male trained attendant

Red describes to me how Pete Norman actually broke down and cried when he confessed it was he who told the authorities about the skylight and showed them where he hid the hacksaw. The only thing he had not confessed was the names of those involved.

In isolation, where he is placed after the trial, Henry Young loses all outward signs of sanity. He reveals the hiding place where those on the escape with Doc had stashed the saw used to cut the bars on the windows. He turns stool pigeon naming guys and various jobs in which they were involved but never convicted and insists on being placed in the dark hole where the daylight can't reach him.

The doctor is on his 9:00 P.M. rounds of isolation before the 9:30 count. He makes the galleries first, the holes last.

When the guard opens the inside door of the dark hole cell containing Henry Young, the doctor steps back in alarm. A distorted expression covers his face as he turns away quickly from the cell. Young's naked white body is carried from the cell, drained of blood like a vampire's victim, the red slashes on his wrists, leg arteries and body standing out like braille, self-inflicted by a lens from his reading glasses.

Following a month of recovery in hospital, Young insists on being placed again in the dark hole rather than a regular cell. It is not until the guard opens his cell during a surprise inspection that Young is finally sent to Springfield as a mental patient. The sight revealed to the guard is bizarre.

Young is lying naked on his mattress which he has stretched across the floor of his cell, his knees, pressed close against his ears, "coping his own joint".

December, 1939

Bill Weaver (AZ-295) and Harry Sawyer invite me to join them in the kitchen. They describe the advantages: a shower every day, the yard every afternoon, all the food I can eat. I point out to them the two disadvantages, Volney Davis and Blackie Audett who are both working back there. "I'll end up taking one of their heads off!"

"Davis says he lost a lot of friendship over the fight he picked with you—says he'd be glad to see you come back and put an end to it," explains Weaver.

"That dog, Audett, he's nothin'," says Sawyer.

6

Alcatraz, 1940

I receive a work change to the kitchen and I am put to work on the steam table in the dining room. Myself and five others have to pick up the silverware and trays, clean the tables after each meal and mop the floor. There is nothing to the job.

The kitchen is like a luxury hotel compared to the mangle in the laundry. The first morning I have two eggs and strawberry preserves for breakfast. My friends Sawyer, Weaver, and Boxhead Brown are working in the butcher shop thus I can have my choice of meat cuts anytime of the day. Filet Mignon becomes a part of my regular diet.

On my third day back in the kitchen, as I'm picking up the silverware, a voice hails me. "Hey Ray, can I say something to you?" I turn around to face the stool pigeon, Blackie Audette.

"Yeah, what do you want?"

"The steward has been watching you. He says you know how to work. Do you want to come back to cook with me for the main line?"

"Talk about gall!" I think to myself as I answer Blackie without enthusiasm. "Hell, I don't know how to cook."

"I'll show you everything there is to know," he persists. "Everyone will help you."

Realizing he's not going to accept a polite refusal, I cut him off abruptly. "No thanks!"

Not long after I refuse to work with Blackie, I receive a message from Volney Davis via my friends in the butcher shop. They tell me he has offered to give me any of the choice food I wish from the guard's dining room where he does the cooking. My response is quick.

"No, I don't want nothing from him!"

The steward approaches me.

"Karpis, do you like working the dining hall?"

"Yeah, I'm alright."

"You're a good worker. You know what you're doing. Do you want to cook? I need someone to prepare the diets for the hospital."

"I'm no cook!"

"Look, I checked your records, you used to be a baker in the state prison but a cook is only a baker with his brains knocked out. I know, I'm a cook and I used to be a baker."

I accept the job.

My friends start to join me up on the hill. Oley, Geary, Ray Miller (AZ-484), and little Chuck Grismer (AZ-479) are soon installed back in the kitchen. Darlino (AZ-478), the fag who I have warned not to mess around with Chuck, who looks about thirteen years old, stands only five-feet one-inch and does not even shave yet, also transfers from the laundry. Young kids coming into a prison are easily intimidated into becoming "girls". Chuck obviously is not a "nic nac". My relationship with him is paternal. I treat him as I would my own son back in Chicago who I have never seen. If he wants to get involved with any of the "tops and bottoms fruit merchants" he can do so on his own terms, not theirs.

Darlino's activities in the kitchen become even more flagrant than they were in the laundry. He works upstairs in the screw's mess but descends to the basement to give out three or four blow jobs a day.

He has just returned from making his rounds of the basement and sits down to dinner when a fly buzzes to a stop on a slice of bread beside his plate. He shoos the fly away angrily and slams the contaminated bread down on the table in disgust, refusing to eat it.

Volney Davis becomes the printer, the best job in the institution. He has no direct boss other than Meathead and is conveniently isolated in the basement of the kitchen.

I take his old job cooking for the guards' mess.

July, 1940

The general population goes on a hunger strike, demanding better food. There is no rule that forces a prisoner to eat although there is one that forces everyone to go into the dining hall for each meal. For an entire week, three meals a day, the convicts file past the steam tables without touching any of the food. The silent protest alarms the officials more than the active and vocal one of 1937.

At the beginning of the second week none of the cell doors open. "You ain't going to work!" announces the cellhouse screw. The guards stop at every cell on each gallery distributing cop-out sheets requesting permission to work.

"I will eat and I will work!" they read. Very few sign the first day but the number caving in climbs to one-third of the population by the end of the second week.

My cell door doesn't open. Neither does Ray Miller's, Oley's, or Angel Face Geary's. "Hey, you didn't open our doors!"

"No you s.o.b.s and we're not goin' to! You ain't working in the kitchen anymore."

We are assigned new cells with the strikers. We are accused of agitating the strike.

Due to the war in Europe, the Alien Registration Act is passed. All aliens must report to the local post office to be fingerprinted for the Immigration Department. Since myself, a Canadian, and five or six other aliens cannot make the trip to the post office, the FBI comes to Alcatraz to fingerprint us for the Immigration Department.

Several desks are set up at the kitchen end of the cellblock. Meathead stands next to the FBI agent who speaks to me, the name Karpowicz on my card means nothing to the stranger.

"Well I guess you've had this done many a time. How many times?"

"What the fuck's the difference. Let's get it done and get out of here," I reply giving Meathead a wink.

The agent rolls the first finger, obviously puzzled. The second finger, no print! After he rolls the third finger, he looks at me suspiciously, then at Meathead, who doesn't say a word but is having a difficult time controlling himself. The agent decides to press my entire hand in the black ink then, thinking I am somehow "beating him," he starts out slowly but slams my hand down roughly on the paper. Still no prints!

Meathead is now laughing out loud at the angry agent. "Goddamn, you're an FBI agent and you don't know who this is? This is Karpis, he don't have no fingerprints!"

"Is that who he is? They told us at the FBI college you couldn't remove fingerprints with an operation."

"Well go ahead and try to get some prints but you ain't goin' to," replies Meathead, "'cause they have us take his prints every year just to see if they've grown back, but they ain't."

I removed the prints when I was on the outside. Doc Moran had first cut the circulation to each finger then shot my finger tips full of cocaine before taking a scalpel and shaving all the layers of skin off each finger, much as you would sharpen a pencil. The operation was a success, my fingerprints never returned. The idea was not to prevent my identification if caught, but to prevent my capture by not leaving a trail of tell-tale prints in every hotel room and automobile.

Two new arrivals in Alcatraz are given cells directly across from mine on Broadway; they are accused of killing a marshal while trying to escape custody. I have long conversations with them on my fingers.

Joe Cretzer (AZ-548) is a master at sign language; both his parents were deaf and dumb. His partner Kyle (AZ-547) married Joe's sister and is also proficient in the art. Joe, in turn, married Kyle's sister. After hours of mute conversation, I learn their backgrounds.

They started out in crime together along with a third partner, all three agreeing they would steal until they accumulated $100,000 each. Then they would stop clean. Unlike many others, their plans worked. They each acquired $100,000 and stopped stealing.

Joe Cretzer bought a hotel in San Diego. Kyle bought a transcontinental trucking line operating big runs from Florida to California. The third guy played the ponies until he was "tapped out" and then came back to Cretzer and Kyle asking them to rob again. They told him "no" but pointed out an easy score where he could pick up forty to fifty thousand easily.

The score was a success but he threw it all away at the racetrack again and was back a second time asking for another easy setup. This time he took a young kid on the job with him who had never made "big money" before. Instead of cautioning the kid, he was so anxious to rush down to the racetrack, he left him on his own. The kid was picked up trying to buy an expensive car for cash. After breaking the kid down the police arrived at the guy's room but he shot himself through the head as the FBI came through the door.

Something in the room connected the dead man to Cretzer and Kyle who had to run out on their legitimate businesses to save their skins. Both were later picked up in different parts of the country. In Kyle's case a youngster ran into the side of his car. Kyle stopped to make sure the kid was alright as a squad car arrived. There was no damage to the youth but Kyle had had a couple of beers so he was taken down to the police station on a routine check where he was identified by his fingerprints.

Both Kyle and Cretzer ended up on McNeil Island doing twenty-five years each. They were due to be transferred the next day when they grabbed a dump truck inside the prison yard, knocked out the driver, and drove through the gate with the load still sliding out the raised back of the truck which shielded them from the bullets as the tower guards emptied their rifles.

Three days later a dog being used in the hunt wouldn't

stop barking at a clump of bushes. Kyle and Cretzer were hauled out of the bushes, taken down to the shower room and severely beaten in the presence of the warden.

Their adventures didn't end with their capture. In the washroom of the court building they tried to wrestle a gun away from the old deputy marshal who escorted them. A large screw bowled them over as the old deputy got the drop on them and stood in the doorway of the washroom, gun in hand, cackling proudly.

"So the old man was too smart for you young whippersnappers, eh?" Then he stiffened slightly before falling to the floor—dead! The strain had been too much, he died as reinforcements rushed through the doorway to his aid.

Now Kyle and Cretzer are in Alcatraz awaiting a murder trial over the death of the deputy marshal.

When the food strike peters out, I return to work in the kitchen. The steward comes over to say hello and explain. "We know you weren't agitating the strike, but we have to lock up any of you guys who might escape whenever there's any trouble in the prison."

DUNKIRK

The end of 1940 has come and a lieutenant on the docks, a red-faced, blue-eyed, healthy Irishman with red hair is made the first Captain of Alcatraz. It's Father Clark's friend, Madigan.

Alcatraz, 1941

The new D block is completed. It no longer resembles its former twin, A block, but instead is completely sealed off from the other cellblocks. The old bars and locks are now remodeled into modern escape-proof cells and the entire flats have undergone a face-lifting. The cells along the flat nearest the large steel door at the yard end of the block are spacious ones designed for "bugs" while at the other end is a series of "hole" cells with double doors to prevent the sunlight from seeping through. There is now a screw on duty twenty-four hours. All these changes were precipitated by Doc Barker's escape.

The first con to be escorted to the new D block is "Swede" Earl Cox (AZ-494). As Swede steps through the door leading into cell 14, the end strip cell, he discovers a welcoming committee. The "goon squad" is huddled inside like guests at a surprise party. They jump out. He struggles, blinded in the dark cell, absorbs blows and falls eventually on the barren cement floor, unconscious.

Swede suffers broken ribs on both sides of his body, most of his teeth are loosened, his eyes are black hollows, his knee is screwed up, his nose is misshapen and one ear is mangled. He has been the sacrificial offering made by the screws to initiate the opening of the new D block.

A strange race is on between the cons at Alcatraz and the armed forces. The military are rushing to complete a string of submarine nets which will stretch across the entrance to the harbor while a group of cons are preparing for an escape. Once the submarine nets are installed there will be a regular shuttle of picket boats checking the nets and watching for debris. If the prisoners' plan, to be picked up by a boat from town, is to work, it must be accomplished before the military congests the channel.

Two of the cons involved are Cretzer and Kyle. Joe Cretzer's sister, who is married to Kyle, is to pick them up in the boat. The third is Barkdoll (AZ-423), and the fourth and last con involved is never identified by the authorities.

Once again the mat shop is the scene of the escape as the four overpower the guard on duty and tie him up along with the rest of the convicts who are not involved in the escape. The other cons are tied up for their own sakes, so no one can blame them for not sounding the alarm or untying the guards after the four have jumped onto the boat which is to rendezvous with them soon outside the window by the water's edge. But, first, the tool-proof bars on the outside window have to be cut.

The whirr of a primitive cutting wheel hums as it bites

against the solid bars. Captain Madigan enters the mat factory following a predictable schedule. He is captured and tied up. A screw who is a truck driver on the island appears—he too is secured.

The whirr of the cutting wheel drones on doggedly.

Next, the superintendent of industries walks into the fracas and joins the group of hostages.

The whirr of the cutting wheel wails impotently against the tool-proof bars.

Lieutenant Weinholt, a Prussian-type disciplinarian, enters the mat shop and, after he is captured tries to argue, in spite of his reversed role, with his captors. "One more word from you and off comes your goddamn head," snaps Joe Cretzer.

The cutting wheel whines, grinds, and snaps. The homemade electrical saw is destroyed. The bars are unscathed. The boat is nowhere in sight. The escape is a bust. The cons make a deal with Captain Madigan and give themselves up.

Across the bay, Edna Kyle sits in a San Francisco jail, unable to notify her husband and brother that she cannot meet them with the boat. She was picked up the day before on a shoplifting charge.

Along with Cretzer, Kyle, and Barkdoll, Sam Shockley (AZ-462) is thrown into D block isolation following the ill-fated escape. Barkdoll asks to see Captain Madigan. "What the hell you got Shockley locked up for? He was tied up with the others, don't you remember? We used your knife to cut him loose."

"Yeah," Madigan scratches his big red head, "I do remember him being tied but, in that case, who was the fourth convict?"

None of the hostages taken in the abortive escape can recall the fourth con involved and none of the cons are talking. Back in his cell, Floyd Hamilton (AZ-523) has a complacent smile on his face. He is the unnamed convict. He and his brother had been associates of Bonnie and Clyde on the outside.

The war is keeping all the industries on the Rock busy. The new industry building is completed.

Captain Madigan is promoted and transferred to the new institution at Sandstone, Minnesota, to become the associate warden.

There is not a con in Alcatraz who wants to help the United States war effort. Sabotage is rampant—razor blades are set in the mangle to shred the expensive linen from the navy ships. Pink and orange dye is thrown in with the white laundry. Fires break out in various industries but always when the cons are up on the hill eating or sleeping; they are set by homemade time bombs constructed from candles and matches.

Cons run the wash out through the drainage system into the bay. When Meathead shows up on the deck of the prison launch trying to retrieve the floating laundry spreading across the waters, he is cheered on by the laughing cons with chants of "Go Meathead, Go!"

July, 1941

The new captain replacing Madigan is Weinholt, an ex-marine, about forty-five years old, glasses, long jaw, strange-shaped head in the process of balding and a mouth full of dentures. Following the escape attempt during which he and Madigan had been tied up and humiliated he swore, "They'll never get me again!"

Today he stands in the center of the dining hall, speaking rapidly with Warden Johnston, when his top dentures fly out of his mouth and slide across the floor. Weinholt runs over, picks them up, wipes them off, and places them back in his mouth then continues talking to the warden over top of the hysterical laughing of the cons eating their meals.

Warden Johnston proceeds to the steam table after the interrupted conversation with Captain Weinholt and tastes the food. Then, as predictable as the rest of the routine in Alcatraz, he wipes his hands and pats his lips with his handkerchief. His neat action always recalls the stories of how he would wave his handkerchief when, as warden of San Quentin, it was his duty to signal the hangman to proceed with an execution.

Sunday, December 7, 1941

The cons working in the kitchen clean up after the Sunday lunch and return to their cells or go out to the exercise yard. Only about three of us are left in the kitchen along with one of the stewards and a guard by the name of Kline.

I'm cooking for the guards' mess, and Kline and I are trying to guess how many guards will show up for the evening meal when the phone on the wall beside us rings. He picks it up.

"Are you sure? Are you sure? Alright!"

As he slowly replaces the phone on the wall I know it has been bad news. His face turns pale and his thoughts are some place far away. My first guess is that he has received tragic news about his family but he turns to me and mumbles in a sort of a daze, "Karpis, the japs have bombed Pearl Harbour!"

Then Kline, who has a son at Pearl Harbour, recovers himself and adds, "Jesus Christ! Don't say anything to the other guys, there's no telling how they might react. I don't want the kitchen torn up!"

I agree to say nothing. Eighty percent of the population is already hoping the Germans will win the war. The other twenty percent is against the Germans only because they are communists and thus support the Russians. I doubt if there are six cons on the entire island who won't be excited and jubilant over the news of Pearl Harbour.

When the other kitchen workers began drifting back to prepare for the evening meal, they are already buzzing with the news. The secret is all over the cell house.

Later that afternoon Volney Davis, myself, and some others sit around the print shop down in the basement, which Davis is now in charge of. Volney is a master at making "home brew" and we sample it freely as we celebrate the news of Pearl Harbour. Our main interest is how it will affect us in Alcatraz. Will they move us off the Pacific coast to inland prisons? Will the japs arrive one day to rescue us? How will our personal lives be changed now that the U.S.A. is fully committed to the war?

Christmas Eve, 1941

Today Christmas packages are given to the cons at Alcatraz for the first time. They contain candy, cookies, and packaged cigarettes which are not available in Alcatraz through the year. All the contents must be used by the end of January or they will be considered contraband. As I sit alone in my cell, the opened Christmas package on the bed beside me, I think to myself, "The war must have these bastards scared as hell if they're starting to treat us cons this good."

Alcatraz, 1942

War activity in San Francisco Bay is increasing steadily. The submarine net is completed across the mouth of the harbor.

One day at noon the kitchen screw nabs me and escorts me to the interview desk in the cell house. I'm drunk on home brew.

"You're drunk eh?" begins Meathead.

"No I'm not!"

"You can't even walk. Try to walk across to the D block door over there." Somewhere on the blurred horizon I see the door leading to the new D block isolation and start for it confidently. As I ricochet off walls, I realize I'm weaving and staggering but I do make it to the D block door. Behind me bellows the hoarse voice of Meathead with laughter. "Now stay right there! Cause that's where you're going for awhile."

Because of the drunken episode, when I get out of isolation, I'm removed from the kitchen and placed down in the mat shop with my old friend and fall partner, Freddie Hunter.

The screw in the mat shop, "Boodhound" Johnson, is a retired twenty-five year veteran of the state prison system who has returned to work for the federal government during the war years.

Saturday Noon

All activity in the mat shop is brought to an abrupt stop.

Meathead interviews us one at a time. "We're closing the mat shop, you won't be working here any more." Meathead hesitates a moment before proceeding. "We're taking you guys over to the laundry, 'cause we're shorthanded since a bunch of those guys went on a strike."

"You know me well enough," I begin slowly. "I know you pretty good. Don't ask me to scab."

"You don't tell me what you're going to do in here!" retorts Meathead.

"No, but I'm telling you what I'm not going to do! I'll work but I won't scab."

"You be at work in the morning!" Meathead concludes the interview.

I'm a few cells from the end of the cellblock where I overhear Meathead's remarks the next morning. "What did them s.o.b.s do? Go to work?"

"They all went to the yard but Karpis—he stayed in his cell," a screw says.

"It would be him! Now watch, every one of those s.o.b.s who were in the mat shop with him will be back in here." No sooner has Meathead made his prediction, than a knock is heard at the door leading to the yard and the other cons from the mat shop file back in, refusing to go to the laundry.

"You bastards!" explodes Meathead. "What the hell did you go to the yard for? Were you afraid to stay in your cells? Get them out of my sight! I want to see the s.o.b. who started all this!"

As I round the corner of the cellblock I'm confronted by seven or eight of the meanest screws in Alcatraz. It's the "goon squad," including Weinholt and Suitcase Simpson. Normally a con out for an interview stands against the C block wall waiting to be called foreward. I start for the traditional position.

"Never mind any of that B.S.! Come over here!" The "goons" part as I walk through them to the interview desk. "Why didn't you go to the yard?"

"I told you I wouldn't scab, now I'm not even willing to go to work."

"Why do you want to do this? You know them guys on strike will cave in and be back on the job in a couple of days."

"I agree, but I'm not doing this for them, I'm doing it for me. I'm no scab. My dad's been a union man all his life. I feel the same way as he does. I'm not working anyplace now. Fuck the work!"

Meathead's voice rises to a screech. "Don't you know there's a war on?" His ridiculous response causes smiles to break out even on the stern faces of the "goons" who hover in a threatening circle around me.

"What's the war got to do with it?"

"Every man has to do his part, our country is in trouble!"

"I'll do my part in the hole, nowhere else." I've pushed Meathead to his limit. I'm as close as I've ever come to being worked over by the "goon squad".

"Mr. Weinholt, Mr. Simpson, do you see this son of a bitch?"

"Yes Mr. Miller!"

"The next time you see this man he'll be working on the mangle in the laundry. Throw his ass in the hole for twenty-one days on a restricted diet—and I mean restricted!" Within half an hour Freddie Hunter, Tommy Nelson, Pendergrast, and Wilmont join me in the new hole cells in D block.

Meathead's idea is that I eat only bread and water for twenty-one days but the cons in isolation celling above my hole cell have other ideas. They receive regular meals in isolation; I get my share of food and tobacco.

The convict orderly leaves the outside door of my cell open when he sees the screw is preoccupied at the other end of the cell house, and a string appears in the open door frame; hanging on the end of it is a package of contraband. The slot on the inside door, which remains locked, is only twelve inches wide and four inches high but, as the food and tobacco is swung in a pendulum motion, I use the trouser leg of my coveralls to hook and haul it into my cell as my benefactor, on the other end of the string, lets it loose.

Isolation, 1942

Toward the end of 1942, either November or December, while I'm still in D block isolation for refusing to scab down in the laundry, Touhy, Banghart and some others make a spectacular escape from Statesville maximum security prison in Illinois. They get hold of some guns and go over the wall, escaping in a car owned by a tower guard. In Chicago they are caught because, with the war on, everyone is suspicious of his neighbour and reporting unusual activities in fear of aliens spying in the country.

When a cell is made up in isolation, days in advance, I know it is not an average incident involving an Alcatraz prisoner. It has to be an arrival from outside who is to be placed in isolation rather than general population. I conclude it must be Banghart.

That evening the outside door opens and someone is placed in one of the bottom cells which is designed for mentally disturbed cons. No one speaks as he is placed in the cell. From my cell I can't see him but I'm curious about who the outsider might be.

No sooner has the cell-house door shut behind the departing screws than a voice begins shouting out, "Hey Karpis! Hey Karpis!"

"Who the hell is that?" I ask.

"It's me! It's me! Stroud. Remember me in Leavenworth? You had the cell right across from me."

Of course I remember him. I was very impressed with him and his birds and often speak about him to other prisoners who know of him. Back in 1936, he had done over twenty years in isolation in Leavenworth. Now, in 1942, he has been suddenly transferred to Alcatraz's isolation unit.

"What the hell happened? What brings you here?"

"That son of a bitch Bennett claims I had a shiv in my cell and that I was planning to kill him the next time he came there. But all it was—it was a phony pretext to get rid of me and my birds. I was a problem to them."

I believe him. Bennett, the Director of Prisons, may not have helped conspire against him but there were many complaints about the extra privileges given to him which other inmates were not allowed. Also he was causing a great deal of trouble over his demands to marry a woman by proxy while in Leavenworth. Perhaps the officials wanted rid of him or maybe another con who he had had a falling out with over in isolation cooked up the story. Certainly after twenty-five years of good behaviour in Leavenworth's isolation unit, it is unlikely he would start to make plans to kill Bennett.

"How is it here?" he asks.

"Not too bad," I reply. "Don't make any mistakes—the place is a madhouse out in general population but things aren't too bad here in isolation. You'll make it alright. You'll get yard privileges and be allowed to play handball. There are some pretty nice guys over here but also a few real bastards."

At these words Swede pops into the conversation, "You son of a bitch, I suppose I'm one of them bastards you're talking about!"

"Yes Swede, you are. Don't butt into this conversation, you fucker, just stay out of it!"

Swede quiets down but not before he threatens to kill me as he has done many times before. I was not referring solely to him when I warned "The Bird Man" of the bastards in isolation. Jimmy Lucas is here as well as Jimmy Groves. I don't realize it but Bob Stroud (AZ-594) will turn out to be as much of a bastard as any of them.

Summer of 1942

Between midnight and morning in D block we hear muffled voices on the roof above us and dragging noises across the ceiling. Anti-aircraft guns are installed on top of the prison. Soldiers man them for the duration of the war.

A special session of the classification committee is held in my honor. It suggests to the Bureau of Prisons that I be sent to

Leavenworth for the duration of the war. "If bombs fall on Alcatraz and Karpis ends up free on the island," they state, "there will be a lot of people killed." Their recommendation is not heeded.

November 1942

Cons working in the industries at Alcatraz are now paid. The industries become a coveted position among those expecting to be released, who wish to build up some money. The pennies mean nothing to me: even if I had hopes of being released I wouldn't depend on the prison system for a grubstake.

Last day of 1942

I get a "call out" in the morning to the dentist's office in the hospital. On the way back from the hospital I am escorted by Ed Stucker, a guard I met at Leavenworth and who escorted me to Alcatraz on the long train trip.

"Ray, why are you hanging around over there in isolation? Everyone is telling Meathead to let you out but he says you refuse to come out."

"That's all bullshit!" I reply, aware that Stucker is feeling me out on the subject. "I'll come out but I won't work in the laundry!"

A few hours later I'm placed on idle status in general population. I hesitate but the screw reassures me. "Don't worry. You won't be working in the laundry! Things are running too smoothly down there, we don't want you around starting trouble."

When I round the corner of the cellblock it's "Bullethead," not Meathead, who sits at the interview desk. Captain Weinholt begins briskly. "Karpis, Mr. Miller told me to assign you to the kitchen." An image of Meathead when he sent me to the hole for refusing to scab jumps to mind—the "goon squad" surrounding me, and Meathead's threats echoing loudly in the empty cell house.

"Where is Mr. Miller?"
"He's busy," is the gruff reply.

Alcatraz, 1943

I spent most of 1942 in isolation because I refused to scab. As I sit idle in my cell for the first week of 1943, I wonder what the coming year holds in store for me.

Basil, the "Owl" Banghart (AZ-595), the famous member of the Touhy mob who I was expecting to see in isolation the day Bob Stroud entered unexpectedly, is brought alone on a transfer.

I'm working in the kitchen when, about 10:00 A.M., Meathead has me brought out to the front where two civilians are waiting.
"These men want to talk to you Karpis," he says. Noticing the look on my face, he adds quickly, "No, they ain't the FBI!"
"I'm the chief inspector for immigration in this area," explains one of my visitors. "We think you should be deported."
"I think so too!" I respond eagerly.
"You don't want to get a lawyer to fight this?"
"Hell no! I've got my birth certificate from St. Vincent de Paul parish in Montreal. The fastest way I'm going to get out of jail is if I'm deported to Canada."
I'm happy when the warrant for deportation is placed in my jacket; however, it reads "when released from custody" so I'm no closer to freedom.

A con begins work in the kitchen. "Moonface" Carolla (AZ-610) is a former syndicate bodyguard who eyes me suspiciously whenever our paths cross. He was escorting Johnny Lazia one evening in Kansas City, Missouri, back in 1934, to a parked car when another automobile came screeching around the corner spitting machine-gun bullets. Moonface, in spite of his bulky body, dove under his own car instinctively but Lazia died instantly, riddled with lead.

The next day the chief of police gave out the story to the newspapers that it was myself and Freddie Barker who eliminated Lazia due to a disagreement over some gambling houses.

April, 1943

When I hear where Freddie Hunter expects to escape from, I can't believe it. The old mat shop again. It's now used for storage since the completion of the new industries building but Freddie and the others plan to use it as an exit to the water.

The others involved are Harold Brest (AZ-467), Jimmy Boarman (AZ-571), and the individual who escaped detection when Cretzer, Kyle, and Barkdoll made their attempt from the same building, Floyd Hamilton.

The plan is similar to the one used by Cretzer, Kyle, and Barkdoll but an electric motor drill specially constructed for the occasion will ensure that the bars on the windows are eliminated beforehand.

I hear the details from Freddie Hunter as I hand him the money he requested sealed in the false bottom of a box of matches. "B-B-Boarman is imp-p-p-patient t-to g-go fa-fast b-b-but the r-r-rest of us w-w-want to w-w-wait f-f-for f-f-fog." The other three work out a compromise with Boarman; he'll wait ten days for a foggy day but, if there is no fog before then, he'll go regardless. The dispute puts pressure on their plans. So, when a fog comes up three or four days later I'm watching from the bake-shop window in the kitchen, and the New York guys pack around me, our noses pressing against the window, like children witnessing the first snowfall of winter.

The fog started after daylight, but it might lift any time now. As the day brightens and I see the water from the bake-shop window up on the hill, I hope they have held off but my hopes vanish as fast as the dispersing fog when I see Bloodhound Johnson run out, peer toward the water, and raise his rifle.

Now I see the two bobbing figures in the misty waters as

the siren sets up a wail at their attempt to desert the Rock. Gunfire sprays down on two men from the towers and rooftops of Alcatraz and army picket boats rush toward the scene followed by a coastguard cutter with a machine gun mounted on the bow. The prison launch rounds the corner of the island and the entire regatta closes in on two men clutching at each other in the midst of the watery turmoil. The Golden Gate Bridge breaks through the milky horizon as if on cue.

Realizing the escape is a failure, I go down to the basement to take a shower. I'm getting dressed when the news reaches me. Boarman is dead, shot in the water. Hamilton is also reported shot and drowned by old Doctor Ritchie who was watching on the yard wall. Brest is wounded and lying in the hospital after being fished from the water by the prison launch.

Freddie Hunter is still missing but believed to be hiding in a cave on the rocky side of the island. Blood is splattered at the entrance to the cave below the mat shop but the screws are waiting for the tide to go out before investigating the interior.

As the launch approached Brest in the water he was holding Boarman in his arms, who had been shot through the head. As the limp body of Boarman was hooked by the belt and pulled up toward the deck of the boat, the belt snapped and the man who was impatient to escape from Alcatraz plunged into the grasp of the vicious undercurrents never to surface.

Freddie Hunter hears the voices of the searchers as they enter the cave where he crouches, neck-deep in water, hidden amongst the debris of old tires floating on the surface. "I hope I catch that s.o.b. in here! I always wanted an excuse to get at him!" Meathead breaks off his threats abruptly as he catches sight of Freddie among the floating rubble and begins blasting wildly with a .45 automatic in the direction of the cowering con. The gun shots and Meathead's curses echo in deafening tones off the cave walls. Meathead jumps on top of Hunter dragging him by the hair from the water, kicking crazily at his twisting body. The other guards have to pull Meathead off the fatigued escapee.

When Hunter and the others began their exit, they overpowered the guard in charge of their work detail in the mat shop. Ironically, who should arrive in the midst of the escape but Bullethead himself, Captain Weinholt. Once again Weinholt is captured and tied up by escaping prisoners. After the four cons slipped from the back window of the old building and scrambled toward the misty water's edge, Weinholt succeeded in working the gag loose from his mouth and began shouting for help. Bert MacDonald (AZ-115), working outside the building, heard his cries for help and ran immediately to the ripsaw beside the building. The scream of the saw soon drowned out Bullethead.

A couple of days after the attempted escape Weinholt makes a round of the now sealed-off mat shop, no doubt recalling the embarrassment of his second capture and promising himself once more that it will never happen again. He stops rigid. In the middle of the deserted building a ghost confronts him, an image from the misty moment of escape a few days before—the deceased Floyd Hamilton, still wet from his return out of the depths of the bay, blocks Weinholt's path. Hamilton, however, is unaware of the captain's presence; he is lying, huddled against the warm radiator, lost in the sleep of a man physically and mentally exhausted.

Bullethead kicks Hamilton into consciousness. "What the fuck are you doing here?"

"I was too cold and hungry down in the cave."

"Cave? Were you in that cave?"

"Yeah!"

"C'mon with me!"

Up in the hospital Dr. Ritchie is given the live body of the man he swore he saw shot and drowned to check over before it is thrown in the hole.

Hamilton mistook the searchlights and picket boats along the submarine net as part of a continuing search for him. He had remained in the cave after Meathead pulled

Hunter out of the water a few feet from where Hamilton watched, concealed behind floating debris. Cold, hungry, and tired, he climbed up to the mat shop to get warm but accidently fell asleep next to the radiator.

August, 1943

It's a Saturday and the five or six guards on the wall are watching for trouble on the yard. None of them notice Ted Walters (AZ-536), the fall partner of Floyd Hamilton, slip from his duties down in the laundry, crawl to the corner of the building, scramble over the fence and drop to the water's edge.

It's a bright, sunny day and it's doubtful if he can swim to shore without being observed, but he never makes it into the water. The whistle blows announcing his escape and, as it does, he slips on the steep rocky shoreline falling to the boulders beneath. He limps painfully along the island's shoreline nursing an injured spine until the screws arrive to haul him back to the cell house.

7

Alcatraz, 1944

The war creates personnel problems at Alcatraz. There are few able-bodied men available for guard duty, the officials running the prison system become more and more desperate and even resort to advertising in the San Francisco papers. Many ex-servicemen wounded in the war are hired and even some ex-convicts last a few weeks, until their records are checked out. These non-professionals are responsible for some unique episodes.

Jack Horner, an ex-diver from the navy, had been brought up from underwater too fast during a bombing at Anzio beachhead. He got the bends. He finds himself in deeper water around Alcatraz and his efforts to stay afloat in the turbulent administration of the penal system seem almost as painful as his navy experience. He is always handing out gum, candy, and cigarettes to the cons, treating them as people and forgetting about the rules. During his last day on the Rock he scolds the other screws in the mess hall: "I'm quitting today! I can see some hope for some of these cons but I can't see no hope for any of you s.o.b.s standing here doing this to them!"

Horner is a big bastard and not one to take any bullshit: no one challenges his opinion.

The barracks for the solders manning the anti-aircraft guns are on the roof of the hospital; their attitude toward the cons is friendly. Whenever possible they throw cigarettes and sandwiches down into the yard and exchange casual stories.

Punch-Drunk Pepper marches along the wall, practicing manual arm movements with his rifle. He attempts, between his private drill practice, to write up the soldiers for fraternizing with the prisoners. The servicemen respond bluntly, "Go fuck yourself! Get away from here!"

The wall screw outside the bake-shop window is hired off skid row. He cradles a machine gun with a twenty-shot clip in his arms. From time to time he stops suddenly, as though a voice had whispered in his ear, and turns sharply as if "throwing down" on someone.

One day myself and the others are yanked out of the bake shop. We are told, "There's a shot came out of this bakery!"

"No!"

"Yes!"

"How? Are there any windows broken?"

Investigation proves that the screw patrolling back of the bake shop had fired the shot accidently. Although he denies it initially, he has no explanation for the missing bullet from his cartridge or the acrid smell of his weapon.

When the first one descends with its deafening drone, I am shocked but it takes me several minutes before I realize there's more than one plane and they are attacking the island. They swarm from every direction and the cons and guards alike scatter under their low nose dives across the yard. One comes so close that the telephone line from the building to the tower is severed in two and torn off its post.

The first hint I have suggesting the onslaught is a harmless military maneuver, rather than the real thing, is the image of Warden Johnston standing on the wall waving frantically at the planes to cease their activities. His shouts are lost in the echoing roar resounding from the buildings. They pay no attention to him. The military reports later that, had the attack been real, they would have lost seven planes but the island would have been completely destroyed.

The "girls" prance onto the yard and the boys begin buzzing. Heads turn; eyes meet. I sit on the stone steps watching the newest shipment of kids from Leavenworth. Their reputations arrived in advance of them. Most were in Springfield before Leavenworth where prison psychiatrists tried bizarre experiments with the youngsters scooped out of the major federal prisons where they were known "nic nacs".

In Springfield they were allowed to wear lipstick, nylon stockings, and to perform "drag shows," all under the auspices of psychiatrists and staff. One of the young arrivals stands out above the others and he knows it. Paul Davis (AZ-577), a fellow kitchen-worker, knew him in Leavenworth when the kid was only about eighteen or nineteen, before he was sent to the Springfield experiment.

"That's the 'China Doll,' I've been hot for her since the first time I saw her in the Big Top!" He points out the youngster with slanted eyes who does look like a portrait of a young Chinese girl although, in fact, Ed Reyes (AZ-628) is a little Mexican kid. He began his criminal career with a six-month sentence out of the army in the disciplinary barracks near Leavenworth. He was soon in trouble and sent to the Big Top, from there to Springfield, back to Leavenworth and now is one of the 300 most dangerous criminals in the U.S.A.

The China Doll gets a job in the cell house, thus every afternoon as I finish my duties in the bake shop, I sit on the steps with my fellow kitchen workers watching him and other cons playing softball on the yard. One day he breaks off from his softball game and everyone watches as he walks over to sit down beside me.

"You're the chief baker, I hear?"

"Yeah."

"Have you got a girlfriend?"

"What do you mean?"

"Hell, you're not stupid," he laughs. "You know what I mean. All us guys in from Leavenworth are 'works'. You know, Paul Davis keeps trying to get me to come back to the kitchen with him, but he don't appeal to me. I don't want nothin' to do with him!"

"No, I don't have a girlfriend."

"Well then we're going to get married and start playin'

house back in your bake shop but I'll tell you right now, I'm strictly a 'girl', no polishing the knob (blow jobs). When I get out, I'm goin' to have an operation and really be a girl!"

I'm flattered, and accept the China Doll's proposition, or as he might prefer, proposal.

Paul Davis has encouraged the stewards and officials to allow the China Doll to work in the kitchen since he arrived on the island, thus when the kid shows up with his work-change slip, it's not surprising that the screw on duty takes it and points in the direction of Davis, as if to say "There's your old man!"

The kid walks past Davis, deliberately ignoring him and comes to sit beside me at the help's table. His first question is, "When can we get together?"

Later that day, Paul Davis descends to the basement print shop. On the point outside the print shop he encounters Harry Brunette (AZ-374) who watches the steps for any sign of a guard. Davis knows the China Doll and I are inside. He's obviously upset, but with the large frame of Brunette, who was once a golden-glove champion, blocking the entrance, he just stomps back upstairs.

Our affair continues for months. As soon as Reyes finishes his work in the dining room, he comes to visit me in the bake shop although usually we use the print shop for sexual action because it is more secure. The China Doll isn't my first prison romance and won't be my last. Most prisoners accept whatever sex is available to them rather than doing without it altogether.

I'm in the basement, washing up. As the coat of soap rinses down my face and I blink the water droplets off my eye lashes, Paul Davis comes into focus. Standing directly in front of me, a homemade shiv extends from his closed fist.

"You son of a bitch—" he starts out.

"Look, are you crazy?" I interrupt hastily, thinking fast. "What's wrong? Do you think I'm having a romance with that kid?"

Primed for action, Davis hesitates when forced to formulate his emotions into verbal logic. "The guys say I should kill you over this!"

"Even if I was romancing with the kid, it's got nothing to do with you or me personally. It's his decision, not yours or mine!"

A few minutes of conversation and Davis hands me the shiv he was going to use to kill me, asking if I'll dispose of it for him.

While the main line eats upstairs in the dining hall, myself, the China Doll, and a few other friends are drinking and talking in the bake shop. Davis, obviously drunk on home brew, breaks into the party. "Ray, if its alright with you, I want to talk to Reyes for a minute alone?"

"Sure," I agree.

The two go to the back of the bake shop and around a corner. Soon the rumble is heard and I shout to one of the other cons, "Get on the point!" As I walk back to investigate, I find a fight which seems somewhat unfair considering that Davis weighs about fifty or sixty pounds more than the China Doll. However, at second sight, I notice both of Davis's eyebrows are cut by the flying fists of Reyes as he systematically tears Davis apart. Blinded with blood from the open gashes across his eyes, Davis is a pathetic sight but continues to fight. I stop the fight then wash Davis up and try to stop the bleeding.

The next morning Davis's blackened eyes and battered face are the talk of the kitchen while the China Doll proudly rubs in his victory by loudly demanding mercurochrome from the screw for his scraped knuckles.

Father Clark, the Jesuit priest who was the Catholic chaplain at Alcatraz, has been serving with the air force during the war. He returns for a half-day visit and stops to speak to me. "I ran into Charlie Fusco, fighting overseas, as well as many other ex-cons from Alcatraz. He asked me to say 'hello' to you. You know Ray, it's a wonder all you fellows didn't end up detesting me. I've learned a lot about human nature and what makes people tick during the war."

Father Clark is right—he has changed drastically from the suspicious personality of the prewar years when he verged on being a policeman. "Tell the guys I'm nothing like I was!"

Christmas Day, 1944

I'm climbing the stairs from the print shop, suffering from a hangover, when I overhear Suitcase Simpson talking casually to another screw in the kitchen.

"Did you have a pretty good Christmas?" asks the screw.

"The best—I got two cartons of Camels," brags Suitcase.

I chuckle to myself—only a month earlier I had five cartons of king size Pall Malls smuggled in to me in spite of the war rationing.

Alcatraz, 1945

Joe Isenburg (AZ-760) is on point watching the steps that lead from the basement to the kitchen above. When the screw's pant leg appears on the top step he instantly knocks a warning to his companions and then stands blocking the door which leads to an ancient freezer stored in the basement. It's a big unused empty box six feet long, four feet high, and four feet wide.

Burdette, a huge screw from Joplin, Missouri, has been transferred to Alcatraz from Springfield where he was one of the "Night Raiders," the Springfield "goon squad". He saw Joe come down to the basement with two friends, "Miss America" and Jimmy Lucas. Knowing Lucas's reputation as a "little girl," Burdette realizes that the pair are in the large rectangular container.

"Joe, get outta the way! I wanta look in that icebox!"

"You big son of a bitch! You ain't about to look in this icebox! If you try there's goin' to be some trouble here!" Joe, standing only five foot, four inches, looks up at the burly Burdette.

"I'll tell you what Joe. I know they're in there! I'm goin' up to my desk and sit down. I want all three of you fellas up there in ten minutes!"

The three cons climb sheepishly out of the basement a few minutes later. Although Burdette, a tolerant type, doesn't report the incident officially, it is soon the talk of the joint and from that day forward Jimmy Lucas is referred to as "Icebox Annie".

President Roosevelt dies shortly following his re-election and Vice-President Truman takes his place. To the inhabitants of two Japanese cities it means atomic doom as Truman gives the orders to drop the bombs; to Tom Robinson (AZ-379), it means a rebirth since Truman commutes his death sentence to life for the kidnapping of Alice Speed Stole and he is returning to the Rock with a new number (AZ-709).

Robinson had originally pled guilty on the kidnapping charge and received only a prison term. He had been working in a garage when Alice Speed Stole discovered him. As he described the events to me, and I believe every word of his story, it was only a matter of time before she had him delivering her car and picking it up for repairs.

He had suggested to her one day, as she complained that the "Colonel" wasn't sufficiently generous with his wealth, that they pull off a hoax and pretend to kidnap her. She agreed and they collected $45,000 ransom. With the money in hand, Tom grew bored with Alice and fled to Los Angeles where he lived with a young girl while he himself became a female impersonator. He was caught, tried, and sent to Alcatraz.

It was not until he hired the famous attorney, Jake Erlich, who wrote the book entitled *Never Plead Guilty*, that Tom Robinson found his life threatened. The lawyer had his original sentence repealed and Tom was returned for a new trial on the kidnapping charge.

This time Robinson told the true story which made sensational headlines but the southern jury refused to believe him even when it was proven that the pair were checking into tourist camps together during the alleged kidnapping. They decided he contrived the story to smear the reputation of a prominent southern lady in an attempt to gain his freedom. They not only found him guilty of kidnapping again, they gave him the death penalty for it.

Roosevelt may have decided to spare the Japanese had he lived, but he never would have spared Tom Robinson because Roosevelt was a personal friend of the Stole family.

Because I enjoy country and western music, I decide to learn steel guitar. Barkdoll teaches me chord construction, inversions, dotted eighths and other theory on paper. I learn fast and become very proficient on steel guitar.

It's years later when a kid approaches me while I'm resting on the grandstand at McNeil Island to request music lessons. He wants to learn guitar and become a music star. "Little Charlie" is so lazy and shiftless, I doubt if he'll put in the time required to learn. He's always in trouble with the officials because he won't shave or get up on time in the morning. He's in the same dormitory as I am so I usually have to wake him or he'll lose his job.

The youngster has been in institutions all his life—first orphanages, then reformatories and finally a federal prison. His mother, a prostitute, was never around to look after him. I decide it's time someone did something for him and to my surprise, he learns quickly. He has a pleasant voice and a pleasing personality although he's unusually meek and mild for a convict. He never has a harsh word to say and is never involved in even an argument.

He and some other kids in McNeil belong to the Church of Scientology, a religious cult which Charlie attempts to persuade me to join. "If you believe strong enough that you can do something, you can do it!" he explains, but I decline his invitation.

When Charlie is getting good on guitar and vocals and also "getting short," he asks me to send him to some contacts in Reno or Las Vegas to get a job. His kind of music is not mine, he likes "rock 'n roll" which is probably in more demand than country and western. Other prisoners, all good friends of mine, are Frankie Carbo, Mickey Cohen, and

Dave Beck who have connections with nightclubs in Las Vegas. I think seriously about using my influence to get him started in the entertainment business.

My decision in the end is to leave him on his own, if he has the talent he'll make it to the top. The history of crime in the United States might have been considerably altered if "Little Charlie" had been given the opportunity to find fame and fortune in the music industry. He later becomes infamous as Charles Manson.

May, 1945

Fire boats in San Francisco Bay shoot out long streams of water, sirens blow throughout the city, the war in Europe is over.

Alcatraz, 1946

As 1946 begins, there is no obvious outward tension but "escape" is once again the whispered word in the cold cells at Alcatraz.

Joe Cretzer is fresh out of isolation where he has been since his attempt to escape with Kyle and Barkdoll. He's a bitter, angry man, predestined to escape, or die trying. I meet him while walking to the library.

"Why don't you come back to work in the kitchen?" I suggest. "We get lots to eat there."

"No thanks! I've got my own plans. I'm goin' to be over in San Francisco eating steaks and drinking champagne!"

I know what he's referring to: another escape attempt. I was asked if I wanted a ticket out but I refused when I heard that Coy (AZ-415) was involved. His lack of judgement, when he used a stool pigeon as a lookout and had to confess to sawing out a bar in the kitchen, convinces me I want no part of anything in which he is involved.

Coy has a reputation as a marksman, having been trained as a sniper in the army. He's thirty-five years old, broad-shouldered, rough and rugged. His job is in the cell house distributing magazines.

In addition to Coy and Cretzer, Hubbard (AZ-645) has come to work in the kitchen strictly so he can be up on the hill where the escape route is planned. He's a mild, quiet-spoken man about thirty-six years of age who wears glasses. Beneath his placid exterior churns a hatred, beaten into him at the same time his confession was beaten out of him following his capture.

An Indian youth, Joe Carnes (AZ-714) has been associating lately with the others. He's a primitive kid; emotional, gullible, and naive. Miran Thompson (AZ-729), serving two consecutive ninety-nine-year sentences for kidnapping and murder, is also involved in the escape attempt.

The sixth participant is poor semi-literate little Sam Shockley who comes from a sharecropper family in Oklahoma. He's the same hero worshipper who was mistakenly suspected as the fourth accomplice when Cretzer, Kyle, and Barkdoll attempted to escape. Sam is a borderline case who should be in a hospital for the retarded.

Thursday is the day. On Thursdays the gun-cage screw enters the new D block, which is now sealed off from the main cell house, to watch from above while the screw in D block searches the fresh laundry for contraband. Thursday is the only day the laundry arrives in D block and, thus, the only day that the cell-house screw is left alone in the main cell house over lunch hour.

May 2, 1946

The majority of cons are down in the industries at work. The only ones left on the hill are the few working around the cell house or in the kitchen. Most of the kitchen guys opt to go out on the yard as they finish their duties although they are permitted to return to their cells if they prefer.

It's a beautiful sunny day. I stand looking out the kitchen windows, wondering whether I should stay in my cell or go out on the yard. Today is Thursday—*the* Thursday. My thoughts are broken by a voice from behind.

"You goin' to the yard Ray?" It's Hubbard, the look in his eyes is disguised behind the sun reflecting on his spectacles.

"How about you?" I respond.

"I'm goin' to my cell," he smiles.

We walk together to the gate separating the dining hall and the cell house. I ring the bell for Mr. Miller, the cellhouse screw (no relation to Meathead), who opens it after a wave from Burdette the kitchen screw, who must signal his approval before anyone leaves the kitchen area.

As I step inside the cell house, the first face I encounter is Coy's. He's casually talking to Miller while making his rounds of cells with the magazines. I make a snap decision. "I'm going to my cell!"

Miller racks back my cell door and Hubbard's. Coy walks with Hubbard to his cell but then, after our cell doors have been closed by the mechanism operated by Miller at the end of the cell house, Coy checks both directions on the deserted Broadway before yelling, "Mr. Miller! Hubbard changed his mind. Now he wants to go to the yard."

Miller laughs good-naturedly as he racks open Hubbard's door, cons are always changing their minds. As Coy and Hubbard round the corner of the cellblock where Miller waits to let them onto the yard, they pounce on him, yank the key ring off his belt and throw him in a cell on the outside of C block. The escape is on!

My cell is along the flats on Broadway only five down from the kitchen end of the cell house where Miller was captured. Coy and Hubbard flash across the top of Broadway, a homemade bar-spreader dangles from Coy's hand. He climbs to the top of the gun cage, spreads the bars, drops onto the third tier of the deserted gun cage and begins crawling toward the D block door beyond which, unaware that he is being stalked, Mr. Burch, the gun-cage screw, watches the search of the laundry below.

Mr. Corwin, the D block screw, looks up suddenly from the pile of laundry he and Louis Fleish (AZ-574) are sorting.

Fleish is the D block orderly, a member of Detroit's Purple Gang. Burch should be sitting on his stool in the gun cage. Corwin yells "What's the matter? Where you at Burch?"

Muffled sounds answer his shouts. Corwin grabs for the telephone on the wall, but a large hand covers his and the voices of Louis Fleish snarls in his ear, "You leave that phone alone!"

The door in the gun cage from D block eases open as Coy slips back into the main cell house armed with the gun-cage firearms. He drops the rifle and the pistol down to Hubbard who whispers loudly once he has secured them, "O.K., Joe, I've got them!"

Joe Cretzer shouts from his cell, "Get this door open!"

Moments later while Coy watches down Broadway for any officials who might enter unexpectedly from the administration end of the building, Cretzer and Hubbard fumble through the eight or nine keys taken from Mr. Miller. None of them will open the door leading to the yard. They enter the cell where Miller is held prisoner and shake it down. No key. I hear a sharp hoarse scream explode from Miller, then silence.

Miller opens and shuts the yard door so frequently, he keeps that key separate from the others for his own convenience. It's always been a mystery to me why Coy didn't remember that. By now Miller has disposed of it and the escape route through the yard is blocked off.

Thompson and young Carnes are let out of their cells and join the other three escapees. They are free in the cell house, armed, but unable to get out. Joe shakes his head at me in disgust.

Then danger! Blackie Audette comes walking through the dining hall toward the cell-house door, behind him, at the other end of the dining hall, Burdette the kitchen screw leans sloppily against the steam tables waiting to signal Miller that Audette can go to the yard. I signal to Cretzer on my fingers.

When Audette reaches the gate to the cell house, he stares at the muzzle end of Cretzer's gun. Realizing what he has stepped into, Blackie starts back toward the kitchen.

Burdette calls him over as he returns, talks to him briefly, then begins to approach the cell-house gate suspiciously as Audette scrambles back into the kitchen. Burdette didn't believe the excuse uttered by Blackie for deciding to stay in the kitchen but he doesn't expect to see Cretzer armed with a rifle when he reaches the barred door. He is captured with a stunned look frozen on his face and thrown into the cell with Miller.

1:52 P.M.

Bristow, the Chief Steward, enters the cellblock from the administration end of Broadway. He joins Miller, Corwin, and Burdette.

A few minutes later, Hubbard is watching in the cell house, armed, when two cons attempt to return from the basement where they have been getting their hair cut. They stop at the top of the steps behind a caged stairway, look at Hubbard, and then behind them at Stucker, the screw in charge of the basement area. Stucker is waiting for Miller to open the door. When he doesn't appear and the two cons return, the basement screw comes to the top of the steps to see what is wrong. After a quick glance, he rushes back to the basement to call the front office.

Released from their cages by their free companions, twelve to fifteen cons pour out of D block. A con comes down from D block to take charge. "Go get the ladder!" he orders.

They congregate under the gun cage exchanging viewpoints about how to get out of the cellblock. The one who has taken charge climbs the ladder to the gun cage, holding his hand over his face to prevent any stool pigeons in their cells from being able to identify him later.

He decides it's a bust. The escapees from D block return to their cells including the mysterious participant from B block who, even I, did not realize was involved. He's none other than Floyd Hamilton who once again evades detection during an escape attempt.

Lageson enters the cell house, rounds the corner at the end of Broadway, is captured and placed in cell 403.

Coy, in desperation, grabs the rifle. He scrambles back to a kitchen window and proceeds to shoot each of the tower guards off their perches. The guards on the walls are forced flat on their stomachs as the bullets buzz past them, but unaware of who is shooting or from where, they remain immobile, unable to reach their telephones for help or instruction.

Sundstrom is next to come down Broadway on his way back to the kitchen. He nods as he passes my cell only a few seconds before walking unexpectedly into a gun barrel.

Phones begin ringing hysterically in the cell house, up in the towers, and back in the kitchen. Unheeded they eventually peter out but shortly afterwards a mountainous figure appears down at the administration end of the cellblock and lumbers heavily toward our end. The bulky form is unmistakable as it storms toward me checking each cell. It is accompanied by a second figure who examines the cells on the other side of Broadway.

As Suitcase Simpson passes by he gives me a dirty look before swaggering around the corner of the cellblock. Instantly his shoulders sag when the forty-five automatic is shoved into his fat gut. Both he and his companion, a big six-foot screw named Baker, are taken captive.

With the cells on the outside of C block overflowing with hostages, another figure slips stealthily down Broadway. Captain Weinholt, his expression hard with suspicion, slides past my cell and into the same ambush that awaited the others. Cretzer greets him enthusiastically. "Good day captain, you son of a bitch! Take off your coat!" Weinholt begins to argue but is silenced by a powerful fist in his face. "Your pants too!"

Stripped of clothing, dignity, and spirit, the captain is whisked to the cells overflowing with his subordinates. "There's one son of a bitch I forgot to shoot!" utters Coy and disappears again into the dining hall. He goes to the window on the opposite side of the kitchen and lines up the tower guard down on the dock in the sights of his rifle.

Oblivious to the events in the cell house Comerford, known as "the sharecropper," is sitting in his tower overlooking the workers on the dock when the leg of his stool is splintered by a rifle bullet which then collapses under his weight. Coy, looking like a clown in his oversized screw's clothing, returns to the cell house. "I've hit everyone of those sons of bitches! We can't give up now."

"Yeah, it's fucked! They'll be in here any minute now," agrees Cretzer. "Go back to your cells, we'll lock you up again."

Carnes and Thompson immediately go back to their cells. Hubbard, Cretzer, and Coy decide to shoot it out to the death. Sam Shockley wants to stay with them but Cretzer convinces the close-to-retarded little Sam to go back to his cell in D block.

No sooner have the three been safely locked in their cells than the siren sends a chilling whistle through the cellblock and over the entire island community. Ironically it is announcing the first official recognition of the jailbreak at the very moment those involved have given up any hopes of escape.

"That's it," sighs Joe Cretzer as he and Coy leave Hubbard with the rifle surveying Broadway for the screws. Cretzer is carrying the .45 pistol as he leads the way to the hostage cells. A few seconds later a succession of shots resounds from the direction where Cretzer and Coy disappeared. When he emerges, Cretzer looks over in my direction and says on his fingers in sign language, "They're all dead!"

Now a hissing noise from Hubbard, who is watching down Broadway. Someone is entering the cell house from the administration end of the building. In his coat and cap, stolen from the screws who float in pools of blood on the floor of the hostage cells, Hubbard starts up Broadway to meet the newest intruder. The rifle lies flat against his body, its barrel blending with his brogans.

Hubbard is now parallel with my cell, his muscles rigid like a western gunfighter. The figure at the other end of Broadway steps slowly into the long corridor. For a moment they eye each other then the rifle at Hubbard's side spins upward in a blurring motion, exploding once only from the hip in a blast which rips the silence. At the other end of the cell house, the target turns and runs for the door leading back into the front offices, followed by echoes of the loud shot.

As the man scrambles for safety, he slams into a beam setting off a gas gun tucked inside his suit pocket. The coat burst into flames and the explosion leaves powder burns on the side of the man's face. As the gate slams behind the retreating figure Hubbard yells back to the others, "That was Meathead!"

Realizing they are dead men, the three mavericks look for a fortress they can call their "Alamo". "Where can we hole up?"

"Let's sell out the best we can!"

"Yeah, we'll take as many of them bastards with us as we can!"

They decide on the utility corridor between the cells of C block. The plumbing and air vents from the cells on both sides are serviced by a utility corridor running between the cells. It's enclosed on the outside and on the roof of the cellblock but open for three storeys inside. They take shelter, and await the inevitable rush of guards: three cons, one rifle, and one pistol.

The first explosion is a shock to everyone waiting inside for the showdown. The rifle grenade explodes against the outside wall of D block and is followed by others in accelerando until the roar is reverberating through our bones. For some reason the officials are bombarding D block unaware that the escape is a bust and the last few culprits are safely sheltered in the C block utility corridor. The artillery attack continues late into the evening as the light grows dim and dies in the semi-deserted cell house.

Out in the yard the main population huddles close to the walls, cold and hungry. They have been brought up from the industries and herded into the stone enclosure for safety.

About 1:00 A.M. there is an outburst of small arms. In the midst of the shooting, I hear a rifle blasting from inside the utility corridor as the screws come charging into the gun cages at both ends of the cell house.

The rhythmic stomp of their boots extends to every inch

of the gun cages, grows loudly up the basement steps, and thumps through the gate from the front offices. The steady drill-like movements can be heard in the corridor between A and B blocks as the screws methodically regain territory lost to the enemy, cell by cell.

"Where are you men at?" The voice is Lieutenant Faulk's. "Are you still alive?"

The answer comes in wheezing gasps from Sundstrom. "We're locked up over in C block on the flats. Cells number 403 and 402." He pauses for breath. "Some in here are dead! Others are hurt bad!"

Faulk's voice snarls murderously, "Where are those sons of bitches at?"

"They're in the servitory between C block!"

"Stay away from the air vents. We'll get you out of there."

The conversation is interrupted by another outburst of firing. On my right two screws dash across Broadway with a stretcher heading for the cells described by Sundstrom. Above them screws are lined along the gun cages, rifles and machine guns sticking out like porcupine quills. Another squad files in from the dining hall were they have secured the kitchen area.

Sundstrom is the first hostage led across Broadway supported on each side by a screw. He's followed by about half a dozen stretchers straining under heavy bodies. Bristow, the steward, walks across by himself. They are taken immediately to fast torpedo boats which rush them to hospitals on the mainland.

The hostages are clear of the cell house. Guards secure all areas but two: the utility corridor housing the last of the desperadoes and D block which they still believe is involved in the escape.

Faulk issues a challenge to the three in the servitory; his voice is calm. "Alright you sons of bitches. You may as well go ahead and stick your necks out now. Get it over with. You ain't goin' to eat or sleep until you have it out with us. You ain't goin' to get off; we ain't goin' t' let you give up. Yer all dead!"

In the silent hours that follow, I fall asleep exhausted. It's the drilling of jackhammers through the ceiling above the utility corridor which awakens me. Three or four holes are drilled along the length of the narrow corridor where the three survivors hold out.

Meathead is now issuing the orders; he calls the men by name: "Coy! Cretzer! Hubbard! Throw them guns overboard and come out with your hands up or we'll kill all of you!"

Silence greets him. "If you don't come out, we'll drop explosives down these holes we just drilled."

"Mr. Miller, there are a lot of innocent men in here!"

"Who is that talking?"

"Hillard!"

"Where you at?"

"I'm in my cell on the third gallery."

"Fuck you! Stay in there. All you s.o.b.s in your cells cover yourselves up best you can."

Three or four minutes later the hand grenades begin to fall. They drop through the holes, rattling off pipes and walls, exploding five seconds from release. The explosions in the narrow corridor echo loudly across the cell house. With each burst the water bounces out of the toilets in the cells. Not all the grenades make it between the cells, some bounce off into the cell house sending shrapnel in every direction. Before the barrage has ended, I collect two matchboxes of shrapnel off the floor of my cell.

When they run out of hand grenades, Meathead offers the convicts a second opportunity to surrender. Again the answer is silence.

Next, tear gas bombs are thrown down into the narrow corridor housing the would-be escapees. Smoke smothers the cell house. I can't breathe, the tears flow from my eyes as I attempt to cover my hands and face with vaseline to prevent the burning, I belch and choke streams of vomit into my toilet bowl.

The vomit flies back from the bowl as a new supply of hand grenades drops into the utility corridor. The concussion bombs dry out the toilets.

May 3, 1946, 1:00 P.M.

"Those bastards must be dead by now!"

"Why don't we find out?"

As screws in the gun cage cover the door at my end of C block leading into the utility corridor, it is unlocked and jerked open. Immediately a shot rings out and a bullet comes from the dark corridor hitting the wall just above Meathead's desk. The door is quickly slammed shut.

In the lull which follows, I hear planes circling over the roof of the cellblock. The Rock smokes like a sinking battleship on San Francisco Bay and a simple attempt to escape is labeled a three-day riot in the mainland newspapers.

2:00 P.M.

State officials in civilian clothes huddle in buzzing groups with guards. Marksmen from San Quentin arrive with machine guns equipped with fifty-shot drums. They decide to riddle the corridor.

A smoke bomb is thrown in and, as the smoke rises from the corridor, the official in charge nods to a waiting marksman. The door is yanked open. Standing five feet from the entrance, the guard empties fifty shots into the corridor in a slow circular motion about three inches in diameter. He nods casually to the guard who slams the door shut. Then they repeat the procedure a second time, as methodically as spraying for insects.

Next the marines arrive. After a reconnaissance, they suggest that a marine sergeant wearing a bulletproof vest enter the corridor with a machine gun. Warden Johnston opposes the plan: "What if they get hold of his machine gun?"

They return to dropping concussion bombs. By the evening a new army shell has been brought over which penetrates concrete on contact. They drop these onto the cutoff below through which runs a tunnel connecting the utility corridor at the administration end of the cell house with the one at the kitchen end. The anti-tank equipment cuts through the concrete like a drill, the shell following it explodes inside.

Friday Evening, May 3, 1946

The outside door leading to the yard, which prevented the escape, finally opens and the guys on the yard, who have been outside all night are brought in and placed, several to a cell, in A block. As they cross Broadway their eyes overflow with tears; they are not used to the lingering tear gas as we are in the cell house.

Saturday, May 4, 1946
10:00 A.M.

Activity begins. Reinforcements from other federal prisons crowd into Alcatraz: Captain May from McNeil Island, Shuttleworth back from Leavenworth. Meathead leads three armed guards down Broadway; his face is livid with burns from the gas gun.

Then the rumors float through the cell house in ghostly whispers.

"They found those three guys and the guns. All three are dead."

Saturday Noon

Warden Johnston escorts a group of newsmen to his island office bragging about the courage of his guards. He releases a list of weapons used during the siege by his men:
1) Shotguns—12-gauge, Remington automatics.
2) Tear Gas Launchers—snubnosed barrel 1½ inches in diameter, mounted on a short stock. Operates on principle of Very pistol. Shoots two types of tear gas shells. One is long range (up to 200 yards), which explodes on contact; the other is a close range shooting gas for 50 feet directly out of the barrel.
3) Springfield .30-.06 rifles.

4) Garand M-1 rifles—.30-.06 caliber weapon of Marines and U.S. Army.
5) Pistols—.45 caliber semi-automatic.
6) Thompson submachine guns, fires 600-800 rounds per minute.
7) Carbines—15-shot semi-automatic weapons, .30 caliber.
8) Fragmentation Grenades—dropped through holes in the roof into the utility corridor in C block.
9) White Phosphorous Grenades—hinder breathing, hurt eyes, and conceal movement.
10) Rifle Grenades—penetrate armor or masonry. Shot into D block via windows and dropped through holes in the roof into the C cutoff area.

The bodies of the three convicts are dragged from the tunnel beneath the C block cutoff area. In Warden Johnston's words, "A pretty good foxhole, but we outfoxed them. Our attack drove them farther and farther back into the bowels of the block. At the end they were deeper in the Rock than any other prisoner ever had been before."

Coy, Cretzer, and Hubbard are found with one rifle and one pistol. Death, according to the autopsy surgeon, was instantaneous in all three cases. Goodsized rifle bullet holes; high velocity bullets.

In addition to the three convicts there are two dead guards, William A. Miller and Harold P. Stites. Miller died in the cell where he had slid the key sought by the desperate mutineers down the toilet bowl. Because he was only slightly wounded compared to the other hostages, he was one of the last to be rescued. He died of shock and loss of blood. Stites was shot by one of his fellow guards as he rushed into the gun cage during the recapturing of the cell house.

Among the injured bodies piled high in the hostage cells were Captain Weinholt and Lieutenant Simpson, two of the most hated members of the Alcatraz "goon squad". Although they both survive they never return to active duty at Alcatraz. After a slow recovery, they become eligible for disability retirement.

Other officers wounded in the escape attempt are: Roberts, Besk (shot in the leg in the Hill Tower), Richberger, Lageson, Cochrane (bullet-shattered arm), Baker, and Oldham. Thompson, Shockley, and Carnes are dragged from their cells and stripped. They are charged with the first-degree murder of Officer Miller and conspiracy to commit murder. On the walls of the hostage cell, their names, along with those of the three deceased convicts, are scribbled in blood.

November 20, 1946

The trial of Thompson, Shockley, and Carnes opens.

December 22, 1946

After fourteen hours of deliberation, a jury of six men and six women returns its verdict at 12:40 P.M. All are found "Guilty". Judge Goodman passes sentences: Death in San Quentin's gas chamber for Shockley and Thompson, and a life sentence for Carnes at the recommendation of the jury.

December 2, 1948, 10:00 A.M.

At 10:12 A.M. Dr. L. I. Stanley, the San Quentin physician listening to the heartbeats of Shockley and Thomspon through the remote stethoscope, pronounces them dead. In the green, octagonal glass and steel chamber with its two straight-back metal chairs, the steel and gas separates the two lifeless bodies from the gawking witnesses.

June, 1946

I lean over to light the oven in the bake shop; it explodes in my face. Momentarily blinded and startled, I instinctively back away from the flames only to discover I'm trapped in a back corner of the bakery, a wall of fire blocking the only exit. The fire hisses and smokes, stretching from floor to ceiling. I can't breathe as the oxygen is rapidly replaced by suffocating blankets of smoke. Oil is splattered over my body and face from the explosion. In a few seconds it will be too late to run. I have to go through the flames and climb three steps to a doorway to escape the spreading fire.

Throwing my hands over my face, I start the dash. Leaping, squirming, I manage to stumble out the doorway only to discover the oil on my skin has caught fire. My right hand is blazing, my nose is on fire, and my left ear is also in flames.

I smother the flames on my nose with my left hand, then those burning my ear, but I can't get the fire out on my hand. As I bash and bang my blazing arm against walls and floors, twisting and writhing in pain, the skin breaks wide open from the abuse but the flames continue to eat away at my flesh. Only when I grab a shirt and twist it around my arm do I succeed in extinguishing the fire. On my way up the steps leading from the basement, I meet a screw who rushes me to the hospital.

The relief doctor bandages me and gives me a stiff dose of morphine; a few hours later Lefty Egan, who had given Warden Johnston the nickname "Old Saltwater," visits me and starts talking but I'm in such a stupor from the morphine, I can hardly follow his conversation. A friendly orderly by the name of Smitty gives me an ice-cold glass of chocolate malted milk because he feels sorry for me. My burnt lips are puffed out one inch thick, but as I sip on the cold drink through a glass straw, I'm thankful to Smitty.

When I first start shaking, Lefty laughs and puts another blanket over me. By the time he places a second blanket on me, he's frowning at the bed shaking beneath me. Alarmed, he calls for the doctor who immediately diagnoses the problem. "He's going into bad shock! Get some more morphine!"

When the newest injection calms me, the doctor questions the MTA severely. "Did you give him the morphine I prescribed the first time? Has he had any other kind of medicine?"

Lefty, standing in the background confirms the MTA's report. "All the spook gave him was a malted milk."

"Malted milk!" screams the doctor, "Don't you know that milk is an antidote to any narcotics?"

I remain on morphine injections, every few hours for several days.

"Karpis, put on your bathrobe, there's someone out front to see you."

It's only been the last few days that I've been able to make the short walk to the window to look down on the yard. With a large scab on the end of my nose, shuffling painfully down the steps from the hospital and out to the visiting area in the cell house, I look a comic sight in my oversized bathrobe. Two FBI agents are waiting to see me.

"What is this?" I ask angrily.

"These fellows want to talk to you," explains Levinson, the screw who has unlocked the front gate for me.

"I don't want to talk to them!"

In the commotion which follows, Meathead is called. "I know how you feel," he says, "but talk to them, see if they can do you some good."

I reluctantly agree to hear them out. They begin with the usual bullshit, offering me a cigarette then asking me to sit down. "No! No!" I respond to both invitations.

"We can help you get away from here!" begins the agent. I know immediately he wants information and believes that, in my deteriorated condition, I might be desperate enough to offer it in hopes of escaping from Alcatraz. I turn to the screw.

"I want to go back to the hospital. Call Mr. Miller!"

"Hot Springs, Arkansas," tempts the agent. "Does that interest you?"

"No, I just want to go back upstairs."

"You don't even want to hear how you might get yourself out of here?" The agent's voice is full of disbelief.

"No!" I conclude the interview.

I learn later that an election is coming up in Hot Springs and the government is desperate to get the corrupt mayor out of office. So desperate, they are willing to make me an offer of freedom in return for incriminating him. I want out of prison but on my terms—not those of a stool pigeon.

Mid-August, 1946

I check out of the hospital and return to work in the bake shop.

Christmas Eve, 1946

Meathead is handing out the Christmas packages. He sends for me but I'm so drunk on home brew I tell the screw to bring it down to me.

Meathead won't have any of that. "No, tell him to come get it himself!"

When I stagger to his desk at the end of the cell house, he regrets his insistance. "Jesus, I should never have sent for you!" Handing me the package, he adds an abrupt, "Merry Christmas!"

8

Alcatraz, 1947

Following the breakout of 1946, several changes are made: Faulk becomes acting captain; intercoms are installed at strategic positions throughout the prison; and the armored plate on the gun cages is made bulletproof.

Screens are placed over the bars on the gun cage. (They make no difference and would never have hindered those involved in the 1946 breakout, but Bennett, the Director of Prisons, had made the recommendation previous to the escape attempt and was furious when he discovered his suggestion was never implemented. As he stormed around the smoke-filled cell house in the aftermath of the escape, his eyes watering from the tear gas, a stranger would have thought the missing mesh was a crucial element.)

Now there are four screws in the cellblock at all times including one lieutenant.

Harry Brunette receives some unexpected news in the spring of 1947. His transfer comes in for Leavenworth and he leaves immediately. I inherit the job of printer, the best job in the institution. I have no boss and am only responsible to Meathead. Barkdoll has the butcher job. We want to get Pappy Kyle back into the kitchen to include him on an escape we are planning from the print shop.

Barkdoll asks Meathead if Kyle can come back to the kitchen; Meathead immediately confronts me. "I'm putting

Kyle back here, but if he tries to get away and it has anything to do with this print shop, you'd better go with him!"

"Don't worry, if he gets away through the print shop, I'll go with him," I joke, but beneath my joke as with Meathead's warning, there is an undercurrent as serious as the one that surrounds the prison island in the middle of the bay.

One of Meathead's last acts as Deputy Warden of Alcatraz is placing Kyle back in the kitchen from where he, Barkdoll, and I plan to escape. Meathead is leaving Alcatraz; he comes back to say goodbye. The three of us are sitting in the print shop when he arrives.

For Barkdoll he has encouragement. "Behave yourself, you'll get something done for you. A lot of people are trying to help you." Barkdoll won favor with the authorities during the attempted escape with Cretzer and Kyle from the mat shop. They are convinced his cool head saved the lives of the hostages on that occasion. Awkwardly, Meathead attempts to give me some hope as well, but I recognize it as bullshit as it spews from his mouth.

"You know Karpis, the old man told me to tell you that when the time comes he's goin' to try and help." Meathead is uncertain of himself, as always, he doesn't know how to say goodbye. He obviously wants to shake hands but is frightened his offer will be refused if he makes it.

He's a far different figure than the healthy specimen who inherited the job of deputy several years before. His gut now hangs over his tightly cinched belt and the traumas of the past years have taken their toll. He's old and tired; scrutinizing him in his decline, I reflect on the effect of the last eleven years on myself. I'm desperate now to escape, there is an increasing irritation to prove myself capable to live again in a world of color, without bars in front of my eyes everywhere I look. Even the knowledge that my desperation can lead to death doesn't scratch my itch.

Meathead's aging form pauses for a second in the doorway before disappearing for the last time. He's bumbled his goodbyes just as he bumbled his existence at Alcatraz, but he's been far more tolerant about the failings and weaknesses of the cons than many would have been.

"I need a clerk! You're the only candidate but it's purely voluntary," Scanland, the Chief Steward, tells me, twisting nervously in my swivel chair in the print shop. I accept his offer and become kitchen clerk, helping him to order the food, and to plan the diet. It's an additional responsibility on top of my obligations as printer but I accept it to gain the experience.

There's much speculation over who will be the new deputy warden. When he arrives he pays us a visit in the same print shop where Meathead sang his swan song. Captain Madigan has returned.

"I never thought I'd see the two of you with the best jobs in the institution," he laughs as he joins Barkdoll and myself.

"I never thought I'd see you back here as deputy," I retort good-naturedly.

"I hear Kyle's back in the kitchen too," he laughs.

"Not because we want to tie you up again," Barkdoll smiles and we all laugh.

Madigan is a man who you have to respect. He's a religious person by nature, never in his many years dealing with the worst criminals in the country have I heard him utter a profanity. On one occasion, when he lost his temper, he blurted "By Cripes!"

All the cons are pleased to see him back as deputy, although many of the screws think he's too soft as a disciplinarian.

The print shop has become a type of private club. Not just any con is allowed back here, but lately Bayless in the bake shop has befriended a young kid, Ekland (AZ-775), who eats up panfuls of fudge which Bayless makes for him.

As Barkdoll and I play our music together, Ekland listens and buys himself not only a guitar but a trumpet too. We have our guitars in the print shop to practice, while

Ekland uses the band room like the other cons in the institution. He learns fast; he has the highest I.Q. of any convict in the federal prison system although he never got past high school in formal education.

Ekland, only in his mid-twenties, has a receding hairline on a funny bulletlike head. He stands only five feet, six inches tall and weighs no more than 140 pounds, but every negro eyes him suspiciously and keeps his distance.

Ekland was dubbed "the Sniper" in the press when he went on a vendetta-style rampage in Washington, D.C., killing as many blacks as possible. As dusk descended "the Sniper" would emerge rifle in hand, on a personal "coon shoot".

His reign of terror ended with his arrest. In the Washington jail he was considered a "bug" because he would spend hours in the exercise corridor "sprinting" from one end to the other. Then, on the way to the courthouse, he sprinted free and remained free until he was later arrested in Atlanta.

It is obvious from the moment he is placed back in the kitchen at Alcatraz that he is an erratic, emotional kid with an inferiority complex. Seldom have I seen anyone so self-conscious. Although he never confides to anyone the reason for his shooting spree, I get the definite impression it was related to a highly personal incident involving him or some immediate member of his family and some negroes.

One day as Pappy Kyle and I are sitting on a bench, near the vegetable room in the basement, Ekland descends from the kitchen. A mattress cover packed with clean rags for the kitchen is located at the bottom of the stairs.

"The Sniper" looks at Pappy and I. Stops. Tugs nervously at a rag hanging from the mattress. It doesn't come loose. Knowing we are watching, he pulls again at the rag which remains stubbornly stuck amidst its companions. Determined to win his struggle with the inanimate object, he places one foot against the bundle and jerks hard, dragging the rag another four or five inches from the mattress. Red with embarrassment, he stoops down, turns around, clasps the piece of cloth securely over his shoulder and pulls with the total weight of his body.

Success! The rag lets loose of the bundle. However, "the Sniper" does a complete pinwheel in the air and lights flat on his back, knocking the wind out of himself. Pappy and I rush over to help him up but his pride is hurt more than his body. He simply has no common sense and is so totally sensitive to other people's opinions of him he is constantly making a fool of himself.

One day while playing ball on the yard, Ekland is on second base. He muffs the ball and looks at the glove as if it is at fault. Again a ball comes in his direction, the same thing happens and he reacts as before. On the third occassion he looks disgustedly at his $20 glove, flings it over the wall of the yard, stomps off the field, and ends his baseball career.

There is no question about his intelligence. One day in the print shop he observes, "You fellows don't have a clock in here, I can make one for you." He makes a "Rube Goldberg" clock. A pendulum hangs on the cord and winds around a central post counter-clockwise until it is completely wrapped, before it begins to unravel in the same steady motion. It keeps perfectly accurate time.

Christmas Eve, 1947

Cherry pie is on the menu. The juice is made into wine by the kitchen crew in preparation for our own "office party" in the cell house on Christmas Eve. Paul Ritter (AZ-526), known as "the brewmaster," has a reputation for making good wine from confiscated materials around the kitchen. He asks, "What will we have for food?"

"Let's take a ham in!" comes a suggestion. Now the problem is how to smuggle an entire ham past the cell-house guard who will be searching everyone on their way back from the kitchen to the cell house.

Immediately there is dissension in the ranks. Half the guys want to carve it into slices and smuggle it cautiously into the cell house in small segments. The other half note the habits of the cell-house screw. He's always "half-swacked" himself and as he shakes you down he has to physically grab hold of your ankles or pant legs to steady himself before standing up straight again.

A small group will go early to the gate, and the men will wait until one of them is on the other side of the screw. Then, while the guard is trying to balance himself before standing erect, one of the cons waiting to be searched will toss the entire ham, football fashion in a foreward pass to the receiver who has already been searched and is waiting for the others before being locked in his cell. The argument over methodology becomes so severe the only solution is to pull straws.

I'll leave to your imagination who wins the straw pull, but I assure you that Christmas Eve is a wild celebration in the cell house with lots of ham and wine. The con taking around the stationary acts as waiter; I had printed up cards reading "From my house to your house".

The drunken party continues until 4 A.M.

It's the middle of the night a few days later. Something wakes me up. I must be going crazy! I know my guitar leaning against the wall just played a simple tune.

Now I hear a shuffling noise on the shelf high off the floor where my Christmas package containing cookies and candies is sitting. I carefully reach for a match box and lob it onto the shelf.

The guitar plays the same tune, in reverse.

A mouse had scampered over the guitar, jumped across to my pants hung carelessly on a hook from the shelf, and reached the package of sweets on the top of the shelf.

Alcatraz, 1948

I step out of the cell house, onto the steps leading to the yard, and into the movies. Columbia pictures has its cameras running as we enter the yard—it's part of a prison documentary being filmed in cooperation with the prison system.

A new jargon is introduced into the prison system as various individuals are given new titles to describe their old duties. Since I'm working in the print shop still, as well as being the clerk in the kitchen, I make lists with the new positions on them: the Deputy Warden is now an Associate Warden; the Chief Clerk is now the Business Administrative Manager; the MTAs, formerly "Male Trained Attendants" in the hospital, are now "Medical Technician Assistants."

These new printing assignments are interrupted each day as Barkdoll, Kyle, and myself plan our escape. We deliberately play our guitars down in the print shop late after the workday is over. The screws get used to our tardiness thus allowing us a few extra minutes on the night we make the break.

The plan is to go through the print-shop window which faces onto the yard. Hunter had drilled through the bars in the mat shop with a homemade drill; I have a real drill in the print shop for drilling holes in the book bindings. Dan Ripley smuggles us some carbon from the movie projector which we hook up electrically to use as an arc. I obtain a steel plate about one-half inch thick to try out the arc but every time the carbon touches the steel plate, the print shop comes alive with sparks shooting crazily through the room as flashing blue lights dazzle our vision. We knock the fuses out two or three times practicing.

Every evening the kitchen screw must shake down the print shop during his inspection tours of the evening. According to regulations, he must check each window-bar to ensure it has not been tampered with. Since the bottom of the print-shop window is at chest level, the only way of properly inspecting each bar is to stand on the stool in the print shop to reach the top of the bars. We need to find out whether he's doing the job thoroughly or whether we can cut the bar ahead of time.

The stool is placed each night at a different place in the print shop but always with the leg on a crack in the cement floor so that we can tell if he's moving it over to the window to climb up and inspect the bars. The stool is always where we left it, the leg exactly on the crack chosen the day before.

George Thompson is back in Alcatraz but ready to be released again. Once more he is willing to bring a boat and outboard motor across the bay to pick us up. We also have water wings and other equipment prepared in case something goes wrong. I'm growing sufficiently desperate, I'm almost willing to jump into the water, something I refused to do with Doc Barker ten years ago. There is a suicidal element in my enthusiasm.

Then one day I notice something which makes me turn suspicious of my partners Barkdoll and Kyle! There is dirt from the shoes of the kitchen screw along the ledge where he is standing as he checks the bars on the window. He has to be using the stool to climb up on the window, nothing else in the room would work. But the stool is always replaced exactly as we left it. Only the three of us involved in the escape know about it. One of us must be a stool pigeon!

I can't believe that either Kyle or Barkdoll would be turning us over as sitting ducks to the officials, but the dirt lies on the ledge. Then one day a guard, who acts as a "connection" is annoyed with me.

"Why didn't you let me turn in that blade? I could have gotten the credit," he announces.

"What blade?" I ask.

"The one you guys hid. Barkdoll told someone else where it was."

I wait for an opportunity and check out the long bench in the print shop. It has lead pipes as a frame and wooden planks for seats. I take the bottom cup off the lead pipe and reach up around the curve. The blade is gone! It would never have been found there. Barkdoll must be the stoolie but I'm always suspicious of prison officials and how they deliberately work at turning cons against one another.

Then Barkdoll convinces me himself. One day as we talk about the approaching escape he announces, "I'm getting out of these plans!"

"Why?" I ask.

Barkdoll explains how many of the officials are attempting to get him released, including one named Walter Gordon, a negro who is head of the "Adult Authority," the name for the state of California Parole Board. I know the real reason Barkdoll doesn't want to stick his head out of the print-shop window—the screws will be waiting to blow it off.

I say nothing to Pappy Kyle but tell him that I too want out and the entire plan is scrapped.

Alcatraz, Warden's Residence, 1948

J. J. Johnston died without knowing that, while he was Warden of Alcatraz, the basement of his home was used by his cook and houseboy as an illegal still and that it was I, Alvin Karpis, who furnished them with the corn sugar used to make the needed mash. There is one day, however, when he almost discovers its existence.

One evening, an hour or so before the Johnstons are to entertain the Birdseyes, of the Birdseye Frozen Food fame, the cook, Paul Ritter, suddenly realizes he has not seen or heard the houseboy, William Montgomery (AZ-509), for over an hour. Descending to the basement quarters used by the two during their working hours, he discovers the houseboy dead drunk on the floor.

He quickly cleans up the mess, conceals the still's opening and drags "Pinhead," as the houseboy is called, into the bathroom. Stripping off Pinhead's clothes, the cook throws him into the tub and turns on the cold water. With the tub half full, he takes Pinhead by the hair and begins frantically dunking his face in and out of the splashing water. It's no use! The houseboy is out cold.

Checking his watch, the cook pulls the plug and rushes back up the stairs to the kitchen where he turns down all the burners and the oven. Softly creeping back down the stairs, he takes another look at Pinhead unconscious in the tub. With the Birdseyes due any minute, Ritter realizes that the situation calls for desperate action. He dashes to the top of the stairs and begins shouting.

"Warden! Warden!"

Johnston sticks his head out of the living room almost immediately.

"What's wrong?"

"I just went down to the basement to use the toilet," answers Paul hurriedly. "I heard groans coming from the bathroom as I came to the door. When I went in, I found Pinhead lying in a tub full of water holding his right side and screaming. I pulled the plug and ran up here to get you. I knew you would know exactly what to do."

Upon seeing the unconscious figure sprawled in the tub, Johnston turns to the cook.

"Yes, yes, you did just right!" and then adds, "A ruptured appendix no doubt. You stay with him while I get the doctor."

The island doctor lives next to the warden. One of the strict rules of the warden is that a doctor should be on the island at all times, not because he is concerned about us prisoners, but because there are numerous prison personnel and their families isolated from medical aid on Alcatraz Island. In just a few minutes Dr. Yokum arrives.

After examining Pinhead, especially around the abdomen, he straightens up from the tub. Giving the cook an odd sort of grin, the doctor announces, "I'll have to operate right away! Stay with him until they come with a stretcher."

This happens around 8:00 P.M., so when the procession comes down Broadway led by the doctor, followed by two screws carrying Pinhead on a stretcher and flanked by cell-house guards, we who live on the flats (as do all kitchen help), are curious and concerned. They all disappear up the stairs leading to the hospital above the kitchen area.

The next day, after the operation, the doctor stops at Pinhead's hospital bed and whispers in his ear: "If I had all the alcohol now that you had in your system when I operated on you, I would have enough alcohol to pickle your appendix and use it as a glaring example of a perfectly normal appendix that was needlessly removed."

The doctor comes from a rather distinguished family of surgeons. He is just one "hell of a swell guy," liked and respected by every con on the island.

Alcatraz, April 1948

"Old Saltwater" is leaving Alcatraz! As we enter the cell house every con has to pass by the blackboard that used to announce news events during the war years. Johnston brings the old blackboard back into the cell house to exhibit the newspaper headlines announcing his retirement.

The Senate has passed a bill making retirement mandatory for any civil servants at the age of seventy-two. Johnston is already over seventy-two and thus he must step down. I realize that the reason Johnston is publicizing his retirement is to dispel any rumours that he is fired due to the riot of 1946.

I recall the political dealings that secured his position as warden and wonder whether he will be guaranteed employment by the federal government as was originally agreed in back-room bargaining.

However, the more immediate question is, "Who will be the new warden at Alcatraz?"

Pappy Kyle brings me the news, hot off the prison grapevine. "Swope is coming as the new warden!"

"Who's Swope?" I ask.

"Trouble! That's who! He'll turn this place upside down within a few months," predicts Pappy, in his nasal Montana twang. "Every joint he has ever been in charge of has ended up in strikes and riots.

"When we tried to lam from McNeil, he was the warden there. After we got grabbed, the screws tore our clothes off and worked us over down in the showers while Swope stood watching the beating."

Swope does not arrive until late into the fall. The ill-feeling between Swope and Johnston is made public when Swope refuses to set foot on the island until the Johnstons leave. When he does finally arrive he brings his wife and the family dog. It is the first time a dog has been allowed on the island as Johnston had never permitted pets during his years as warden.

The couple who operates the lighthouse on Alcatraz Island falls under the jurisdiction of the warden of Alcatraz. They have long wanted a dog to brighten up their isolated existence so when the Swopes arrive complete with family pet, they are delighted.

Immediately they purchase a big-eyed, long-eared puppy in a San Francisco pet shop and board the prison launch with the squirming bundle balanced proudly between them.

"Sorry no dogs are allowed on the island," announces the officer in charge of the prison launch. "Warden's orders!"

"No! No!" responds the lighthouse keeper's wife amicably, "those were Warden Johnston's orders. We have a new warden now, Warden Swope."

"That's just the warden I'm talking about. Warden Swope! He gave orders that no one was to bring any pets on the island."

"There must be some mistake. Swope has a dog of his own," argues the lighthouse keeper.

"There's no mistake!" is the blunt reply.

Convinced that there is a mistake, the lighthouse keeper asks for an interview with Swope.

"Those are my orders," confirms Swope. "No one is to have a dog on this island!"

"But why not? You have a dog yourself!"

"Well I'll tell you what," Swope informs the surprised couple, "when I start operating the lighthouse and you become warden of this island, you can have a dog and I can't. Until then, no dog!"

Everyone in the kitchen is scrubbing and polishing for days in anticipation of Swope's first official inspection. Scanland, the chief steward, is nervous and jumpy when he ushers the new warden into my print shop in the basement.

"This is Warden Swope, Karpis!"

My eyes fall on a short, aggressive bundle wrapped in a $300 suit, topped off with a wide-brimmed $100 Stetson hat which announces that he is out of New Mexico. Glancing down at his feet, I see the shiny toes of a pair of boots poking out from neatly pressed trousers. His squinting slate grey eyes are inspecting me in return.

"How long have you been working in this print shop?"

"What are your hours?"

"You're the first printer I ever met who wears a white shirt!"

He spits out his questions as fast as his eyes dart around the room. They tilt to the ceiling, pan to the door, and focus on the bars covering the windows. Scanland, on the defensive, explains the reason for my white shirt rather than the traditional blue uniform. "Karpis is also my clerk up in the kitchen. In fact he has more duties around this kitchen than any of the other inmates."

"Maybe he's too busy, maybe he should take a rest!" comes Swope's sharp reply.

I think to myself, "This don't sound like a good start with this son of a bitch!"

"I'll be seeing you often," are his parting words. "I'll be back in this kitchen quite a bit!"

He is true to his word. Every Friday he descends on the paranoid chief steward and the disinterested kitchen staff. Swope leads the "Snoop Squad" followed closely by the doctor and the captain, the latter carrying a clipboard on which he notes Swope's every displeasure.

Election Night, 1948

No one believes Truman has a chance against Dewey, including myself. We cons believe that when the Republicans win the election, they will close Alcatraz down on economic grounds. It would be cheaper to place the 300 inmates of Alcatraz in the best hotel suites in San Francisco with full room service. If Alcatraz is closed, we'll be transferred to another federal prison from which escape will be easier.

Lieutenant Robinson is working the midnight to morning shift and as he comes down Broadway just before midnight, I call out to him, "How badly did Truman get beat?"

"Beat! Hell, it's not over yet! They're still running neck and neck!" he shouts back.

His answer puzzles me. I know Dewey must have been declared President of the United States by now. What puzzles me is why Robinson, who is usually a friendly sort, doesn't want to tell me.

As I lie back in my cell pondering the attitude of the guard my thoughts drift back to a political argument I once had with a judge in a speakeasy in Kansas City. My opponent was a political hack, fortunate enough to be on the coattails of Bos Pendergrast.

The judge and I had exchanged viewpoints over a few drinks before, but on this occasion the debate got out of hand. I was upset over a fifty-cent fee for a driving licence newly instigated by politicians and the outspoken abrupt little judge was attempting to rationalize it. His logic might sound good at a political meeting or rally, but I had watched him enter the speakeasy every night and noticed the two armed hoods who were assigned by the manager to protect and escort him while he was in the bar. I knew who owned the bar and I had my own views about where the fifty cents paid by every driver was going.

The crusty judge, who was drinking heavily, could hold his liquor but even sober he had no finesse. Eventually, as our tempers rose and the level of the liquid in our glasses diminished, we ended up yelling insults at each other.

"You don't know anything about politics!" he chided me.

"You'd be surprised who I know in politics!" I hollered back. His bodyguards were moving nervously. Tony, the manager, who knew who I was, interceded and broke up the argument.

When morning arrives in Alcatraz, I am astonished to hear that the little judge from the speakeasy, Harry Truman, is reelected President of the United States.

Father Clark has returned to his duties as Catholic priest in Alcatraz following the war. Due to his persuasions and personal contacts, many famous personalities visit Alcatraz to break up the monotonous routine of the prison. I meet Cary Grant, Franchot Tone, Jack Bickford, Bing Crosby, and Joe E. Brown.

We eventually hear the news about former warden J. J. Johnston. He is appointed Special Assistant to the Attorney General for the West Coast. The position is specially created for him, the political agreement which secured him the position as warden at Alcatraz and guaranteed him a government job for the duration of his life has been honoured, thus circumventing the mandatory retirement bill.

Christmas, 1948

As I file into the dining hall this morning, I witness a sight never before seen inside these walls. Her soft scent, which has not aroused my nostrils for more than twelve years, reawakens strange emotions long forgotten. In the middle of the mess hall stands the first Christmas tree ever to be erected in Alcatraz.

Alcatraz, January, 1949

Swope declares war. It's personal with him. He is determined to break up the happy carefree life enjoyed by all of us back in the kitchen. We, in turn, are equally determined to keep our comforts:

Unlimited Food—we have our choice of the food supplies and can prepare appetizers whenever we crave them rather than being regimented to strict meal hours like the general population or the guards.

Buckets of Booze—we have all the ingredients and utensils to prepare home brew. Never is anyone working in the kitchen forced to go without liquid comfort. The challenge is to avoid becoming an alcoholic.

Free Sex—plentiful opportunities everywhere. The basement is a labyrinth of vegetable rooms, showers, freezers, and storerooms, where homosexual delights are exchanged freely and frequently. The brazen homosexuals in the kitchen flaunt their wares to the point where they have become notorious throughout Alcatraz. The eight cons who work on the steam tables serving the main line at meal hours attract hoots and whistles from the boys in the mess hall. When Pappy Kyle takes his place behind the steam tables with them, the general population labels them "Pappy Kyle and his all girl band!"

The blatant antics of the kitchen workers with their utter disrespect and lack of concern for Swope, vex the little warden into desperate attempts to establish order.

I have to admit we probably have arranged for ourselves the best existence possible in Alcatraz. The only drawback is, "Who wants a life in prison on *any* terms?"

Bergen and Faulk have been taking turns as acting captain but neither of them is Swope's choice for a permanent appointment. Instead he imports an outsider for the job.

"Ray you'll never guess who the new captain is going to be. Pappy tells me it's going to be Tahash!"

Dan Ripley (AZ-344) has told me about Tahash. Dan is a colorful character who cut out one of the most profitable criminal careers in the history of the United States, yet remains an unknown to the general public. He is one of the few unsung antiheroes of North American crime. Although he never made the headlines, he did make more money than Dillinger, myself, or anybody I know in the bank robbing business.

It was Dan Ripley along with "Old Fitz" and several others who took off the famous Lincoln, Nebraska, bank robbery which netted them over a million in Liberty Bonds and over one hundred thousand in cash—not to mention several other large scores around the country.

Ripley and Clyde Nimerick (AZ-848) were bank burglars torching their way into bank vaults in the dead of night when fate turned against them. A dog, being walked by its master, dug up their concealed torches in a field. The owner of the animal alerted police and when the pair, along with two other partners, showed up for their tools, they found themselves surrounded by police. The other three were shipped off to Kansas to stand trial for a bank burglary, but Ripley was positively identified in Indiana as the thief who held up a local filling station. Ironically, he was innocent of the filling station robbery but received ten to twenty years for it, and was sent to the Indiana Reformatory. He escaped immediately.

While waiting for his friends to serve their sentences in Kansas and rejoin him to continue their night work under torch light, Ripley took to robbing banks in dangerous daylight. His new career proved so successful, he did what every con talks and dreams about but never accomplishes—he retired to South America.

In Bolivia he became fluent in Spanish and married into a rich land holding family where he became lord and master over thousands of square miles of ranch land. The six-foot, two-inch Irishman reminisces in the grey shadows of Alcatraz of his luxurious Bolivian existence. His blue eyes shine with life as he recalls his role as judge and jury in all the disputes between the Indians who lived on the ranch and looked upon him as a feudal lord.

Revolution interrupted his comfortable life. His wife's family contracted to supply all the beef to the Bolivian soldiers but unfortunately chose the losing side in the revolution. Ripley slipped out of Bolivia, across the Andes, into Chile with barely his life—he left behind his wife and sons.

One day, months later, he sauntered into his old hangout back in the United States and took up stealing. He saved his money and was boarding a ship for Peru from which he intended to fly across the Andes and return to his family in Bolivia, when he was plucked off the gangplank and sentenced to two consecutive twelve-year sentences. It was then that he first met our new captain at Alcatraz, Tahash.

"Tahash is the son of a bitch who's responsible for me being here at all! He and two screws out of Lewisburg, Pennsylvania were transferring me to Leavenworth. My hands were cuffed but they didn't have leg irons on me. I waited my time, until the train was leaving a small town where it had stopped for water in the middle of the night. As the train picked up speed, I stood up, as if to stretch my legs, ran for the window and smashed headfirst into the darkness beyond. As I came to a rolling stop along the edge of the tracks, I couldn't see for the blood running down into my eyes from cut glass and cinders in my forehead. Still, I felt certain I could disappear before they could stop the train to look for me. But that cocksucker, Tahash, is like a goddamn bulldog. He jumped through the broken window and landed a few feet behind me."

I know Ripley well and I know it took a good man to stop him. After Tahash deposited him in Leavenworth, Suitcase Simpson picked him up and brought him to Alcatraz. On the train to Alcatraz Dan asked Simpson for a pencil and paper. When Simpson produced them, Ripley produced two $1,000 bills and one $500 bill. "Write down the serial numbers of these bills and put them in my account when we reach Alcatraz."

Simpson was dumbfounded. "How did you get through two prisons without anyone finding that money on you?"

Ripley was no fool. By surrendering the money voluntarily, it remained his property. If it had been discovered in Alcatraz when they gave him a finger wave up his ass, it would have been confiscated and lost forever.

Years later, after Ripley served his sentence, he left prison a rich man, not so much because of the few thousand he saved but due to the United States Government. During the war, the U.S.A. was badly in need of Bolivia's tin mines. They gave over one-hundred-million dollars to the Bolivian government to ensure its support but one of the minor conditions of the government was that Americans were to be compensated for all property they had lost during the revolution. Ripley received about $50,000 thanks to Uncle Sam. When he was being transferred to Leavenworth, with only a few months left to serve, he told me, "They have a detainer on me in Indiana where I first escaped from that phony filling station robbery, but I'm buying my way out of it with the help of an expensive lawyer."

It cost Ripley twenty-five thousand but once he was released to the Indiana authorities, he had the detainer in Indiana dropped and walked out of prison a rich and free man.

Several months later Father Clark returned from his offices in the city. "Ray, I was talking to a friend of yours. A man came to my office in Los Angeles, announced himself to my secretary as "Mr. Simon" and, when I received him, it turned out to be Dan Ripley with a young bride on his arm, young enough to be his daughter. He asked me to say 'hello' to you when I returned to Alcatraz."

As I said, Dan Ripley was probably the most successful bank robber in the United States back in the 1930s but his name would mean nothing to the average citizen, whereas Baby Face, Machine Gun, Pretty Boy, and the other dead losers have become legends.

Barkdoll and I eat together and then walk out to the yard where we relax in the hot sunshine. He falls asleep until three o'clock when the whistle blows indicating we should all come in off the yard to prepare for supper.

Barkdoll looks at me through bloodshot eyes clutching his chest. "I've got a bad pain, right here!"

"Hell, it ain't nothin'. Probably something you ate," I reassure him.

"Tell the steward I can't come in right now. I don't feel too good!"

From the kitchen I watch two guards escort Barkdoll to the hospital. One of them is passing by me half an hour later on his way through the kitchen to the screw's dining hall. "That's too bad about Barkdoll," he remarks.

"Yeah, he's up in the hospital," I comment.

"No, he's dead! He had a heart clog or a massive blood clot as close as the guys in the hospital can figure. He turned black as coal before he croaked!"

The rumor circulates around Alcatraz that I poisoned Barkdoll because he had turned stool pigeon on us but I, of course, vehemently deny it.

Swope makes his presence felt all over the island with both guards and cons. Down in the industry buildings he upsets established patterns of behaviour which have existed for years in Alcatraz. He orders the doors off the men's lockers so he can see what is inside without opening them on his inspections. They can keep only one pair of work pants instead of three. They must stand at their work areas at all times even when they have no immediate work to do. He outlaws the makeshift showers which exist in every industry.

Many of the screws switch to the "prison industry service" to get out from under Swope. This means that they remain in the industries at Alcatraz but are no longer considered guards and thus are not ultimately under the jurisdiction of what appears to be a megalomaniac.

By the end of the summer, Swope's antics prompt retaliation. There is hardly an industry on the island that has not experienced minor strikes and sabotage. The waste and damage resulting from reaction to Swope's petty rules costs the government thousands of dollars.

All the new shipments of cons into Alcatraz are now topheavy with negroes, most of them military prisoners on minor convictions. Regardless of race, new arrivals at Alcatraz feel obligated to prove how tough they are because Alcatraz is the "ultimate prison". Everytime a new shipment arrives there are weeks or months of fistfights.

For some reason, the negroes usually stage their outbursts in the mess hall. The theory among the more prejudiced whites, is that the "spooks" know the screws quickly break them up and thus neither participant is seriously hurt. A pitcher of hot coffee smashed into a black face or a tray full of food crashing down on a dark curly head are common sights at dinner hours. If you are eating near the section of tables reserved for the negroes, there is a good chance food will be flying in your direction once the fight is underway. The punishment for fighting in the mess hall involves a flat 500 days loss of "good time".

So far the fights are segregated, white against white or black against black, but as the negro population increases and as Swope's repressive regulations continue, frustration festers and it is only a matter of time until race turns against race.

Swope's "snoop squad" degenerates to a "one man shakedown" by the warden himself. The doctor and the captain, who used to accompany him, each excuse themselves on some sort of pretext. Nevertheless, every Friday, Swope swoops through the kitchen and notes the most miniscule of violations. He has Bristow remove the table used by the kitchen help because he disapproves of them relaxing between their duties.

As the kitchen clerk, I have my desk in the corner of the kitchen and whenever he makes his rounds, I see to it that I am behind it, working. One day he stops beside me. "Looks like you're awfully busy Karpis."

"Yes warden, I am. I don't even have time to bullshit I'm so far behind in my work!"

My answer is disquieting to him. I can see he is itching to order me away from my desk so that he can search through the drawers for contraband but he doesn't get up the nerve. It's just as well he doesn't because the guys in the kitchen had noticed long ago that the one place exempt from his search is my desk and every Friday they stash their illegal possessions with me until the warden is finished his rounds.

The politicians are agitating to deport all foreign-born prisoners rather than feed and clothe them in already overcrowded prisons for years prior to deporting them. It is good news to me because, being Canadian born, I'll be certain to be deported when my sentence is served, unless another jurisdiction in the U.S.A. has placed a detainer on me requiring that I be turned over to them when my time is up in Alcatraz.

Even aside from the latest political rumblings, I shall be eligible for parole in the summer of 1951, only a couple of years away now. It's time to discover whether or not there is a detainer on my record out in the front office.

The records clerk is a son of a bitch, so I wait until he is on holiday for a few weeks. His replacement is Baker, a screw who was shot during the 1946 riot and he assures me that there is no detainer on my record other than the deportation one which is exactly what I want. I am pleased with Baker's news but would have been less so if I could have predicted the future.

A large negro walks up to the handball courts and, rather than wait his turn, pushes in front of the cons waiting to play the winner. The other cons are white and before long fists are flying. The white cons playing horseshoes nearby notice the fight between the whites and negroes and quickly jump into it using their horseshoes as weapons. More negroes join their fellow to even up the match and, before the guards have noticed, there is a racial riot on the yard.

Iron horseshoes are biting into skulls and the growing hurricane of white and black bodies begins to turn red as blood splatters across the yard. "Wildman" Willie Vasilick (AZ-614) comes running from the other end of the yard, snapping the shovel from the horseshoe pits and whirling it crazily around his head as the sharp edges just miss severing many black necks from their bodies. By now the guards on the walls are shooting frantically in the air in an effort to quell the rioting mass of cons while reinforcements file rapidly into the yard.

When the commotion subsides bodies of black and white are scattered, moaning and twitching, over a bloody red carpet. There are so many knife wounds on both sides that from now on the knives are used only once a week in the dining hall and a very rigid and precise count is initiated to ensure they are returned. None of the authorities thinks to check the knives used in the guards' mess and, since the guards' mess is open to the kitchen help all day, no one wanting a knife in Alcatraz goes without one.

Swope, insensitive to the real causes of the mounting tension, orders that the horseshoes be removed from the yard.

LeRoy McGary (AZ-712) talks to himself a good deal of the time in his cell. He's ignorant, brash, and over 200 pounds, mainly muscle.

I'm sitting by the wall on some cushions, watching the ball game in front of me quietly taking the afternoon sun on the yard when I first spot Joe Baker (AZ-1305) stalking up behind LeRoy, a baseball bat raised above his head. LeRoy, intent on playing a bridge game, doesn't see the other negro behind his left shoulder.

Baker brings the bat down with a powerful blow on the side of LeRoy's skull. No sound is uttered. LeRoy merely collapses at Baker's feet. Joe prods the back of LeRoy's head which wobbles on the end of the bloodstained bat.

The screw on the wall "throws down" on Joe with a machine gun and the yard screw rushes in his direction but Baker, oblivious to their reactions, kicks at LeRoy's limp head with his boot. As reinforcements arrive to escort Joe off the yard only one thought is racing through my mind—"How can I get out of being a witness during the murder trial?" While we're waiting for a stretcher to arrive, a strange thing happens.

LeRoy's body begins to quiver, it moves, it rises, it stands upright.

Another negro, "Peaches," has come out on the yard after the incident—he has no idea what happened but LeRoy turns to him. "Who all hit me just den?"

"Hit you? Ain't no brother hit you!"

The wall screw hollers down to a confused LeRoy, "Can you walk up to the gate?"

"Sure I's can walk up der."

I can't believe it as LeRoy covers the distance and climbs the steps to the cell-house entrance. "A delayed reaction to a concussion," is my personal diagnosis. "He'll be in hospital for a week."

I'm wrong. LeRoy struts into supper, his left ear four times its normal size, painted bright with mercurochrome but not even bandanged.

9

Alcatraz, 1950

Warden Swope censored a letter from a woman in Los Angeles to Robert Stroud seeking advice and describing the symptoms of her pet bird. Swope's sharp sarcastic reply informed the woman that Alcatraz isn't an information center on ailing birds.

The bird died. The woman packaged it in a box and sent it to Swope. When the press got hold of the story black headlines read:

SWOPE GETS THE BIRD, BUT LITERALLY

and copies of the woman's letter as well as Swope's reply are included in the story.

McIntyre (AZ-826) is cooking fish on four griddles as "The Devil" enters the kitchen behind him.

"Hi Mac! How you doing today?"

"Yeah, I'm doing alright warden but I'd like to ask you something?"

"What is it Mac?"

"What did you do with that dead bird the woman sent you?"

Swope retreats to his rigid defensive stance with hands clasped behind him, leaning forward. He didn't realize until now that the bird story was known to the convicts who can't legally receive newspapers.

"I'll tell you what I did. I gave that bird a decent burial

which is more than I'll give any of you bastards if you die in here!"

Ed Stucker, the big screw on duty, confides in me one afternoon after four o'clock. "Don't tell anyone, but my brother is coming here as the new captain to replace Tahash. Keep it under your hat though, because before long he's going to be the new associate warden!"

I'm both skeptical and curious about this news. Madigan is presently the associate warden. It's a bad sign to me because it indicates a widening rift between Swope and Madigan.

Nova Stucker arrives as the new captain, he's decked out in Stetson hat, expensive grey suit and black shoes. He looks strangely familiar and then it occurs to me he's a dead ringer for my old bank-robbing partner, Freddie Barker, who along with his mother Ma Barker, was shot dead by the FBI.

As Swope escorts Stucker through the kitchen he whispers to him after passing me by, "That's Karpis!"

They both turn and look back in my direction. Upon their return from inspecting the kitchen basement, they approach me. Swope introduces us, kidding on the square. "Here's the guy I want to show you, captain. He's the one who's really running the kitchen. The steward just thinks he's the boss around here. Ain't that right, Karpis?"

"Look, I don't run nothin' but my mouth around here," I retort, "and I'm gettin scared of doing that too much!"

We all laugh. As they leave, Bristow, who has not even received an introduction to the new captain, comes up beside me at the steam tables in the dining hall and comments, "Boy, I sure don't like the look of that character. He wasn't acting too friendly!"

The next day Nova returns, now in his double-breasted uniform, and walks over to where Bristow is sitting at his desk. "Get up!"

Bristow is dumbfounded.

"Yeah, that's what I said, get up!" Bristow stands up

by reflex more than by notion. Nova takes the rubber pad off Bristow's chair, walks over to the garbage and deposits it into the can. Bristow turns even redder than his normal alcoholic hue.

"You don't need no cushions around here in the future," remarks Nova as he leaves the kitchen. I think to myself, "This is the beginning of the end!"

Nova also takes the cushions from the guards on the walls and in the towers but then he and Swope go too far. He tells the guards to remove their stools from the towers altogether. They rebel forcing Swope and Nova to back down and leave the stools in place.

The "trouble shooters," a pair of screws who Nova used in Leavenworth to break up any trouble spots in the prison, are transferred to Alcatraz on Swope's orders and placed in the kitchen. Their names are Hughes, a husky but flabby little screw who stands about five feet, eight inches tall, and Larkin, a dumb but rough customer from Kansas who is part Indian.

"Old Man" Piere, next to Bristow, the chief steward, is second in command in the kitchen. He's a civilian employee and is in charge of the butcher shop.

One day the main line has beef hearts for dinner but "Old Man" Piere notices when the shipment arrives that there are not enough for the main line, the screws' mess, and the kitchen help. Sensibly enough, he decides to give the guards a small steak and the kitchen help a hamburger to ensure there are enough beef hearts for the main line.

I am helping him out in the butcher shop when "The Devil" himself storms in. "Piere! What the hell is goin' on here? The guards upstairs are eating steaks when your menu says beef hearts! You know that guards and convicts are supposed to eat the same meal."

"Normally they do," explains the old man as he continues to go about his work in the butcher shop, "but we didn't have enough beef hearts to go around."

At this moment Piere happens to open the large walk-in

freezer which is used for storage. Swope's eyes fix on a box full of what he thinks are beef hearts in the storage unit. He explodes into a rage of insults and accusations which takes the old man by surprise.

"Mr. Swope, sir—let me explain—you're mistaken—"

It's no use. Swope is in the midst of one of his temper tantrums and no one can interrupt him. As he concludes, he stomps back upstairs and out to his front office where he dictates a letter to his secretary Bertrand.

Bertrand is sent back to the butcher shop to deliver a copy of the letter to "Old Man" Piere. The letter is addressed to Washington with a copy going to the Culinary Department and it tirades against Piere in insulting terms and rants on about the pounds of beef hearts that Swope discovered in the butcher shop while the guards were being fed steaks for dinner.

"Old Man" Piere reads the letter and invites Bertrand, the warden's secretary, over to the storage unit. He points to the object of the warden's displeasure and explains, "These are kidneys, not beef hearts. I have to save them up gradually from quarters of beef until I have enough to make kidney stew for the boys."

"Why the hell didn't you tell the warden that?" demands Bertrand.

At this point I burst out laughing. "No one here could have said anything to him in his condition," I explain to Bertrand. "'Old Man' Piere certainly tried his best to—but no one could talk to him. You can see those kidneys are not beef hearts."

Bertrand is concerned. "I'm going back to explain this to the warden before he sends those letters to Washington and gets you in unnecessary trouble. Once the letter goes out Swope will never back down."

Half an hour later Piere receives a telephone call from Bertrand in the front office. "I tried to explain to the warden but he just says, 'I said they're beef hearts and that's what they are! And that's the end of it!' "

Larkin and Hughes, the "trouble shooters," are on their day off. Gregory, a large easygoing Swede who stands six feet, four inches tall is the relief officer. It's only a few days after the "beef hearts" incident but Swope comes charging on a dead run back to the kitchen in search of some trouble and is frustrated at finding nothing to complain about.

He's on his way out, about ten feet past the steam tables in the dining hall, when he looks over his shoulders and halts abruptly. Walking back slowly, he calls the large guard from the kitchen into the dining room. Gregory saunters out—he doesn't give a damn about Swope or anyone else.

"Mr. Gregory, why hasn't that syrup been cleaned up that is under the steam table?"

"Well I don't know," replies Gregory unconcernedly, "but let me take a look." He strolls over and peers casually under the steam table then reports back to Swope. "That's not syrup under there, warden."

"I said it was syrup!" insists Swope, "and it's syrup!"

"We didn't have hotcakes today," reasons Gregory, "so what would syrup be doing out here? Even if we had served hotcakes, syrup is never dished out from the steam table."

Nevertheless, in an attempt to pacify the furious Swope, Gregory reaches under the table and sticks his fingers into the mess on the floor. "I told you it wasn't syrup, sir and it ain't syrup. That's rusty water! You'd better send a plumber in here to fix the steam pipes, they're leaking."

Swope leaves the mess hall mumbling insistantly to himself, "It *is* syrup! It *is* syrup!"

We are wondering what new insanity will overtake Swope but no one can predict his next move. Swope orders some surplus paint available from the government.

Up until now everything, with the exception of the flat white on the walls, is covered traditionally in grey aluminum paint. When the new paint arrives, he has the entire cell house repainted in a new color—the bars, the lock cages, the walls, the light fixtures and the doors are all covered in two layers of shocking pink paint!

Next Swope reads that colors have a psychological effect on individuals and orders the inside of each cell repainted in bright colorful shades—green, red, orange, lemon. The only problem is no one has his choice of color so most of the cons are upset by the change rather than being soothed.

A shroud of secrecy prevails over an emergency meeting of the top brass in Alcatraz. No one knows why the meeting has been called by Swope. Everyone in the warden's office is staring expectantly at Swope in anticipation of a monumental announcement. Twitching with excitement, Swope produces a shiny article in the palm of his hand. "Do you know what this is gentlemen?"

The collection of experienced federal prison officials stares in puzzled bewilderment. Swope's eyes flash victoriously as he unravels the piece of tin foil and spreads it out flat on his desk. "Now do you know what it is?"

Again silence. Then a voice hesitantly volunteers—"It looks like—like a gum wrapper, warden."

"No!" snaps back Swope. "It's more than just an ordinary gum wrapper. It's contraband!"

There is nervous shuffling in the the assembly of officials as they look awkwardly at each other in an attempt to avoid the warden's darting eyes. At this moment Swope reaches into a desk drawer and withdraws from it a brown envelope with the official Alcatraz letterhead decorating it. Dramatically he empties the contents of the envelope onto his desk.

"See this! See this!" he shouts in squeaking tones as he shovels up handfuls of the gum wrappers allowing them to fall through his fingers back onto the top of his desk. "I picked each of these gum wrappers from a hollow pipe down in the industries. Someone had been depositing them there for months. There are hundreds of them!"

Then, checking himself, his voice deepens—"Gentlemen, someone is smuggling chewing gum into Alcatraz. There's a leak in our security. Contraband is sneaking past us!"

The conclusion of the meeting is rapid. Swope demands tighter security following his great discovery of the gum wrappers. It's Bertrand, the warden's own secretary, who tells me, in secret, about the meeting. "The man is going insane!"

Madigan, the associate warden, secures for the inmates the small recording facilities in the basement of Alcatraz. Swope and Nova Stucker both consider the enterprise a waste of time but it proves to be very popular.

It enables the cons to record their own voices or a song, played by themselves and their fellow inmates, which can be sent to their wives, children, parents, and friends across the country. The discs cost only fifty-cents each and the practice becomes so popular hundreds of dollars worth of discs are being used every week. There is a long waiting list to use the equipment which enables men who are not inclined or able to write letters to maintain a personal contact with loved ones.

One day as I and my musical companions are recording a version of "Steel Guitar Rag," we are interrupted by a visitor. It's Bennett, the head of the federal prison system from Washington, D.C.

"Karpis, is that you playing? I've never heard that song knocked out so well. Would you send me a copy of it?"

I accommodate Bennett and send him a copy of "Steel Guitar Rag" by Public Enemy Number One Alvin Karpis, backed up by the cons in Alcatraz.

Swope's restrictions and petty regulations continue to annoy the cons in the industries and to lower the quality of the food being prepared in the kitchen.

There is an epidemic of bombings in the laundry and in the glove factory. Tens of thousands of dollars worth of material is destroyed by homemade bombs constructed of match heads and candles and timed to explode into flames during meal hours or after the cons are safely locked away for the night.

In any other prison in the country, there would be riots in the mess hall over the quality of the food but, with the cannisters of nauseating gas hanging over the dining-room tables and guards toting machine guns in the cage over the entrance and along the outside of the mess-hall windows, the resentment is controlled—but only for the present. There is a time bomb set to explode in Alcatraz which is burning slowly through the emotions of the inmates.

Euphemisms are instituted at Alcatraz. The D block isolation is renamed the "Treatment Unit". The "hole'" is now the "Special Treatment Unit" and the "bread and water" fed to the cons while in the "hole" is a "restricted diet".

Every year there is an art exhibition on the streets of San Francisco. The artist conducting classes at Alcatraz, with the help of Father Clark and Madigan, arranges to have Alcatraz inmates exhibit their work along with other local artists.
 The publicity in the newspaper is overwhelming. Many of the cons sell their work for as much as $350. The entire experiment is a great success—almost.
 Paul Ritter, the con cooking in the warden's house, reports that Swope and his wife are furious because Madigan and Father Clark's photos appeared in the newspapers in connection with the event while Swope had been overlooked by the press.

The two "trouble shooters" imported by Nova from Leavenworth to "clean up" the kitchen have only encouraged sabotage. They brag about how they are going to teach us how things are done in Leavenworth but, due to their list of petty rules, the cooks forget to put salt in the beans, the bakers neglect to add sugar to the cake, the coffee machine is "accidently" turned off, so that when the main line arrives the coffee is cold, the trays are dirty, and the pile of rejects by the main line builds up until there is a shortage of trays halfway through meal hour.
 Larkin, the larger of the pair, literally runs from the bakery to the cooks in the kitchen to the mess hall shouting, "Line, Line!" At that order, the cons working on the steam

tables take their places ready to serve the meal to hundreds of hungry cons fresh from their jobs in the industries. Larkin is always overexcited and on the run.

One day he dashes into the bake shop hollering and comes charging out again on his way back to the kitchen. His voice rises in a long scream of horror and surprise which sticks in his throat as he ludicrously slides halfway down the hall on a slippery surface of spilled grease. The scream culminates in a groan where he lies in a crumpled heap on the kitchen floor. His wrist is broken in several places and he is moved, in agony, to the hospital amidst the unconcealed and uncontrolled laughter of the jubilant cons.

His partner, Hughes, the sex specialist who is constantly on the prowl for homosexual activity, has become a comical figure. The joke is that he's so anxious and excited in his attempts to discover two guys in action, his pants are bulging at the crotch half the time he's on duty. He never succeeds. Then, about a week after the "accident" which his partner had run into, Hughes doesn't show up for work. We are all curious. Then, the truth comes out. Hughes has been committed to a mental hospital in San Francisco.

After Larkin recovers from his broken bones, he asks for a transfer back to Leavenworth and we never see either of Nova's "trouble shooters" again.

Alcatraz, January 1951

The new year, 1951, begins with a bang. Bristow, the alcoholic chief steward, collapses morally under Swope's insistence that he limit the budget in the kitchen. He serves cheap, unattractive meals which are usually non-nutritious as well. Bristow's dream for many years of becoming chief steward disintegrates into a gutless existence where he stays within Swope's budget, collects his pay cheque, and rushes home every evening to his wife, Irene, and a bottle. Bologna is served all too often for meals, the milk is watered, and the menu shows no imagination or effort. There is a steady dull diet repeated every ten days in a predictable pattern.

The fuse is short and burning fast. Alcatraz is ready to explode and the food becomes the issue. Bristow introduces a new dish which he calls "Macaroni Milanaise". It consists of forty pounds of macaroni, a couple of cans of tomatoes, a can of ketchup, and chopped up green peppers and onions. The "meat sauce" is thirty pounds of which two pounds are beef and the balance is suet. As soon at it begins to cool, the grease rises to the top, three inches thick. Poor meals, merely a source of annoyance to a free man, can generate anger and frustration in a convict who has no control over what he is expected to eat.

The cons wait patiently until the "macaroni milanaise" falls on a Wednesday during the ten-day menu cycle. Wednesday is the associate warden's day off and no one wants Madigan blamed for what is to happen. The responsibility will fall on Swope and Stucker.

Aware the moment has arrived, I leave my work area in the kitchen and walk over to the locked gate separating the mess hall and the kitchen to watch the action. The key to this gate is placed in the gun cage above the mess-hall entrance before the main line arrives to ensure that the cons are confined in the dining room with armed guards on the catwalks outside the windows.

Without warning it begins. Two cons run up each side of the center isle tipping over every table in the dining hall. The "macaroni milanaise à la grease" flies in all directions, splattering cons and guards alike. Trays, silverware, plates and bread pudding are flung across the room as the multitude of bodies struggles to keep its footing on the greasy floor. The more intelligent cons in the room sit down and refuse to slip or slide in the rolling mess of food decorating the mess hall. Everyone in the room is sprinkled with macaroni from hair to shoes.

"Alright, back to your cells!" shouts one of the screws in the dining hall.

"Go fuck yourself!" comes the reply. "No one is leaving here until we get a proper meal! And don't you try to leave either!"

The last sentence is a threat against the screws caught up in the chaos of the mess hall. At this moment, however, reinforcements arrive to grab the ringleaders who upset the tables. They are quickly escorted out of the mess hall and hustled over to isolation in D block. One of them, Penska (AZ-774), is screaming above the commotion at his colleagues, urging them to attack the guards as he is being dragged through the macaroni and out the door at the other end of the hall. The sliding door locks tight behind his exit cutting off his tirade of insults.

Bristow has joined me at my ringside seat, safely situated behind the barred gate leading to the kitchen. We watch together as the guards attempt to convince the hundreds of stained and shouting cons to return to their cells. The screws move awkwardly across the grease-laden floor like men walking across an ice rink without skates. Everytime one of them slips and plunges into the debris surrounding him loud cheers explode from the inmates.

"You may as well go to your cells," reasons one of the guards. "There's nothing left to eat!"

Bristow turns to me. "Ray, they're going about this all wrong."

"What are you talking about? The cons have tried everything else, this is all they have left."

"No. No. I mean the screws," he explains. "We should offer to feed them."

"How can you feed them? There's nothing left to eat. And if there was something to eat, the dishes and silverware are floating around in that sea of macaroni out there."

"I could boil some eggs," suggests Bristow.

Now I lose my temper and start yelling at him. "Why don't you give them some of your goddamn bologna while you're at it. That'll really make them happy! This is your fault. If you had the guts to stand up to Swope and tell him to go fuck himself there would be no complaints about the food."

My attention switches from the stunned Bristow to the gate at the other end of the mess hall which has just opened to admit Swope and Stucker into the congestion of macaroni and emotions. They stand about ten feet inside the door protected by machine guns on the alert in the gun cages.

"Listen to me men," urges Swope. "Go to your cells. No one is going to be punished—unless they deserve it."

His appendix brings a storm of booing, hissing and swearing from the angry inmates. Stucker turns to Swope. "They ain't going to listen to you warden. I'm going to have the gas bomb dropped on them!"

"Not while I'm here!" declares Swope as he splashes his way out of the hall, leaving the problem with Nova Stucker. Stucker, left in authority without any support from Swope makes his way across the dining room to where Bristow and I are standing. He moves like someone who has just put on a pair of roller skates for the first time. His awkward movements and near slips are orchestrated by the laughter and hooting of the men in the mess hall. I move away from the gate to allow him to speak with Bristow in private. As Nova Stucker begins his precarious journey back across the dining-hall floor Bristow is visibly alarmed.

"It looks like he's going to turn on the gas. We'll all get sick to our stomachs in here," whines Bristow.

Nova stops at the other end of the hall to make an announcement. "You might as well move out of here. There's nothing to eat! If you leave now, we'll get you something to eat after we clean up this mess. Go back to your cells! No one has been hurt yet!"

Slowly, a few at a time, the cons pick themselves up and make their way back to their cages. The numbers leaving are few at first but increase steadily until the hall is clear. With the cons back behind bars Nova opens the gate leading to the kitchen where we have been trapped since the riot began.

"I'll start boiling eggs and slicing bologna for sandwiches," Bristow shouts to Nova.

"What!" exclaims Nova, "Give them sons of bitches eggs? Let them drink the water in their cells, that's good enough for them. They won't starve to death. Clean this mess up before breakfast in the morning."

Penska, the con who was screaming at the others in the dining hall after he and his friends overturned the tables, becomes depressed over the fiasco not turning into a riot and no one else joining in the revolt. While in isolation he cuts himself around the armpits and groin arteries with a razor blade and dies.

Shortly after the riot in the mess hall, Bristow is busy writing at his desk. He solemnly seals the letter in a brown envelope and waves down Stucker as he passes through the kitchen on his rounds. "Would you take this out to the front office for me?" asks Bristow in a subdued voice.

"Well why can't you take it out there yourself? What is it anyway?"

"It's my resignation," chokes Bristow with emotion. "Read it if you want."

"Why should I want to read it?" responds Stucker coldly as he places Bristow's soul-searching letter in his pocket and walks, disinterestedly, from the kitchen. Bristow breaks down, sobbing like a child.

"Ice-Box Annie," who replaced me as kitchen clerk before the riot, is transferred to Leavenworth and "Old Man" Piere is made acting chief steward until a replacement for Bristow can be found. Piere comes to me immediately.

"Ray, you know I don't know one damn thing about this paperwork. But you do, you know all about this work. You've been around this kitchen for ten years now, you know it better than anyone else. Why don't you do it for me. Be my clerk!"

"If I do," I explain, "I want to do it in my own way. I don't want any interference from anyone. You just sign the papers I give you."

"I'll agree to that," he bargains.

I take the paperwork back to my cell to work out a new menu and ordering system. I know the prices already. I change everything. Instead of six or seven items consisting of inedible slop, I cut it down to three or four items of good solid food each meal. I stay within poundage allowed and also within the budget but manage to feed the guys well.

After four weeks, Swope calls Piere out to his office. When the old man returns he confides in me. "Swope wants to give me the job of chief steward permanently."

"Why?" I ask.

"He showed me dozens of letters he has received from the convicts asking that I be kept as chief steward instead of just acting chief steward. The letters said they've been fed better since I took over than at any time previously. Then Swope told me he had checked up on me and discovered that I've been feeding the guys for less than Bristow by two cents per meal."

"Are you going to take the job?" I ask.

"Hell no! I can't take it! You know damn well I ain't doing this. I don't know anything about this work. You're the one who's doing it all and if you get mad at me for some reason and quit I'll be left up shit creek. I don't want to be chief steward—I just want to keep my job!"

The feud between Swope and Madigan breaks into the open. In his latest attempt to flaunt his authority, Swope, a Protestant himself, issues orders that no guards or employees are to attend Father Clark's Roman Catholic services held for the convicts every Sunday. No such orders are given out in respect to the Protestant services. The newest regulation instigated by Swope is obviously intended as a slap in the face to Madigan who never misses one of Father Clark's services. Madigan is a strongly religious man. In fact I never swear in front of him out of respect.

Swope is not satisfied with his decree. He sees to it that no Roman Catholic guards are on duty during Father Clark's services in case they might take part. It's Swope's petty retaliation because he was left out of the publicity surrounding the art exhibit run by Madigan and Father Clark.

Back in the days when Johnston was warden, the associate warden had been given two days per week of holiday rather than just one. Meathead never took the two days.

When Madigan arrived as associate warden, he had voluntarily continued in the tradition and took only Wednesday as a holiday. Now he insists on taking Sunday as well in order to attend Catholic services in San Francisco.

However, back on the Rock the battle continues. Nova Stucker stops Father Clark at the boat dock when he arrives on the island one Sunday and insists on searching his belongings and person.

It's about 8:00 P.M. and I'm sitting in my cell on Broadway. I have the strangest feeling that I've forgotten something but I can't remember what it is. Then. I hear footsteps approaching.

"Here's Karpis, right here in this cell!"

The voice is Swope's; the visitor with him is U.S. Senator Langer, "Wild Bill" Langer, a politician from North Dakota who is known for his dedication to duty and sympathy for convicts. He is chewing on his trademark, a cellophane wrapped cigar; he never smokes them.

"Hello, Karpis."

We exchange polite greetings and small talk then he asks more seriously, "Is there anything I can do for you?"

Thinking for a moment, I reply, "Maybe there is, I'm eligible for deportation this summer."

Langer's eyes flood with warmth and understanding. "The hell you are! Listen, write to my office in Washington and tell them that I told you to write, mark it personal. Give me a rundown on what you would do if deported, where you would go, if you have a job to go to and so on. I really want to know about this."

Swope fidgets in the background. "Senator, I want to show you how clean we keep the kitchen here at Alcatraz and I know you don't have much time."

Swope's words remind me of what I forgot earlier. As the pair disappear down Broadway, an image of the butcher shop flashes in my mind.

Earlier this afternoon, as we prepared for supper, "Old Man" Piere ran out of cheese and shouted frantically to me, "C'mon Ray, lets go cut up a few more pounds of cheese!" Using the meat grinder in the butcher shop we quickly ground up the necessary cheese. As we finished, the old man turned quickly to return to the kitchen.

"We can't leave this machine covered in cheese," I reminded him. "Don't you want to clean it up?"

"Hell, I can't do it now. I have to get upstairs and finish the meal. And I can't leave you here alone because Swope has given specific orders never to leave any convict alone in this butcher shop."

I knew this was the truth. In fact Swope is so certain someone will attempt to break out of the butcher shop, he has installed an extra set of bars across the windows.

"Remind me to clean it up after supper. Just throw a clean cloth over it for now."

We both forgot about the cheese. Remembering now, I keep my fingers crossed that Swope and Langer won't include the butcher shop in their inspection.

My hopes fade as I watch Langer and Swope on their return trip down Broadway. The senator is walking briskly and frowning, while Swope is panting along behind looking apologetic.

"Old Man" Piere gets the story straight from "The Devil" himself the next morning. As Swope was showing the Senator through the kitchen and stressing its cleanliness, he ushered him into the darkened butcher shop and turned on the lights. "What's under this sheet?" inquired Langer casually.

"That's the meat grinder," announced Swope proudly. "It's always kept snow white and polished clean!" Punctuating his brag, Swope jerked the sheet off the machine. Immediately both men were attacked by hundreds of surprised cockroaches. The startled insects swarmed up their pant legs and over their suit jackets. They swatted and slapped at the invading armies in vain. Only by escaping the butcher shop did they rid themselves of the last of the cockroaches squirming up their sleeves and hiding down their shoes. Alcatraz is infested with millions of cockroaches. Normally, they are seldom seen during the day but under the cover of darkness and with the unexpected treat of a cheese meal, they had congregated that evening on the grinding machine.

The next time Swope sees me he makes his point. "Karpis, I heard what you told Langer about your eligibility for deportation soon. I wonder how he would feel about helping you if he knew you were the one responsible for leaving that cheese out for the cockroaches that attacked him."

As long as I remain on the Rock, I can never be released from prison, not even on a deportation order. First, I must be transferred from this fortress, reserved for dangerous public enemies, to a regular federal prison. No one receives a direct parole from Alcatraz.

My name goes before the classification committee in Alcatraz to see whether they will recommend me for a transfer to McNeil Island, another federal prison. Madigan and Father Clark are both members of the large committee deciding my future. Shortly following the vote, Swope comes back to the kitchen to speak to me.

"Karpis, I guess you heard that the classification committee voted to have you transferred to McNeil Island." He pauses to let the news sink in, then adds vindictively, "Yeah, they recommended you but you wouldn't have liked it up there anyways."

His message is loud and clear, although disguised. The recommendation of the committee has been refused. I am to remain at Alcatraz.

"Have a seat, Karpis."

"No, I'll stand. What did you want to see me about, Mr. Austin?"

"As you know, in addition to being the librarian here, I'm also the secretary for the classification committee and acting parole officer."

"What does that have to do with me?"

"Don't you realize that you're almost eligible for parole? It's my job to help you fill out your application form."

"Is there any information you need? Should I contact the Canadian authorities?"

"No, no. Everything's in order. The Canadians agree that you're a citizen. They'll accept you."

"Well then I don't have any problems, except getting up there."

"I don't know about that, you *might* be wanted in Missouri."

"For what?"

"For shooting the sheriff down there!"

"No, I've got a letter from the records office here in Alcatraz saying I'm not wanted down there. There are no detainers on me from Missouri."

"Karpis, I understand that you told Mr. Austin yesterday that you have a letter from the records office stating there are no detainers on you from Missouri. Do you have such a letter?"

"Yeah, I've got that letter, Mr. Sundstrom."

"I'm the records clerk and I never signed any letter like that. If it doesn't have my signature on it, it's no good. How did you get the letter?"

"One day, a while back, I was trying to straighten up my affairs. I wrote out to the records office to ask if there were any detainers on me. There were none!"

"Whose signature is on the letter?"

"I don't know. Up until now I thought it was yours, but you claim you never signed such a letter."

"I'll bet I know whose signature it is! There's only one man who relieves me when I'm on holiday and that's Mr. Baker. But that letter is not binding on me."

It's the middle of August when Austin and Sundstrom come back to visit me in the kitchen. Sundstrom does the talking for the pair. "Karpis, I've got some real bad news for you!"

"What's that?"

"You remember we were talking a few weeks back about you and that detainer business. Well, a detainer came in on you from Missouri just yesterday. They want you turned over to them if we release you."

"Alright," I reply.

"Alright! Wait a minute, you don't seem upset. Do you

have any idea why they would slap a detainer on you now after all these years?"

"Well, I imagine you know more about that than I do."

"No, I don't know anything about it," he lies. "They just sent it. What are you going to do about it?"

"You just let me worry about that!"

As the pair of vultures retreat from the kitchen, my thoughts are bouncing off the inside of my skull. The "beef" in Missouri is twenty years old. They tried unsuccessfully to have me turned over to them when I first arrived at Alcatraz but that was fifteen years ago. Now on the eve of my eligibility for parole, comes a detainer. How did they know about me? Who in Missouri has a grudge against me that's twenty years old? The coincidence is too great. There is no danger of being found guilty of murder after twenty years but with any kind of detainer on my record my application for parole will be turned down automatically. There's only one obvious conclusion. Someone in Alcatraz wants to prevent me from obtaining a parole. The question is—Who?

I ask to see the detainer on my record which arrived from Missouri but they refuse to let me see it.

I request to see Madigan, the associate warden, and explain to him my desire to see the detainer.

"Ray, why are you so anxious to see it? I know the detainer is there!"

"I want to see what date is on it. I want to know *when* the warrant was issued."

"What will that prove to you?"

"It will prove whether it was issued after I spoke to Austin or before. If it's after, I want to know how long after because if I'm right in my suspicions, I'm going to take someone to court over this!"

"Well, I'll see what I can do."

Saturday morning. Swope is in San Francisco. Sundstrom is not on duty. Madigan sends for me, pulls the warrant out of his pocket and hands it to me. "Take your time."

The first thing I notice is the date. It's dated two weeks

after I spoke to Austin which gave someone in Alcatraz time to get in touch with Missouri and ask for the detainer to be placed on my record. The second thing I look at is the name of the person who filed the complaint. Such a person must be an eyewitness to the crime and must have "personal knowledge" that I am guilty. The signature is that of the sherriff's wife who was at home the Saturday morning her husband was shot.

Madigan interrupts my thoughts, "I'm going to tell you something, Ray. I've been looking into this matter myself. You go right ahead and fight them right down to the wire! You've never been indicted on this matter. Not even fifteen years ago when they wanted you turned over to them.

"One thing more, don't talk around the institution. No one needs to know I showed you this warrant."

I agree and keep my word but it's the last time I see Madigan for many years. Swope finally wins out. Madigan is transferred from Alcatraz and Nova Stucker is immediately promoted to associate warden. I remember the conversation I had with Nova's brother in which he predicted how Nova would arrive as captain then be promoted to associate warden.

I obtain a lawyer in San Francisco who has a reputation as a strong protector of civil rights—his name is Grupp. When he arrives, I explain what I have learned about the Missouri business and the connection with the Alcatraz authorities.

"Do you think you can prove this?" he asks, incredulous.

"Yes, I'll prove it to you within the next thirty days."

"If you're right," he comments, "the officials here at Alcatraz are breaking the law. Soliciting detainers is illegal, it's a two-year felony charge!" As Grupp leaves, he is enthusiatic and eager to act on my behalf.

I immediately have $500 transferred from Chicago to my account in Alcatraz in order to cover the initial legal expenses. Next, I learn through connections I have in the prison that there has been considerable communications between the warden's office and the Missouri State Police, between the warden's office and the prosecutor's office in Missouri, and between the warden's office and certain individuals in Missouri. Now I know I'm on the right track. "The Devil" himself is behind the whole business. Austin and Sundstrom are only stooges.

The obstacles to proving what I suspect are massive. I'm confined to a few square feet behind bars on an island in San Francisco Bay. All my letters or communications to the outside world are censored by the very officials who I must prove have broken the law if I am ever to have the detainer lifted from my record. If I don't have the detainer removed I'll never be eligible for parole.

My dilemma seems hopeless. My only protection is to have several individuals on the outside working on my behalf. If I place all my confidence in one and he lets me down, I'll be lost.

First I write to Missouri and hire a lawyer, Esco Kell, who replies, "I was the county attorney here for eight years and I never heard of this case. I'm surprised to hear it would be revived at this late date."

I then write to Senator Langer who responds immediately and who recognizes my plight. He says, "Keep me informed of any developments through your attorney in Missouri by registered mail."

Finally, I write to my sister in Chicago and I have her contact a top lawyer there who I hire to keep his eye on the other two lawyers in case they make any errors in judgement or procedure.

Now, I again request that Grupp, the civil rights lawyer in San Francisco, visit me. He arrives and I show him the letters from my Missouri attorney and Senatory Langer, and tell him, "When the time comes, I want you to get me into court in San Francisco. I'll have everything ready for you in ten days. How much will you charge?"

"I'm not sure how much work could be involved here," he hesitates, "maybe $350 at the most."

"I'll give you $500 just to get us into court. I'll give you $1,000 if you win the case." Grupp is delighted as he leaves the visiting area.

It's necessary for me to notarize copies of all the material and information I send to my lawyer in Missouri. The person acting as notary at Alcatraz is the associate warden who is now Nova Stucker. He reads all the material I send to him and then comes to visit me.

"Karpis, I've never tried in all my years in the prison service to dissuade a con from fighting a legal battle but I'm warning you right now. Stop! Drop the whole thing! You can never win. This is a hot potato. You're accusing government people here. They can't let you win. You're just going to get yourself all twisted up."

"You mean I can be tried for murder and hanged in Missouri over this but the government can't be embarrassed?"

"I'm only warning you because I don't want to see you get in over your head. Take my advice, get out now!"

I refuse to abandon my legal rights and Nova no doubt reports back to Swope, the man who has just promoted him as associate warden to replace Madigan.

After assembling the material, I package it, place a letter to my attorney in Missouri inside the package and put in a request to have it sent to him by registered mail.

The next day I receive a withdrawal slip from my account in the front office. It's for two dollars to cover the cost of registering the parcel and placing air mail postage on it. But I don't receive a receipt from the post office with the registration number on it. I don't think too much about it until I don't get a response from my lawyer. I keep waiting until I finally receive a letter from him telling me he has been waiting also.

"I received your letter indicating you were enclosing the material and sending it by registered mail but I have not yet received a registered package—only the letter."

Now I am suspicious. How could my lawyer receive the letter I placed inside the package but not the package itself. I remember I never received the registration slip from the post office at Alcatraz.

I put a request in to speak to "The Devil" himself, and

Swope grants me an interview. His desk is set up inside the cell house at the north end of A block. As I round the corner I see him turning on the recorder he keeps in the desk drawer and checking the alarm button on top of his desk.

"What can I do for you?" he asks jovially, between a set of white teeth guaranteed to make a shark envious.

"A few weeks ago I sent a registered parcel to my attorney and I wanted to know why I haven't received the registration slip from the island post office."

"What do you want it for?" he asks suspiciously.

"I need it. Where the hell is it?"

"We put it in your jacket out front for safekeeping."

"I've sent registered mail before. I always got the receipt from the post office the next day."

"Why do you need this receipt so badly?"

"My lawyer never received the package I sent to him with material for him and Senator Langer. I need the registration number so I can complain to the post office authorities. If you want to keep the slip in my jacket, just send me the number. I think someone has been tampering with my mail."

The warden's face is bulging out in purple and red shades as he spits out his conclusion to our interview. "You know what I think Karpis? I think you're barking up the wrong tree!"

Needless to say, I never receive the receipt. Realizing I can't trust the mail service at Alcatraz, I ask for an interview with my lawyer in San Francisco. I am notified when Grupp arrives on the island but I'm kept waiting in the visitors' area.

"Where the hell is my lawyer?"

"He's coming. The warden is talking to him first."

Eventually Grupp arrives but it is not the same enthusiastic civil rights crusader who I spoke to previously, he is nervous, fidgeting with his tie clip, looking at his watch frequently even though he has just arrived and there is a long wait before the next boat returns to San Francisco. Shaking, he offers me a cigarette.

"A lot has happened since I last spoke to you," I begin. "I've got all the information I told you I would have and more!"

"You know, I've been giving this some thought since I was last here, Karpis. If you go through with this you're going to have everyone in the prison system down on you. Maybe you should think about this a bit longer."

"I'll tell you, I've already thought enough about what I'm going to do. I'm going through with this whether you handle it or not! All you have to decide is yes or no! Do you want my case or not?"

"Don't get burned up. Take it easy. Let me explain something to you. I've been talking to Warden Swope. He offers you an ironclad guarantee that if you drop everything here and now, the detainer will be dropped from your record within thirty days."

"Do you know what kind of a madman you were talking to? Do you have any idea how his mind works? Did it ever occur to you that he can tell you that. He can tell me that. He can actually do it. But, I'm sitting in this little cage over here not in your expensive office in San Francisco and there's not a goddamn thing in the world to stop him from placing that detainer back on my record in a year from now unless I have legal protection. I can't rely on his whim, never mind his word for it."

"I can't take your case Karpis but I want you to know that personally I believe you will be performing a public service if you go through with it. This kind of thing should be stopped!"

As Grupp retreats from the visiting area I think to myself, "You slimy coward! What have you got to lose in this? How did Swope scare you off?"

"Ray, a lot of stuff came in from the bureau in Washington about you today—from Bennett's office. There are photostats of everything as well. You'll probably get something in the mail today.

"The photostats, too?"

"No, they'll be placed in your jacket out front."

That night when I return to my cell, the missing contents from my registered package are sitting on my bunk. I wrap them up again, with another letter to my lawyer explaining how they had been sidetracked to Washington, and mail them. This time he receives them.

Senator Langer, who is the minority member of a subcommittee on prisons, sends me a letter explaining how he called Bennett, the head of the federal prison system, to his office to explain why my correspondence had been tampered with. He also tells me that my lawyer in Missouri complained to his own senator who contacted Langer and also asked Bennett to his office to explain the incident. Bennett assured them both that such a situation would never occur again and that he would notify the officials at Alcatraz to follow the law governing the correspondence between lawyers and their clients in prisons. I know now that it is open war between me and Swope.

Christmas Eve, 1951

The kitchen workers have their own holiday tradition every Christmas Eve. The majority of us get drunk on home brew. In an attempt to stop us, Swope assigns "Fatso" Mitchell to watch the kitchen and sends us his salutations in the form of a special "shakedown squad" who arrives unannounced and makes a "toothcomb" search of the kitchen.

Fatso watches as the "shakedown squad" begins its systematic search of the kitchen and basement areas. They are very thorough, picking up containers of wine found in cleverly concealed positions around the kitchen, but it's not until they reach the basement vegetable room that they hit the alcoholic jackpot.

One of the squad climbs up on top of a ten-foot-high potato bin and after digging and probing into the layers of potatoes, lets out a victory whoop. "I've got it! I've got it!"

Home brew is filtering through the potatoes and dripping out on the basement floor as he yanks the wooden bucket back and forth in his efforts to drag it up from beneath two feet of potatoes. As he descends with his prize, Fatso is smirking happily.

"There'll be no drunks staggering around here this Christmas!" he brags, as he examines the three gallons of home brew which has been hauled from the potato bin. He immediately calls up Warden Swope and tells him the home brew is on its way out to the front office.

A sober silence descends on the workers as they continue to prepare for the evening meal. Fatso walks about the kitchen, proud of himself. When the main line is outside the gate leading to the mess hall, several hundred deep, hungry for the evening meal, Fatso calls out, "Line!"

Instead of eight inmates rushing from the kitchen to take their places on the steam table, ready to serve up the meal, there is no response in the deserted mess hall. Fatso trots back to the kitchen only to discover the cooks have not even placed the meal on the steam table. The cooks, the steam-table crew, and most of the other cons around the kitchen are so drunk they either can't hear Fatso or don't care whether they hear him. They are laughing, pushing, kidding, and in general enjoying their Christmas Eve party while the noise from the hundreds of cons waiting to be fed outside the dining hall rises in protest. Fatso has no time to discipline anyone, he resorts to trying to humour the pack of drunks into serving the meal.

In their own, slow, staggering, slap-happy time, the kitchen crew responds and, in an obviously inebriated condition, greets the line of cons as they file into the mess hall. A few of the boys back in the kitchen have collapsed in corners or under tables. One of them is curled up inside the dishwasher. Several of those on duty serving the meal to the main line have bowls full of home brew from which they sip in open defiance. When the main line discovers that some of the pitchers of coffee on the dining-room tables contain home brew, they join in the celebration without alerting the guards. Fatso is sweating profusely and attempting to keep a semblance of order. If he puts anyone on report,

Swope will be as angry with Fatso for being unsuccessful at detecting the party before it got out of hand, as he will be with the cons.

Fatso and the "shakedown squad" underestimated us. We had arranged for them to discover the bucket of home brew in the potato bin. The main portion of the home brew was deep down in the bottom of the potato bin supported steadily between two layers of boards covered over tightly by stretched sheets. We knew once they found the "decoy" bucket at the top, they would never go to the trouble of digging through eight more feet of potatoes and, if they did probe, they would only think they were hitting the bottom of the bin when they came to the boards protecting the other buckets of brew.

New Year's Eve, 1951

It's a tradition in all federal prisons that on New Year's Eve the cons raise hell late into the night. At Alcatraz, the party antics were prevented until around 1945 or 1946. At that time the guards formed a union and when the officials found they would have to pay dozens of guards double overtime to be in the gun cages keeping order on a holiday, the officials decided to put up with the harmless noise.

With Swope's consistent interference in every aspect of life on the Rock, the tension is at a new high as the evening begins. Celebrating the New Year is a useful release of energy which is probably healthy under normal conditions, even in prisons, but this New Year's Eve the party gets out of hand. Following the habitual demonstrations of hollering, shouting, screaming, banging on bars and stomping of feet, a vicious, serious note emerges from the overture of strained vocal cords. The inmates work themselves into a hypnotic frenzy of protest against Swope as they divert their efforts from harmless noisemaking to deliberate destruction of cells and petty attempts at arson. Guards are pelted with bars of soap if they come within range of the caged criminals. Containers of shoe polish, supplied to cons since Johnston's days as warden, are set on fire and thrown out into Broadway to burn in defiance of Swope's regime. Water does not extinguish the flames and no guard wants to try snuffing them out at the risk of being bombarded from the cells on either side.

The flames licking Broadway are only small foreshadowings of what is to come, but Swope ignores the warning and solves the problem, he thinks, by declaring shoe polish will no longer be issued to inmates.

10

Alcatraz, New Year's Day, 1952

The events of New Year's Eve have not eased the tension—it's more evident than the smoke lingering in the morning light. Even the guards can taste it, everyone is breathing in the anxiety.

During breakfast I observe four screws on the catwalk outside in place of the regular single guard. In the deadly silence the silverware taps in steady rythmic patterns like jungle tom-toms beating out a signal. Not since the days of the rule of silence back in the 1930s has the mess hall been this lifeless.

On the yard, after breakfast, the talk is aggressive.

"Let's turn over the tables at lunch!"

"Let's grab the screws in the mess hall and put ropes around their necks."

"Yeah, we'll kill the bastards if there's any shooting."

If asked, no one could articulate why he is angry or what he hopes to gain. The noon meal is a repetition of the solemn silent brooding and there are even more armed guards visible along the catwalks.

The regular weekend movie is scheduled for the afternoon. I seriously debate whether I should opt to remain in my cell. Convicts stampede as easily as a herd of cattle. Any small incident could turn into a riot if the screws start shooting up the theater, no one will be able to find shelter from the onslaught. I decide to chance it.

We pack in, shoulder to shoulder; the film begins. At

first it seems as if the projectionist forgets to turn on the sound. With the cons motionless and mute the colored film unfolds in dramatic silence, only the hum of the projector floods the crowded room.

It's an Alfred Hitchcock flick called *Vertigo*, filmed in San Francisco. It begins with a harness cop chasing a guy across rooftops, jumping from roof to roof. After many narrow, suspense-filled moments of near misses, emphasized by cut shots indicating the long distance to the hard pavement below, the cop in pursuit loses his hold on one of the jumps between buildings, and his death scream smashes onto the eardrums of the jolted Alcatraz cons.

The last cries of the falling cop are lost in the explosion of whistling, clapping, laughing and cheering that washes through the multitude of rigid bodies like a tidal wave and cleanses the tension from the room instantly. Due to that one short sequence, courtesy of Alfred Hitchcock, Swope gets a reprieve. The unusual sight on the screen of a cop losing, and the criminal escaping, completely erases our aggravation.

Swope is lucky this time, but he has planted the seeds of rebellion and, although the film gives him a postponement, his intolerance and repressive measures guarantee an explosion in the near future.

Today Whitey Franklin is finally released from isolation where he was put for attempting to escape in 1938 after killing Cline. He's assigned to the kitchen and Nova Stucker asks me to keep my eye on him since he is emerging into a very different prison than the one he left thirteen years ago. Very few of his old acquaintances remain at Alcatraz with the exception of myself and Pappy Kyle.

Father Clark makes a farewell visit.

"I'm leaving this place, Ray. Ever since Mr. Madigan was forced out by Swope, the warden has given instructions to Nova Stucker that I'm to be searched every time I arrive on the island.

"The only ones not afraid to be seen talking to me are the cons. The word's out that I'm on Swope's blacklist.

You're on his blacklist too, so watch out for the maniac. With the court case you're pushing against him in Missouri he's liable to do anything, and the man is dangerous."

Thinking about Father Clark's warning, I speak to Pappy Kyle and we give our illegal cash, hidden in the kitchen, to Cook (AZ-710), the harelipped orderly in the main cellblock who is the banker in Alcatraz. "The bank" is a cell in A block where Cook's cleaning equipment is kept. Only he has access to it. As a trusted orderly in the cell house Cook moves around freely when everyone else is locked up. The $500 which we have between us is safer with him if anything prevents me from getting to it back in the kitchen.

Immediately following breakfast we are called out, one at a time, to the interview desk on the north side of A block.

"Sit down, Karpis," barks Nova Stucker. "Until further notice, you are not assigned to the kitchen. We're reorganizing things back there. It will take a week to ten days. At that time, if you or anyone else want to come back under the new setup, you'll have to put in a request. If you decide to apply for the job we may or may not accept you. If you don't put in a request you'll be assigned another work detail elsewhere in the prison."

He is acting as if it will be a great privilege if we are accepted. I tell him, "I don't know that I want to work in the kitchen any longer. I've been back there for too many years."

"Oh you wouldn't want to work any other place Karpis. I'll talk to you in a week or so."

After the third day, they run out of the bread we had baked. The screws can't bake, so we have packaged bread from town, much to our delight. The guards, who used to be assigned merely to watch us work, are now employed usefully. Fatso Mitchell is sweating over the pots and pans and looks an unhappy sight in his rubber boots and large rubber apron. The screws who are now replacing the bread, the coffee, or the water on the tables during the meals are given a rough time by the cons. They especially resent serving the negro tables but the blacks enjoy their discomfort.

"Hey, mudderfucker! Where's dat water at? I's thirsty!" If they ever attempted to make such demands to the white cons who used to serve the tables, they would have been told, "You want water, you black son of a bitch? Here's water!" and then they would have been belted over the head with the whole pitcher of water. The guards, however, can't put themselves in the position of starting a fight or creating a disturbance, so they must put up with the abuse. Three of them quit, rather than work in the mess hall.

Two weeks after the purge the officials complete the reorganization. The cell-house screw hands out request slips to all the former kitchen workers. No one takes one.

Nova Stucker now panics. If we don't return to the kitchen work no other cons will "scab" on our jobs but on the other hand the guards don't want to be kitchen workers, they are already near revolt over the duties. Since the government will never approve hiring of civilian help for the kitchen due to the expense of so many salaries, we are Nova's only available labor source. His brainstorm, where he imagined us begging to be reinstated in the kitchen while he decided who would be accepted, has backfired. Now he has to beg us to return to our duties. Not wishing to lose face he changes his original orders and this time, as we are called individually to the desk beside A block, his message is strong and clear, although his desperation can't be disguised. "Come back to work in the kitchen or go to the hole!"

No one goes back to work. By 2:30 in the afternoon, we are all in the hole. Since the general population supports us entirely, none of the other cons take our positions. Stucker tries to persuade the negroes to break the strike. Up to now, no negro has worked in the kitchen and the reason Swope ensures new shipments have a majority of black prisoners is that they never go on strikes. Of course, in later years the same will not be true of negroes in the federal prisons but it is true of the majority of them up to this time in Alcatraz. The spokesman for the negroes replies, "Sure, we'll go to work der, after dis strike is done cleared up."

"No, no. We want you back there now!"

"Sure youse do, but soon as dat strike is broken and

dem white mudderfuckers comes back t' work, youse'll throw us out."

Shortly afterwards, I am called out of my cell and confronted by Bergen, who is a calm, even-headed captain. He says, "How you feeling, Karpis?"

"I'm alright."

"How long do you guys plan to keep this up?"

"Us guys! What did 'us guys' do? Why are we in the hole? We were told we no longer worked in the kitchen. Why not throw everyone else in the hole for refusing to work there? We aren't on strike, we were fired!"

"Yeah, yeah, I know that's what happened. It was badly handled but the thing now is what are we going to do about it?"

"We? I can't do nothin'. I don't care about it. It's not my problem."

"Well you can't stay in the hole the rest of your life, Karpis."

"No, I don't intend to unless I die in the next couple of years."

"The next couple of years!"

"Yeah, I need a rest bad. Settle this the way you want but count me out."

"We have to do something here and fast. Did it ever occur to you that you might be up for transfer one of these days?"

"Don't give me any of that crap! You tell all these guys if they behave, they'll get a transfer. Do you think I'm new on the block?"

"Look Karpis, if you agree to go back to work, Kyle and Banghart will join you and then the rest will follow like sheep. You're the leader. We had a meeting last night and Warden Swope told me that he promises you a transfer out of here once the kitchen is back in order. You know a transfer is the first step to a parole. Haven't you been in prison long enough? This is your chance to get out!"

"Well that sounds alright except for one thing. I wash my face every morning and to do that I have to look in the mirror. If I got a transfer on the conditions that you suggest,

I'd never be able to face myself in the mirror. You tell the warden that he has his nerve to ask me for favours when he's gone out of his way to place that detainer on me in Missouri."

The hole is uncomfortable. Bread and water. No smokes. Cold. Damp. Five guys cave in and go back to work. They have to be housed up in the hospital. The traitors wouldn't survive out in the cell house; the other cons would murder them. They all have guarantees of transfers the moment the strike is over.

Since all five are from the south and have declared loudly on many occasions they would never work with negroes, someone suggests that it would be a good idea to have negroes go to work in the kitchen in order to shame them out. The idea amuses the negroes if we strikers in isolation accept the scheme. The majority think it's a good idea but the five back in the kitchen swallow their pride and prejudice. They work beside the blacks.

The "goon squad" marches into D block and straight up to the third gallery cell of Butterfield (AZ-1051). As they pass my cell I can see they are intent on hurting someone. Their faces are grim and emotionless. A large polack lieutenant is the first one to burst into Butterfield's cell. As the convict is thrown on the steel floor of the cell, the full 250 pounds of the lieutenant is behind the heavy knee that comes down on the youth's chest. Blood flies out of his ears, nose, and mouth as he nearly dies from the blow which crushes his breastbone. They drag him past my cell toward the hospital.

Gradually the guys in isolation give up and return to the job until there are only five of us who have not put in request forms to return to work in the kitchen. We remain in isolation for over a year due to our stubborn attitude.

The kitchen affair at Alcatraz becomes the scandal of the prison service. Nova Stucker gets the blame, loses his position as deputy warden, and is transferred to another prison. Swope's choice as his replacement is Larry Delmar, a "Hell on Wheels," who was the deputy warden at McNeil Island.

Isolation, 1952

Back in 1951, I made the decision to fight the court case in Missouri against the detainer placed on me before attempting to take Swope to court in San Francisco for illegally soliciting the detainer. I instructed my attorney in Missouri to hire a court reporter to take down the proceedings and make copies of them. In those days the courts did not keep records of court proceedings—if either party wished to have a record they had to hire someone at their own expense.

While I sit in isolation, I am well aware that part of the reason I am here is because I chose to fight the case rather than accept any of Swope's offers or deals. The results of the court case in Missouri I receive are disappointing—I have lost. The judge has ruled that the detainer can remain on my record. My lawyer tells me, "Sorry, I don't know what else I can do."

But I notice that although the detainer remains, I have obtained the evidence necessary to prove Swope's duplicity. In the transcripts from the trial it becomes obvious that the entire business was precipitated by Swope.

The testimony by the widow of the sheriff, who had been shot down over twenty years ago, indicates that she was asked to place the detainer on me by a lieutenant in the Missouri Highway Patrol, after he was contacted by Swope. She refuses to change her mind, convinced apparently that I am the one who murdered her husband.

When my lawyer, who used to be the prosecutor himself, questioned the present prosecutor on the witness stand, the evidence against Swope becomes even more incriminating.

"If you had Karpis here right now, would you put him on trial?"

"If I had the evidence I would."

"You know you have no new evidence. What prompted you to get involved in this case after twenty years?"

"I have a vivid recollection of a letter I received from Warden Swope of Alcatraz in which he described to me how

Karpis would be coming up for deportation consideration soon and that there was a possibility he might get favorable action. On the other hand the warden explained that if a detainer were placed on him there would be no possibility for parole."

During my long hours of inactivity in isolation, I read through the Supreme Court decisions available from the library in Alcatraz discovering that it is a rare situation for an accused criminal to demand a trial. If someone does demand to be tried, he is entitled to a quick and speedy trial or immediate dismissal of the case if there is no evidence.

I instruct my lawyer in Missouri to demand that they try me for murder using the Supreme Court ruling as a precedent. This time the judge instructs the widow and the prosecutor to present a case in ten days or remove the detainer. Since there is no evidence for a case and because they will be liable for all expenses if they lose the case, the detainer is removed.

My lawyer ensures that the judge, on dismissing the detainer, does so "with prejudice". This means that it can never be reinstated again.

When the results of the second trial arrive everyone at Alcatraz knows that I have beaten Swope and proven his interference. The screw delivering the letter from my lawyer says, "I think you're going to find out that Santa Claus came early this year."

In theory, I am now in a position to take Swope to court on a charge of "soliciting a detainer". However, when I attempt to arrange for a lawyer to press the charges in a San Francisco court, my letter is returned with Swope's scrawling penmanship across it. "Tell Karpis I said no!"

When I ask my lawyer in Missouri to send me copies of both trials so I can distribute them to Senators Langer, Bennett, and other interested officials, he takes several weeks to reply. When his letter does arrive it is obvious someone has convinced him I am some kind of troublemaker who should be content that the detainer was removed. He tells me that the girl who kept the court records for the hearings moved from town and thus he cannot obtain a copy of the second hearing at all and the copies of the first which I already have are the only ones available.

I know that if I were free to travel to Missouri, I would find the missing court reporter quickly enough. I know, too, that I've been sitting in isolation now for more than a year on a flimsy pretext invented by the Alcatraz authorities. Already it is obvious that due to the embarrassment I have caused everyone, there is no point in applying for a parole for at least five years even though I am eligible and there are no longer any detainers on my record. I am practical enough and experienced enough to know that a prisoner should never expect justice. Swope holds the power of life and death over me. I decide to drop the entire affair while I'm still alive. It might already be too late.

The five of us who remain in isolation because we wouldn't return to the kitchen are gradually released back into general population after fourteen months of punishment. Livers (AZ-876) goes to work in the hospital, "Bigsy" Gilford (AZ-926) is the next one out followed by Banghart, then Pappy Kyle who is given a job in the clothing room. I am the last one left in isolation due to the fact that Swope believes I am the ringleader, but I've been given the job as orderly which is a certain sign that I'll soon be released.

As I sweep the gallery one day, my broom comes to rest against a pair of highly polished boots. Following the neat press up the trousers I come face to face with Delmar, the new deputy warden. I stop sweeping to give him the opportunity to pass but he doesn't move.

"What's going on here, Karpis? Don't you want out of isolation?"

"I haven't thought about it," I lie. "What's the big deal out there?"

"If I turn you out, will you go?"

"Like I say, I haven't thought about it. I don't care much one way or the other."

"Yes or no? Do you want out?"

"Let me think about it for a minute. I don't want back

in that kitchen, I've had my share of the library, I certainly wouldn't want to work around the cell house and I would hate to work in the industries."

Delmar thinks about what I have just said and then bursts out laughing. "That only leaves one place, doesn't it? Down in the clothing issue with your friend Kyle."

"Now you mention it," I reply, "Yeah, I would work down there. It ain't important though, I'm alright here."

The next day I am turned out of isolation and given a job in the clothing room with my old friend Pappy.

Although I don't realize it immediately, I am let out of isolation just in time to be involved in one of the wildest weeks in the history of Alcatraz. A caged animal turns mean. If you taunt it deliberately, it becomes dangerous. Most of the violence inflicted on cons by other cons is probably explained by this simple fact.

Lieutenant Severson earned the nickname "Utah" when promoted from McNeil Island to the position of warden in a Utah State Penitentiary. He lasted only a month before the joint rocked in riot. Now he's back working for the federal system but still remains a walking catastrophe. We are so used to his blunders, we assume that when he places a new shipment of cons on Fish Row without segregating the blacks from the whites, it's just another of Utah's errors. But the Tuesday morning shift arrives and no change is made, we now realize "The Devil" is up to his old pranks. Swope is introducing integration.

"Wildman" Willie Vasalick, the same one who ran the length of the yard to join in an earlier squabble between the blacks and the whites on the handball court, cells next to me. By Tuesday night he's hanging on the bars of his cell shaking violently in loud protests. There are many other outspoken anti-negroes screaming their objections to the guards and the new arrivals.

"White guys don't cell next to niggers here!"

"Get those black bastards over with their own kind!"

"Tell Swope if he wants to sleep with a spook next to him he's welcome to but we don't go for that crap in here!"

The newcomers are mainly a mixture of negroes and white trash from the South. Once the southerners realize they are being used to alter a standing tradition in Alcatraz, they begin to act up. The anger and resentment spreads—the cons start raising hell and a few end up in the hole but for the most part Tuesday night is a vocal affair.

My own feelings are mixed. I know Swope is only using the integration as a further test of how far he can force us into submission. On the other hand, I recognize that the negroes who have arrived on Fish Row have probably got more class than the white trash beside them. I started my prison experiences years ago in a state system where integration was in full force so the concept is neither shocking nor upsetting to me.

Still, my instincts warn me that the mixture of white and black in the explosive atmosphere of Alcatraz will bring disaster. I try to calm down "Wildman" Willie as best I can but I know Swope has gone too far this time.

Like everyone else I am caught in the middle, there is no place to hide. The choices are clear. Side with Swope and the negroes or side with the whites. I stay still, like the majority of white and negro cons, and hope that the authorities will work out some type of compromise.

By Wednesday night, the hole fills up with protestors. Bottles of black ink are smashed across the fading pink walls inside the cell house and run like blood down towards our doors. There's a not-so-hidden prophecy for the warden in the Rorschach-like blots forming on the walls of Alcatraz.

The waiting list to get into the overcrowded isolation block grows longer each hour as resentment spreads through the cell house. Following supper some demand to be placed in the hole rather than cell on Broadway next to negroes. They are carried bodily to their cells, struggling violently all the way, and thrown roughly inside.

People have to be educated to integration, not subjected to it. The artificial and autocratic atmosphere of the prison only intensifies the emotional reactions. Swope's actions incense the population but, by now, it is impossible to expect him to back down on his decision. Ironically, when I was in the kitchen, we used to always cell on the southern flats of Broadway next to the entrance to the mess hall, with black inmates across from us. That was a practical and accepted location for us, thus no one objected.

The negroes, who have no say in the new arrangements, are being used as pawns by Swope but they are enjoying their role and replying to the whining whites in increasingly bold and humorous jingles:

> *White boy, white boy, with your cell so fine,*
> *Your asshole stinks the same as mine!*

I am in constant discomfort from streams of pain in an infected elbow. If I sit or lie down it is unbearable but when I stand the pain subsides. Every second day I visit the hospital for treatments. It is difficult to say which worries me most, the impending disaster around me or the unending discomfort within.

Thursday's supper in the mess hall is a nervous experience. On one side of the dining hall fierce defensive eyeballs pop out under deep black frowns as the negroes feel the power of resentment seeping across the center isle. On the white side of the room, the tension is equally tight as silent stares across the tables catch other eyes, as if to say, "How shall we do this? Turn the tables over first and then jump on these black sons of bitches or jump on the niggers and forget about the goddamn tables?"

The guards, the machine guns, the gas bombs overlook the scene fully conscious of the confined energy. Miraculously, we make it back to our cells for the evening before the eruption.

First comes the spontaneous hollering and arguing with the negroes.

"You white mudderfuckers tink youse better den us, you ain't nothin!"

"Just try to come around here and cell on the galleries, you black bastards, you'll go over the edge in ten seconds!"

The point of neutrality is past. One white guy in all of Alcatraz sides with the negroes, his name is Consolo

(AZ-988). His negro friend is shouting encouragement in the growing din but the insults from the whites are drowning them out.

Lights out for the night acts as a signal—the roof just about blows off the cell house. In the explosion of noise and debris, paper, drawing boards, domino boards, and other personal articles fly across the corridors. The shelves along the backs of the cells are torn out, smashed into sharp fragments, and become dangerous projectiles. Toilet bowls are broken apart and fragments ricochet off cell-house walls and bars.

From the art supplies in various cells come bottles of turpentine, remodeled into Molotov cocktails. As they land on the coveralls and broken boards tossed into the corridors, the entire mass begins to blaze and savage forked flames lick their way slowly through the cell house and creep toward cell doors.

The screws are unable to put out the fires for fear of being hit by flying debris. Within ten minutes the smoke is suffocating the cons on the flat and rolling in grey clouds up to the tiers. Red Winhoven (AZ-829) suffers a heart attack but his choking gasps for help are ignored by the guards who are not about to open any cell in the midst of the rioting. Cries come up from the lower cells hidden below clouds of smoke. "We're all going to suffocate down here if we don't get rid of this smoke!"

"Plug up your toilets! Keep your foot on the flusher and let them overflow! That will flood out the fire!" shouts a con.

Everyone overflows his toilet and the salt water from San Francisco Bay comes flooding into the cell house.

Grasping my infected arm and attempting to wipe the tears from my smarting eyes I struggle to the rear of my cell and press down on the toilet flusher. The water quickly overflows and starts to creep across the floor in the direction of the snapping flames as if it recognizes a natural enemy by instinct. Once the flooding begins the pressure keeps the water running even when I remove my soaked foot from the peddle. It's the same all over the cell house.

Uncontrolled torrents of water gush out of each cell,

mingle with the streams from neighboring cells, and overflow from the tiers onto Broadway. Fast-moving rapids of seawater plunge down the staircases at either end as the entire cell house fills with a cooling swirling tide which gradually extinguishes the flames.

But, after the fires are drowned out, the water continues to rise and flood. The debris floats across the cell-house floor and we discover the entire building is on a slant as the currents rush in the direction of the dining hall and kitchen, overflowing down the staircase leading to the basement.

The roar of the falling, swirling, rushing water is heard above the clamour of the cons, as it plunges in Niagara-like arcs from the second and third tiers into the deepening lake now covering the main cell-house floor.

The waters wash away and cool the fires burning inside the cons. There is little left to break, burn or flood. We wait, subdued, for the next act in this bizarre drama to unfold in the morning light.

Although the water stops running and drains off into the basement by morning, the cell house overflows with eighty or ninety screws. They systematically move in squads through the rubble left in the wake of the fire and flood.

When the cell house orderlies refuse to clean up the mess, "goon squads" select cons and escort them over to A block where the cleaning equipment is kept in "the bank". The cons rebel and are worked over before they are thrown back into their cells.

The captain speaks to the negroes who volunteer to clean up. Consolo insists on helping them but he is warned by the other whites celling near him.

"Don't come back to this cell! If you do, you're going over the gallery. Go over and cell with the rest of the spooks. Your skin is the only white thing about you." Even the screws realize Consolo will be dead if he returns. They change his cell.

When the cell doors rack open after breakfast to allow us to go to work, no one steps out of his cell. No work! The entire population is on strike.

The morning is quiet but after lunch the boys in isolation stage a mini-riot of their own all afternoon. The authorities give up on their policy of one man to a cell in isolation—five or six cons crowd each cell. Every time the door to D block opens to allow new columns of reinforcements to enter, the cons jump up and down on their bunks and bang their bunks on the floor until you can swear they're rattling the very foundations of the Rock.

After supper, the general population comes to life again, and joins into the commotion precipitated in D block. The rioting continues another night although there is little left to throw out on the galleries.

In the darkness of my cell, with my infected arm stabbing pain, I move about uncomfortably doing my share to add to the avalanche of hysteria from the cages piled three storeys high. As I smash my steel bed against the cold cement floor with my good arm, the only thing in my mind is survival. I just spent an unnecessary fourteen months in isolation due to my "special" relationship with Swope. Plagued now by physical ailments, I hope only to survive the riot.

Gas masks and riot guns protrude from the impersonal grey forms packed shoulder to shoulder inside the tight gun cages as we parade into the mess hall for breakfast on Saturday morning. The uniformed figures hidden behind the ugly masks suggest an eerie threat as they wait and watch in anticipation of the expected outburst. The meal ends without incident.

When I return from the hospital and the treatments, I am a little surprised to discover Lieutenant Severson waiting to unlock the door to the cell house. Usually a screw looks after such petty duties, not a lieutenant. Utah greets me with, "Well Karpis, here we go again!" My immediate fears are Swope has found an excuse to label me a ringleader in order to get revenge for my victory over him in court.

"Am I going into the hole?" I ask.

"No! No! I mean 'more trouble.' "

"Yeah, I've been around Alcatraz longer than most anyone," I reply somewhat relieved. "There's never a dull moment."

Alvin Karpis (AZ-325)

Robert Stroud (AZ-594), the "Birdman of Alcatraz"

"Scarface" Al Capone (AZ-85)

"Machine Gun" Kelly (AZ-117)

John Paul Chase (AZ-238), partner of "Baby Face" Nelson

Volney Davis (AZ-271)

Roland Simcox (AZ-1131)

Joe Bowers (AZ-210), killed April 27, 1936

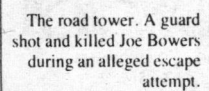

The road tower. A guard shot and killed Joe Bowers during an alleged escape attempt.

Mat shop. On December 16, 1937, Roe and Cole disappeared from the mat shop.

Ralph Roe (AZ-260)

Ted Cole (AZ-258)

left: Jimmy Lucas (AZ-224). right: Rufus Franklin (AZ-335). On May 23, 1938, Lucas, Franklin, and Limerick killed officer Cline during an escape attempt but Limerick was shot to death and Lucas and Franklin were recaptured.

In an escape attempt on January 13, 1939, five inmates broke out of D block isolation. Doc Barker was killed; the other four were recaptured.

Doc Barker (AZ-268)

Henry Young (AZ-244)

left: **Dale Stamphill (AZ-435)**
right: **Rufe McCain (AZ-267)**

Ty Martin (AZ-370)

In April 1943 four cons tried to escape the island. James Boarman was killed in the water; Freddie Hunter (Karpis's partner), Harold Brest, and Floyd Hamilton were recaptured.

James Boarman (AZ-571)

Harold Brest (AZ-467)

Freddie Hunter (AZ-402)

Joe Cretzer (AZ-548)	 Bernard Paul Coy (AZ-415)
 Marvin Hubbard (AZ-645)	 Miran Thompson (AZ-729)
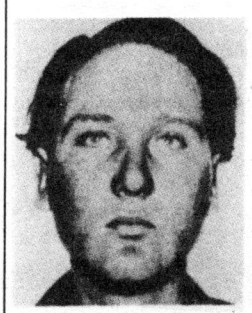 Sam Shockley (AZ-462)	 Clarence Carnes (AZ-714)

left: Warden Johnston
right: Bennett, Director of Prisons

Associate Warden Ernie Miller shows burns from a gas grenade. The explosion occurred during the 1946 escape attempt.

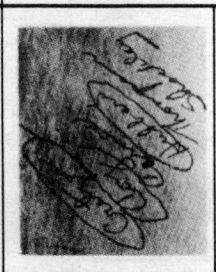

Six cons attempted to escape on May 2, 1946. Three were shot to death; two were later executed. Two guards were killed. The names of the six inmates were scrawled in blood on the cell wall by a wounded officer.

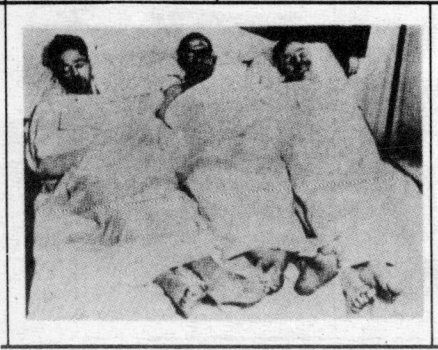

The bodies of the three convicts on a slab in the morgue

Escape attempt, June 13, 1962. Frank Morris and the two Anglin brothers cut through the walls of their cells and disappeared, never to be recaptured.

Frank Lee Morris
(AZ-1441)

John Anglin
(AZ-1476)

Clarence Anglin
(AZ-1485)

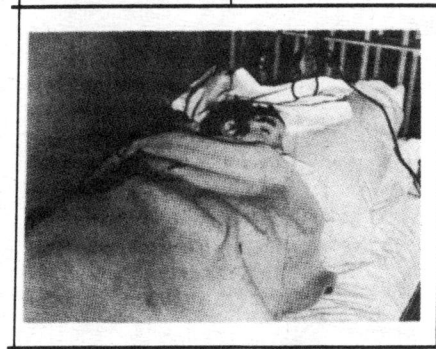

Dummy heads were left in the cells

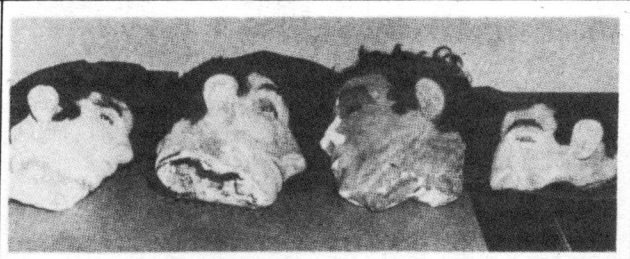

Plaster of paris heads used in the escape

After thirty-three years in captivity, Karpis was released. He is shown below in recent years participating in a CBC television interview before his death in 1979.

"How do you think this one will end up? We can't let you guys run around without working forever. When are you guys going back to work?"

"As soon as Mr. Delmar and Warden Swope clear this mess up."

"You're pretty well known around here, Karpis. Everyone knows you aren't afraid of the hole. You're well respected. Why don't you find out if there are any suggestions as to how we can square this thing up. What do you guys want?"

"Hell, I don't want nothin', I just want to go back to work as soon as you clear everything up."

"All of you are involved. When you go out on the yard, talk to the guys—find out how this can be cleared up."

I speak to Pappy Kyle about how far we should go in supporting the strike.

"Ray, if we get ourselves thrown into isolation over this, we'll be left holding out while the rest of these no good bastards cave in as they did over the kitchen thing." I agree with him.

Every time I go to the hospital for the ever increasing pains in my arm, Severson is waiting at the bottom of the steps leading back into the cell house with his persistent questions.

"How can we stop it? What do you guys want?"

The yard is dangerous even during normal times. Anything can happen in the arena if you let down your defenses. Many inmates choose never to venture out into that no man's land. On Saturday, I speak to about half a dozen of the guys on the yard who have a good deal of influence around Alcatraz. I tell them how Severson has been needling me to come up with some suggestions from the cons. They tell me, "Some of those guys over in D block ain't had a goddamn thing to do with this trouble. Tell Severson if they turn the guys out and leave the other ones in till they're ready to let them out, it could help us get back to work."

"I'll tell Utah what you've said and he can tell the captain—but I won't tell him who I've been talking to," I reply.

Severson is waiting as usual when I go to the hospital for my shots. I tell him, "Look, I know you guys don't make deals but I did ask around as you suggested. The best I can figure out, there are many guys in isolation who ain't had a fuckin' thing to do with this strike. If you'll turn them out you might calm down a lot of the excitement."

"How will we know who they are?"

"I'll get a list for you."

"I'll inform the captain, Karpis."

Monday morning the cell doors rack open as usual. "Everyone out to work!"

As usual only the negroes go to work. Then my door opens independently and I am taken around to the corner of the cell house where the interview desk is located.

Captain Richtner sits at the desk. Delmar, the Associate Warden, stands ominously in the background and Lieutenant Severson is right beside the desk, avoiding my eyes. Richtner speaks for all three. "You know Karpis, we suspected you were mixed up in this. Now we know it. You're trying to give us orders about who will be let out of D block. Are you trying to get your accomplices out so you can really wreck this place?

"I'll tell you something, Karpis. We'll do this our way, not yours! These guys would have all gone to work this morning if it hadn't been for you. The lieutenant will take you to D block—he already knows what to do with you over there." Richtner was the only one to speak. The interview ends abruptly.

On the way across the cell house my mind is moving faster than my feet. I've been had! Swope set me up! Severson says nothing from the time we leave the desk to the time we arrive at the large steel door, leading to isolation where he turns me over to the guard in charge of D block.

"Take off your clothes!" I'm ordered. I remove my clothes and wait for the guard to hand me the garments usually worn in isolation. Instead he says, "O.K. Karpis, come with me!"

Completely naked, I follow him down the wet cold corridor in isolation, past cells containing five or six men each. Some of the prisoners are as naked as I am, others wear underpants or shirts. We continue to the end of D block where the "hole cells" with solid doors are located and past them to the most barren and desolate of any confinement in Alcatraz, number 14, the "strip cell".

"Hit 14!" bellows the guard beside me as he unlocks the outside door and the screw up in the gun cage pushes the electric lever which opens the dark entrance to the "strip cell". A second door inside the first is opened and I am thrust forward into the empty box.

The double doors block out all light even in the middle of the day. The walls and floors are steel, nothing else exists in the small cupboard-like space except a hole in the floor which is the toilet. A guard flushes it from outside the cell. Otherwise, nothing. No bed, no blanket, no book, no shelf, no sink—nothing but the pathetic initials and dates scratched on the walls by former occupants.

Standing naked on the damp steel floor, I hear the doors lock behind me and realize that if I had the ability to raise my infected arm as well as my healthy one to my side, I would touch both walls and that I might walk about three steps before colliding against the wall at the end of the cell.

Even in the solitary confinement of the "strip cell," I am supposed to receive one subsistence meal a day. The bread and water diet has been replaced by a dixie cup of mush prepared by Stoddard, the new steward. He collects the leftovers from the main line—beets, carrots, spinach—and washes them thoroughly until the salt, minerals and nutrients are drained from them. Then he mashes the entire concoction into a sickly looking puke that is more liquid than solid.

However, no water and no slop arrives on the first day. Likewise, I receive no food or water the second day. There's no room to pace in the tiny cage and the cold chills crawl up my legs from the salt water on the floor. If I sit or lie on the floor my infected arm drives me crazy with pain. It seems to hurt less if I am standing so I spend most of the time on my feet. As the hours pass slowly, into days, my teeth begin to chatter uncontrollably. It is the fifth morning when the door to my cell opens. It's a screw with the MTA from the hospital on his rounds of D block.

"Are you alright, Karpis?"

"If I was alright I wouldn't have been coming to the hospital for shots every second day for over a month. You know that! You know I've never been on sick call unless I had to be and sometimes not even then!"

"We can't give you any shots for your arm while you're in here."

"I don't expect any shots, I just don't want any foolish questions!"

As the MTA slips sheepishly from the cell, the screw casually remarks, "By the way, Karpis, you're getting water every day aren't you?"

"You son of a bitch! You know damn well I'm not getting any water. Where would I get water? The only water in here is the salt water seeping in off the floor on the flats."

Feigning a look of surprise, he replies, "You mean to say you haven't had a drink for the four days that you've been over here?"

"You know fuckin' well that I ain't had a goddamn thing to eat or drink! You know the whole goddamn story, you son of a bitch! Don't come to me with your bullshit!"

In a few minutes, the screw returns with a large half-gallon jug of water filled to the top. "Here, drink all you can of this. You must really be thirsty!"

I know better. I was raised in Kansas where the temperatures reach 105° in the summer. Too much water in my dehydrated condition will make me sick. "You bastard, you ain't doing me no favour with all that water. You just want me to get sick. You tell that s.o.b. who sent you in here with it that all I need is a cupful." His face flushes red with embarrassment as he realizes I am aware of what they are trying to do to me in my weakened condition. He's not bringing me water as a favour any more than he was responsible for depriving me of it for five days. He's only following orders.

After that episode, I receive a dixie cup of water and slop once a day, but nothing else.

I eat only a portion of the slop they hand me each day in the dixie cup. Just enough to ensure they don't force feed me. I have a dread fear of them forcing their way into my cell and ramming tubes down my throat. Just the thought of it makes me gag. Not once in the twenty-two days I spend in the "strip cell" do I take a crap.

At first I keep track of the days by listening for the cell counts. At regular times through the days and nights they look into my cell to be certain I am still alive. It turns into a bad dream, a gigantic hallucination. Nothing seems real any longer. Days seem like nights and nights seem like days. At intervals sunlight floods into my eyes leaving me blinded as I grope for the dixie cup and force myself to swallow half the contents.

An insane idea takes possession of me. They must never discover me lying down or sitting. Whenever I hear the outside door being opened, I struggle to my feet. My head is in a constant spin and I am now oblivious to the pain in my arm.

"Can you walk out of here on your own?" The voice of the screw is far away and vibrating in almost undistinguishable syllables.

"Sure I can!"

"Well try it."

As I wobble independently into the blinding daylight I strike headfirst into the door left ajar for my exit. I can see why the screw had his doubts. He leads me the rest of the route from the "strip cell" to a long cell on the flats which already contains three other cons. I am given a pair of coveralls to hide my bony frame. Inside the cell I notice two mattresses on the floor side by side which the four of us can use by lying across them sideways rather than lengthwise. The only con I recognize in the cell is Ernie Lopez (AZ-697). A suspicion rushes into my mind but I don't speak it aloud—"Why are they being so kind to me all of a sudden?"

"Have you had a dixie cup yet today?" asks Ernie.

"I don't remember," I answer honestly. "Have you?"

"No," he replies, "I think they are going to give us our first meal over here for more than a month. You got out of the strip cell just in time."

About an hour later the chuck wagon rolls into D block. On the menu is boiled potato, macaroni and cheese, and spinach. It's the only time in my life that I eat spinach although I give most of the meal away. My stomach has shrivelled to such a small size, I can't take more than a few bites before I'm full.

The cons in isolation are still riotous even after a month of solitary. With the cells overcrowded it's not too solitary but the food is rationed and the majority of the cells have been destroyed to the point where there is no plumbing or comforts such as bunks. Richtner and the "goon squad" run fire hoses out onto the flats and spray us all down during the night to drown out the screams of protest.

"This is nothing," shouts Ernie as we huddle in the rear of the cell, away from the jet of water. "When the main cell house heard that you had been thrown into the strip cell as the ringleader twenty-two days ago they went wild. The joint rocked all night and they even threw their shoes out of their cells after setting fire to them." In spite of my drenched clothing and crippled arm, I sleep soundly the balance of the night on my few feet of mattress.

In the morning I have a visitor. He enters D block and comes to stand directly in front of my new cell. It's "The Devil" himself. Swope does not go past my cell and does not stop in front of any other one. We stand eye to eye. I see the warped twinkle glow behind his eyes as his mouth twists into a sly grin. Although he says nothing before leaving as abruptly as he appeared, his smile has said it all—"You son of a bitch, I've taught you not to try to take a warden to court."

Like all prison strikes and riots, this one simmers down with time. Slowly, a few at a time, the cons drift back to work in the industries. "Back to work" is one of the conditions if anyone wants out of the unbearable conditions in the overcrowded cells of D block. Another condition for release from isolation is a cell on Broadway beside the negroes. Although guys are still arriving in isolation regularly, there are now two or three giving up the protest and returning to population for every new arrival. The population in isolation thins out and I'm transferred to a cell of my own on the second gallery.

Delmar, the associate warden, takes the brunt of the blame and is forced to resign from the prison service. Swope receives a communication from Washington. "Why didn't you have the radio installed as you were told to do years ago?"

I conclude that Swope has mislead Washington about the cause of the rioting. No one in Alcatraz is objecting to the lack of a radio or a commissary this time. Although the press never reports it as such, it is a straightforward racial riot. If Swope is not reporting the actual cause to Washington or the public, it is most likely because the forced integration is his own idea.

The screw is looking straight ahead as he strolls past my cell in isolation and slyly passes a slip of paper between his fingertips into my hand in a secretive gesture.

I unfold it to discover a typewritten copy of a telegram from my sister informing me of my father's death. Letters from my sister follow describing how my father, who had been a painter most of his life and consuming fumes from his hard labor, died of lung cancer. Her letters dwell on her own guilt at ushering him to a hospital against his wishes as he declared he would never return home alive and begged to be left at home.

I brood over the disheartening news, my sister berating herself, my failures as a son and the heartaches and trouble I caused our parents all my life, and then realistically push it all from my mind and ask my sister not to refer to our father's death again in any of her correspondence.

Alcatraz, 1953

No one in Alcatraz, neither guards nor inmates, slept last night. Gregory, the big screw in charge of isolation, stops at my cell this morning. "You guys get any sleep last night?" he asks.

"Hell, no! If you screws think that us 'hardened criminals' are trouble, how would you like to have 300 cons like that handful who kept us going all night?"

"I'd hand in my resignation inside of twenty-four hours," he admits in a tired, hoarse voice.

Last night was a strange experiment. It is never attempted again.

A large group of teenagers, being transferred to a reformatory in Oklahoma, was passing through San Francisco. In the case of large transfers, it is a common practice to put them up at various jails or prisons along the way, but never at a maximum security institution such as Alcatraz. In this instance, someone came up with the bright suggestion that the cells in A block, which are rarely used because they have not been converted to tool-proof bars, could house the kids overnight.

They paraded the gang of them into A block and threw them, two or three to a cell, into the ancient cages. The cells are not equipped with bunks, so each of the young inmates was given a mattress for the night. Some slop was shoveled into bowls back in the kitchen and brought around to the cells to be dispersed amongst the youngsters. The authorities reasoned that the children would be so tired from the long day of traveling that they would quickly fall to sleep. In a pig's ass they would!

The steel and concrete of old Alcatraz groaned under their stomping feet and the barred windows ached from their shrill shouts of excitement at being inmates of the most notorious prison in America. They were the wildest, craziest pack of kids I've ever seen and they were determined to make their one night stay in Alcatraz memorable. To them, this was one of the greatest treats of their lives, like the first night they slept away from home with friends, and they intended to "party" all night.

The gruff, experienced guards of Alcatraz tried to quiet them. Suggestions that they would need their sleep for the long trip ahead of them were barely audible over the din. Louder threats by the screws demanding they end their shouting and hollering were ignored. An organized attempt to discover a few ringleaders and cower them into obedience was met with gleeful laughter and only increased the throbbing tempo now echoing through the cellblocks.

Behind our bars, we listened with amusement at the frustrated attempts of our keepers to keep order. Under normal circumstances most of the cell house would be complaining because they couldn't sleep, but not in this case. If anyone tried to speak, the other cons would shout them down with cries of, "Keep Still! Keep Still! so we can hear what they're saying." "Kids" and cons were shouting messages and greetings back and forth across the vibrating old structure.

Finally one of the lieutenants brought out the strap and after showing them the size and weight of it, gave them a lecture on the damage it could do to a human back. The kids listened with relish to the descriptions of skin being torn from bone and immediately sent up a chant. "We want the strap! We want the strap!"

Of course the lieutenant had no intention of using the strap on any of them, let alone all of them. With his bluff called and the racket growing louder he retired in disgrace.

One foolish screw tried to threaten them by suggesting he would throw them in a cell with a dangerous public enemy for the night. Now the youngsters were making every kind of weird demand imaginable.

"We want Scarface Al Capones's autograph!"

"We want to talk to Old Creepy Karpis!"

"We want to cell with Machine Gun Kelly!"

The fact that most of the "big name" criminals they associated with Alcatraz were no longer here, did not prevent their playful demands.

The noise was rocking the entire island and even the families of the guards who live on the island could hear the loud uproar. More and tougher guards entered the children's cell house to try to quell their rioting antics.

"You see those stairs," indicated one deep-voiced guard after he had succeeded in getting their attention. He was pointing at the stairs which were seen from the cells in A block and which descended under the cell house to the "dungeon" below. Many a hardened con had had his spirit broken down in the "dungeon".

"These stairs lead to *the dungeon*! This is where we put Alcatraz cons who give us trouble. It's dark, it's wet, it's cold, and it stinks of rot and decay down there. There are skeletons in that dungeon of prisoners tortured to death by the Spanish when Alcatraz used to be a military fortress centuries ago. The rats down there are as large as alley cats and devour human flesh. Now, if you don't quiet down for the rest of the night, we're going to throw the whole lot of you down in *the dungeon* until morning!"

There were a few seconds of silence when he concluded and then the response came in unison and grew louder on each syllable, "We want in the dungeon! We want to say we spent the night in Alcatraz's dungeon! We want to tell everyone we slept in the dungeon."

Well, Jesus Christ! The whole cell house was in stitches.

The guards tried one last threat. They hauled out the fire hoses and aimed them up at the jeering and taunting multitude of young "criminals". "Quiet down or we'll turn the hoses on you!"

Cheers came down from the mass of eager faces pressed against the bars. "Yea! Turn on the fire hoses! We want the fire hoses! We want the fire hoses!"

No further attempts at intimidation were made by the authorities. They must have finally realized they were only encouraging greater outbursts.

All night long, until the morning sun came to wish them on their way, the youngsters kept Alcatraz in a state of chaos. By morning both cons and screws were glad to see them gone. No one had slept, but no con was upset about it.

If the Rock ever came close to cracking under pressure and sinking into San Francisco Bay it was during "the night of the children."

Someone special is to visit isolation. A screw orders, "Everyone up and dressed! If you have blankets in your cell fold them neatly."

We stand by our cell doors, as ordered, and the electrically operated steel door, leading from the main cell house, swings open. I recognize both visitors almost immediately.

The first is James V. Bennett, Director of Prisons, from Washington, and the second is a feeble old man who is only a weak imitation of his movie screen personality. It's Edward G. Robinson, the epitome of the 1930 gangster.

As Bennett ushers his aging guest along the flats in front of our cells, I see the gun cage at the end of the cell house filling up with reinforcements of armed screws. Bennett and Robinson have not made it halfway down the cell fronts when the booing and shouting begins.

The boys in isolation have no more discipline than a bunch of crows on a telephone wire. It's for this reason that the warden, the associate warden and the captain rarely visit isolation now, it's simply too embarrassing for them.

Finding their progress blocked by the catcalls and insults hurled in their path, the pair cut their tour short. The happy smile across Edward G. Robinson's face indicates he's enjoying the tirade but Bennett makes an undignified exit with a scowl on his face.

When I hear that the new associate warden used to work at Springfield, the "bughouse" of the federal prison system, I expect him to be a brutal sadistic asshole. The complaints of inmates in mental institutions are never taken seriously by anyone thus the custodians in such hospitals treat the patients worse than regular prison guards would ever get away with.

The first time Latimer arrives in D block to inspect the boys in isolation, there is a hushed silence. He enters the cell house alone and proceeds along the flats in front of our cells. His lonely footsteps are the only break in the supersaturated tension. Over thirty pairs of eyes, shadowed behind bars, follow his every movement as his own eyes expertly scan the cells.

Halfway down the cell house, he throws down the

cigarette he's smoking and crushes it beneath his boot. Nervously he lights up another. Then the silence is smashed by a lone voice—"Ain't he a funny lookin' son of a bitch!"

The entire crew of cons collapse into uncontrolled laughter. Even the screws have a difficult time holding back their chuckles. The spontaneous outburst, which degenerates into more specific attacks on his anatomy, takes the new associate warden by surprise. He is visibly shaken and attempts to retain his dignity. The second cigarette, only half-finished, hits the cement floor and is immediately smothered under a flat sole as he takes out a third one in the same movement and fumbles in a pathetic attempt to light it.

A young kid named Butterfield yells out, "Hey look it's Mortimer Snerd, the Walking Turd!"

The nickname meets with instant approval and applause as others add their comments:

"You couldn't give him a better name!"

"Maybe this dummy posed for that block of wood when they carved the real Mortimer Snerd!"

From that day on, whenever Latimer enters D block, he is greeted with the gleeful salutation, "It's Mortimer Snerd the Walking Turd!" although in common references to him among cons he is called simply "Skinhead" because he has a large bald portion on the side and top of his head which is a different hue from the rest of his skin—probably the result of a burn or accident. He never fails to get in a nervous tizzy over the name-calling and gives the guards hell if they don't take down the names of the cons who taunt him.

The scene of Latimer's first visit is a direct contrast to a similar scene years ago in the same isolation unit. Just as the cell house is now in ruins following the rioting, it was also a mess on that day back in 1942. Today the walls of isolation are splattered with the sickly green mush that they serve us in place of food; on that day in the past the walls were running with spaghetti and meat sauce.

The associate warden at that time was old Meathead and he came charging into the cell house like gangbusters—"If I ever find out which of you cocksuckers is responsible for the mess on these walls, I'll break him in half with my own hands!"

"Why you big, soft, sow-bellied son of a bitch," called down Pappy Kyle from his cell on the galleries, "I'm the one who threw that out. Now, what do you want to do about it!" Instantly the entire cell house had broken into catcalls and insults against Meathead similar to what we gave Skinhead. Meathead, however, had reacted in a very different manner than our newest associate warden. He broke out laughing at the abuse, danced a little jig to the further amusement of the cell house and sang us a little jingle:

*Sticks and stones
May break my bones
But names can never hurt me!*

before he went out, laughing over his shoulder as he left, "Fuck you sons of bitches!"

I crouch in the rear of my cell trying to draw on a squashed cigarette. Ten packs were smuggled into D block today in the binding of an encyclopedia from the library. At other times they come in with the laundry hamper. Seldom is anyone who wants to smoke without cigarettes, even in the hole.

In the background, I can't help but hear the noise echoing from the bandroom in the basement where the showers and laundry are located. It's easy to deduce that the negroes are using the bandroom—their brass horns can be heard across the bay in San Francisco. Also they hit more sour notes than anyone else, not because they are worse musicians but because they are more interested in jumping around, swaying their bodies to and fro, falling on their knees with their backs arched in catlike motions, their heads thrown back and, on balance, putting on more of a visual show than a musical one.

When the racket in the basement stops abruptly for the day I decide to stop smoking. It takes too much of the pleasure away when I have to hide in corners and puff on flattened or broken cigarettes. I give up smoking for the duration of my stay in isolation which turns out to be about fourteen months.

11

Alcatraz, Isolation, 1954

Pappy Kyle is sent back to general population—I am the only one left of the forty-two occupants in D block who was sent to the hole for participating in the riot. Most of the young punks who scream the loudest for strikes and riots are the first to whine their way out of isolation. They beg the "man" to let them out, promising to stay out of trouble. The sniveling bastards even accept cells on Broadway with the negroes in order to get out. Forcing whites to cell with blacks on Broadway started the riot and now many of the guys who participated in the chaos who have been put into isolation three or four times have swallowed their pride to get out each time.

"It's time you woke up," I tell myself, "you can't break into the hole every time some new guys get excited. They all crawl out with their tails between their legs while you get left behind because of your stubborn pride. In four or five years they go home and you're left here in Alcatraz still being punished over their complaints. Straighten yourself up!"

I've been in isolation for over a year for allegedly being the ringleader of the riot which all but destroyed the cell house when I have an encounter with "T. U." Moore. The "T. U." is his nickname because he works in the "Treatment Unit," the new euphemism for the forty-two isolation cells in D block.

"T. U." Moore was a marine and worked at Lewisburg, Pennsylvania, before coming to our island. He is a real policeman and hated by most of the inmates although he thinks he is the best guard in the cell house.

He tells me one day, "You know the guards overheard what you told the other strikers over here in isolation when they were threatening to mutilate themselves in protest. Your comments about how you would cut one of the screws or officials before you cut yourself are written down in your jacket out front. Some of the guards think you should be kept over here indefinitely."

"Fuck them! I live here, they come and go. This is my home, I'll live the way I think I should, not the way they want me to."

"T. U." walks away from my cell and continues a strange game he plays. He likes to turn on the air conditioner which is connected to each of the hole cells in order to freeze the poor bastards inside. In defence the cons collect toilet paper every time the guards change and by moistening the paper they stick it into the one-foot by eight-inch wire mesh screen on the back of the vents in the cells. The wet paper hardens and acts as a cement, keeping out the air. As the cold air backs up in the ventilator shaft it produces a rumbling noise which has brought the defensive maneuver of the cons to the attention of "T. U." Moore. Now everyday he spends hours tearing the paper out of the ventilator openings with a handmade hook he invented for the purpose. He is going to all this work and trouble in order to be able to turn the cold air on the convicts who are already miserable in the holes. He refuses to issue them any more toilet paper and writes notes to the other screws telling them to withhold it.

I'm furious with his petty attitude and, as he begins his work on the ventilators, I begin "low rating" him with loud shouts, "You son of a bitch! Ain't you got nothin' better to do than tear paper out of mesh screens? What poor excuse for a man are you?"

When he finishes he comes up to my cell. "Hey Ray, you don't have a goddamn bit of respect for me, do you?"

"Well I don't know why you're putting it on a personal basis," I reply, "but now that you ask me, let me tell you something. For me to have respect for someone, con or screw, he has to have self-respect. If he don't have self-respect, why the hell would he expect me to have any for him? Anybody who would spend hours a day doing what you've been doing the last few weeks with those goddamn hooks you made to keep those guys from getting warm in them holes—you couldn't have any self-respect. So no! I don't have a fuckin' bit of respect for you!

"I'm going to tell you something else," I add, lowering my voice to a whisper, "get up here close to the bars so you can hear me."

By the look on his face I see that he suspects I'm going to grab him by his necktie. I grin. "No, no really. I want to tell you something."

He comes up close and presses his cheek against the bars of my cell.

"I don't know if you know this or not," I begin, "but God's got a funny way of working around people. You can't be religious anyhow, a guy like you couldn't believe in God or you wouldn't do the things you do over here, but God gets back at people who do mean things to others. Maybe not directly but He gets them—sometimes through someone else in their family. Often the member of the family who is suffering doesn't even know what is going on or why they are being punished."

"Jesus Christ, Ray! Don't say that! Don't say that!" His face is a shocked white and he looks over his shoulder as if he expects to see God in D block taking notes.

"What's the matter?"

"I ain't going to say what's the matter but don't be saying that. Don't tell me anything like that. O.K., I'm goin' to quit takin' the paper out of there," he promises in a hoarse whisper.

"There's a hell of a lot more you'd better quit doing too," I warn, seeing that my words are effective.

He leaves. Nothing more is said but he throws away his hook and never turns on the air conditioning again.

Three days earlier I had spoken to a relief screw who

was filling in for "T. U." Moore. "Where's 'T. U.'?" I had asked.

"Don't say anything to these other guys," he cautioned me, "because they all hate him and would only yell and scream at him if they knew of his personal troubles. His twelve-year-old daughter was struck down with polio. He and his wife are at the children's hospital in San Francisco visiting her. She may die!"

I had not broken faith with the guard who confided that information to me, I never mentioned it to any con.

Less than a week later "T. U." once again approaches my cell. "Listen Ray, if I ask Deputy Latimore if you can be the D block orderly, will you take the job?"

"What about the guy who has the job now?"

"He's going out in a few days."

I am secretly delighted because the orderly has the freedom to roam around D block but I answer cautiously, "Okay but only if you continue acting like a human being as you have been the last little while! Quit screwing those guys around in the hole. Quit trying to be so goddamn efficient seeing that we don't get what we're not supposed to have. We ain't got nothin' over here anyhow but you're trying to make doubly sure we don't get anything. Yeah, I'll take it, but I don't think Skinhead will let me have the job."

In a couple of days he brings me the news. "Yeah, Mr. Latimer says he's going to let you have the job!" This is strange because I've never had any conversation with Skinhead since he became deputy warden at Alcatraz. I wonder why he would agree to give me a prestige position of trust in D block. Anytime he visits D block, I busy myself at the rear of my cell as he passes by and thus we have never spoken a word to each other.

On the other hand, Skinhead was not deputy when I had the legal battle with Swope and it is because I exposed Swope in open court and proved he was breaking the law that I'm in isolation. Everyone in the prison is by now aware of the way the officials "set me up" and tossed me into isolation over the riot when the true reason for them punishing me is that I went to court in Missouri and proved Swope's duplicity.

"I'm sitting on the end of my bunk when Skinhead and "T. U." Moore stop in front of me. Immediately I get up, go to the rear of my cell, and begin brushing my teeth to avoid them. I have never spoken to the new deputy and don't intend to start now. Over my shoulder I can still feel the pair watching and waiting on the other side of the bars. "Goddamn, how long do I have to brush my teeth?" I wonder to myself. Eventually they depart but "T. U." returns alone.

"Ray, Mr. Latimer knows you don't want to talk to him about anything. He asked me to inform you that your mother died."

"O.K.," I reply and walk back to my sink to get a drink of water. "T. U." takes the hint and leaves.

When people you hurt are alive you don't think of making amends. Her death shakes me up because she had always been good to me in spite of everything—unlike my father with whom I always argued. I was always generous with money and treated her well but she didn't need my money, I would have made her much happier if I had stayed out of trouble.

Now it's too late, she's dead, there is no way to make amends; if I dwell on the matter it can only lead to depression.

Curley Thomas (AZ-687), one of the inmates in isolation, is probably one of the most dangerous paranoids ever to be housed in Alcatraz. He killed a couple of fellow inmates in a prison in Washington, D.C., and another one in the medical center at Springfield, Missouri. I never understood how, in spite of his violent background, he was given the job of negro barber. Segregation is in full force in the barbershop. White convicts cut the hair of the white inmates and black barbers work on the negroes. They have separate days to use the barbershop.

Curley has had many fights with other negroes while at Alcatraz. He tried on several occasions to kill unwanted or outdated lovers still annoying him with their attentions. He is a "little girl" and much sought after by the negro population. One day he took a homemade shiv into the mess hall and went after a large negro with it. It was obvious that he was not grandstanding but meant business. There were other incidents and Curley spends much time in isolation over his fighting and loving.

Unlike the large lips and flat noses common to the majority of negro convicts, Curley has slim, even features and an extremely light complexion. He is good looking, small, and has curly rather than kinky hair. He is always clean and neat in appearance but suffers from a slight Narcissus complex.

Most of the black convicts try "to make" Curley so it was no surprise when a large negro named Barsock (AZ-884) began chasing him. Since the war years, we all received a Christmas package of candies and cake once a year. The previous Christmas Barsock gave his Christmas package to Curley in an effort to woo him. Finally Barsock realized he wasn't going to get much for his sacrifice and there was ill-feeling between them over it.

It was during the noon hour that Barsock, large, black, and muscular, went for his haircut. Little Curley was the barber. There was no outward sign of the friction between the two as Barsock took his place in the barber chair and Curley wrapped the white cloth comfortably around him with the finesse of an experienced hair stylist. Curley then walked slowly over to his work stand and picked up the shears. As he returned to the barber chair he walked around it as if surveying Barsock's hair before trimming it. Then, without warning, Curley drove the shears through Barsock's heart.

The big man lunged out of the barber chair, stood for a moment in dazed disbelief at the red blood gushing from the white linen where it remained nailed to him by the shears, and fell flat on his back dead!

The guard in the barbershop in his panic forgot about the alarm button and began shouting frantically for help.

Curley remained calm, walked over to Barsock's body

tangled in the crimson-stained barber's sheet. Kneeling down beside his deceased victim, he placed a tender farewell kiss on the motionless lips.

When he stood up again, Curley returned quietly to stand beside his work bench and waited nonchalantly for the guards to come and get him.

Saturday morning and "T. U." Moore meets me with a smile on his face. "Karpis, can you be ready to go in ten minutes?"

"Where?"

"To general population. First I'll have to send you downstairs for a shower and a clothing issue."

"Wait a minute," I caution, no longer trusting anyone, "I want to know what cell you're going to give me. I'm better off staying here than going out there and refusing a cell. Then I'll only end up back here in the hole. I want to know where I'm going to cell before I go out of here."

The exasperation shows on his face as he replies, "You know something. If it was anyone else I would tell them it ain't none of their goddamn business. You either come and take your chances or stay here! I won't tell you where you are going to cell, but I'll tell you it sure as hell ain't going to be on Broadway. That warden wouldn't have you on Broadway for love or money!"

"What the hell are you talking about," I challenge him. "He's making everyone who goes out of here cell on Broadway."

"Well not you. You'd have the whole place in an uproar inside of ten days. No, you ain't going on Broadway, even if you want to. Take my word for it!"

Like the routine for all prisoners being released from isolation (Treatment Unit) in D block, I march down to the basement where I trade in my "T. U." coveralls for an issue of clean clothing with my number on it—AZ-325. Before dressing I take a shower (the showers are still located in the basement directly in front of the clothing issue) and afterwards I am taken to my new cell. As it turns out, "T. U.'s" word is good. I am not placed on Broadway but given a cell on the outside of B block directly across from the barbershop.

On Monday morning, I stare thoughtfully at the barbershop area recalling the blood-splattered remains of Barsock lying on the floor when my vision of him is suddenly eclipsed by a youthful face with a happy smile on it. I have just blinked the newcomer into focus when a second young head pops up beside the first. The two kids are strangers to me: they arrived at Alcatraz during the last year while I was in isolation.

"Are you really Alvin Karpis?"

"Did you used to be the leader of the Ma Barker Gang?"

"I heard you were a good friend of Baby Face Nelson—is that true?"

"What was Al Capone like when he was here in Alcatraz?"

"How many banks did you rob with Pretty Boy Floyd?"

"They say you were the ringleader of the riot in here a few years ago."

Their questions come like rapid-fire and, being only an hour out of isolation, I'm somewhat overwhelmed by them. It soon becomes obvious that they are great "crime buffs" and that I am a celebrity to them. In the weeks and months to follow, the guard is continually chasing them away from the front of my cell.

Both are about twenty-one or twenty-two years of age, and each stands over six feet. They are "fall partners" from an army detention barracks and are serving forty years each. They work around the cell house and always come by my cell with more questions about the old days and my former associates. Even when I am on the yard talking with friends, they show up in the middle of a private conversation with their unending questions.

"What kind of a guy was Dillinger? Could he drive a car good?"

"Could Machine Gun Kelly really write his name in bullet holes on a wooden fence? Have you ever seen him do it? Did he ever tell you he did it?"

Roland E. Simcox (AZ-1131) is by far the more aggressive of the pair. He has a heavy face, is good looking, weighs about 200 pounds and is a child of the fifties, straight out of *American Grafitti*. His hair, honey blond and curley, slopes back into a "ducktail" on the back of his neck and flows up from his ears on top of his head in "jelly rolls". His pride and joy are two carefully trained curls which hang over his forehead almost to his eyebrows. Simcox is vain. Whenever he walks on the yard he can't keep his eyes off his own chest and biceps. His T-shirt is usually rolled up over his shoulders to reveal his muscular arms.

His partner, Edward H. Gauvin (AZ-1134), is not as strong or muscular as Simcox although he stands as tall. His light, almost soft complexion is enhanced by a pair of dark alert eyes and a head of black hair which he combs straight back and high on his head. He has as much hair as many women and this along with his feminine features give him a "chorus boy" look. He is younger than Simcox, has even white teeth, delicate lips and nose, and (although he doesn't act like an outright homosexual) it is assumed by many that he and Simcox are lovers. The two are inseparable and it is understood by everyone in Alcatraz that no one should "mix into this affair." I know the first time I see Gauvin's innocent face in front of my cell that he will end up getting in a lot of trouble in Alcatraz or getting a lot of other people in trouble.

Alcatraz, On The Yard, 1954

I sit talking with Pappy Kyle. High on the steps overlooking the yard, we both recognize that Simcox and Gauvin are in the midst of a passionate argument up by the handball court. At one point in the oral exchange, Simcox loses his temper and slams his fist into the kid's mouth. Even from the distance where we sit, I see the blood trickling from the corner of Gauvin's mouth.

My first reaction is to look at the screw on the yard but

he hasn't noticed the incident. The wall screw, however, does and he starts hollering to his counterpart who doesn't hear him because he is at the other end of the yard, near the baseball diamond. Without warning, Gauvin takes off in a dead run in the direction of the yard screw.

"What the hell! I'm sure that kid isn't running to that screw," I comment to Pappy as we sit watching the drama. From our vantage point above the yard, the entire show is like a silent movie—only the plot is real and the outcome unrehearsed.

Simcox knows what the kid is running for. He takes right after him, trying to catch him, but doesn't quite make it. The yard screw thinks they are running a race across the yard, as is the custom at Alcatraz among friends.

By the time Simcox gets to the other end of the yard, Gauvin reaches down and straightens up with a baseball bat between his hands. Simcox is so close on Gauvin's heels, the whirling bat bounces off his back harmlessly as he grabs it from the kid's grasp. Gauvin is trying desperately to regain his weapon from Simcox as they struggle together.

The wall screw calls into the main office for help while the yard screw, finally aware of what is happening, stands by helplessly. He is not about to step between two angry inmates and a baseball bat. Who can blame him?

As their bodies revolve, the emotions of Simcox and Gauvin unwind although what words they gasp in whispered tones to one another remain their secret. The bat, held high and erect between them at first, droops and then relaxes in Simcox's grip until, the moment of passion over, it hangs limply, touching the ground. The guards move quickly and escort the pair to isolation.

Many of the screws are angry because I'm released from isolation. With the exception of a few weeks between the time I spent in isolation over the kitchen strike and the long stretch I've just finished over the racial riots, I haven't lived in Alcatraz's main cell house for almost three years. There are many changes. It doesn't seem like the old Alcatraz to me anymore.

First, with few exceptions, the faces of both cons and

screws are new to me. Not only has the prison filled up with young kids like Simcox and Gauvin who regard me as some sort of antique but there is also another drastic change. When Swope discovered that the negroes work when the whites go on strike and that they can be relied on to clean up the mess after the riots, he continued to deliberately fill Alcatraz with blacks. Racial prejudice, in existence before, is nearing the point where racism is bubbling and boiling. With the types of pressure exerted by Swope, a riot is bound to explode again, even more violent than before.

There are only seven or eight white guys celling anywhere on Broadway now due to the shortage of cells since half the population is now black. Broadway looks like a flock of crows perched along a country road. It's entirely black, three tiers high. The whites cell on the outside of the cellblocks. I recall the early days when there weren't even enough negroes to make up one table in the dining hall. Now it's a split mess hall with blacks on one side and whites on the other and trouble lurking somewhere in between.

Swope forces whites to cell on Broadway beside or across from negroes as punishment but he has never been foolish enough to precipitate another riot by placing a negro in the outside cells which are the exclusive white suburbs of Alcatraz. If the negro population grows any larger, he will have no inside cells left and when that day arrives, I'll be looking for a place to hide because people are going to be killed by the dozens when the racial warfare breaks out in earnest. The year ahead promises to be a deadly one.

When I go to the yard I feel out the direction the racial issue is heading so I'll be able to get out of its way. My conversations with various cons on the yard cause me much concern. "Am I just out of isolation in time for another race riot?" I ask bluntly.

"Sure as hell! The more of them come in, the more brazen they're gettin'. There's bound to be a war if more of 'em keep comin' in."

"Do you know where or when?"

"Out here on the yard and when we white guys want it, if we have any choice about it."

"What's it all about? Why is it going to happen?"

"Wait till you've been out here for a while and you'll see the difference in the attitude of these black bastards since the place is overflowing with them."

I don't want to get a fractured skull, a shiv in my back, or another few years in isolation when Swope decides to name me as the ringleader! Dark clouds are gathering on the horizon and there is no shelter in sight.

It's Saturday, the day before Christmas, 1954, when I notice a sharp pain in my right side. At first I ignore it, but as the day goes on, it becomes more painful until I am forced to call a guard and have him escort me to the hospital. They can't figure out what the problem is in the hospital but on Monday they take an X-ray.

"Goddamn, you've got a kidney stone! No wonder you're hurtin'! How the hell have you been puttin' up with the pain? It's stuck in that tube between your kidney and your bladder."

They put me on morphine immediately for a few days until the X-rays reveal that the stone has dropped into my bladder. Then they insist on keeping me in the hospital until I piss it out. After a week I still haven't recovered the stone for them and I don't care if I do.

"I ain't hurtin' no more, let me out!" I insist. They release me from the hospital and as I return to the cell house Fatso Mitchell greets me.

"I didn't realize how sick you were back before Christmas, Karpis. Happy New Year! It's 1955 now."

"Ray, my father and sister are coming for a visit tomorrow. They've read so much about your career as Public Enemy Number One and heard so much about you from me, they want to see what you look like. When I'm talking with them, you come past with your library wagon to say hello."

The next day as Pappy Kyle is visiting with his family, I roll my wagon full of books past that end of the cellblock and stall in front of the visiting area. After a cursory glance, the guard ignores my presence.

I wave at the sister and father who respond happily. They feel honored that I should take the time to say hello.

For me it is also an honor. Kyle's sister is the first woman I have seen in nineteen years.

Alcatraz, Clothing Issue, 1955

When Simcox and Gauvin go to work in the clothing issue they come into contact with a catalyst which is to cause one of the deadliest explosions in the history of Alcatraz. The catalyst is "San Quentin" Smitty.

San Quentin Smitty takes an immediate liking to young Gauvin and the kid seems to return the interest, to the chagrin of Simcox. When San Quentin is put in isolation, the tension relaxes, but then Gauvin also is thrown into isolation. Simcox finds himself left alone back in the clothing issue and begins to get suspicious while his friend Gauvin and San Quentin are together in D block.

Several months pass with "kites" going back and forth between Simcox and Gauvin. In the kites sent back to Simcox, Gauvin talks about how he is trying to get out of solitary without success. Simcox goes to his superior in charge of the clothing issue and asks him to intercede with Skinhead in order to get Gauvin released and back into the clothing issue. The guard speaks to Skinhead and reports back to Simcox. "Why are you so anxious to get Gauvin out of D block?"

"Because he's my friend and he wants out!"

"No he doesn't! I spoke with Skinhead and several others over there and they tell me the kid doesn't want out. He's staying at his own request."

With the shock of this information, Simcox feels molten emotions churning inside his system. In his kites he sends accusations flying in Gauvin's direction—curiosity and suspicion boil up inside Simcox. On the surface he is cold, solid, and impassionate but, beneath the outer shell, his emotions rise steadily until, determined to discover the truth about D block, he erupts one day on the yard.

Pappy Kyle and myself are walking up and down, as is the custom on the yard, talking as we walk. I hardly notice Simcox appear on the yard. He stands overlooking the scattered groups of cons playing handball, baseball, horseshoes, or just walking for exercise. As we approach him he comes down from the high steps until he is only a few steps from the ground level as we pass.

"Have you seen 'Shortgrass'?" he asks abruptly.

"No, I haven't seen him. He's probably working back in the cell house," I answer noticing the vacant empty look in his eyes.

"He's probably shacked up in a cell sucking on a black cock!" adds Pappy with a laugh as we continue down the yard.

Shortgrass, Glen C. Crawford (AZ-1108), is probably the most unpopular prisoner on the island. He is a Texan sharecropper about twenty-six or twenty-seven years of age doing time for car theft. He was well-liked when he arrived at Alcatraz because he loved baseball and was a good catcher. Immediately he joined one of the yard teams but now no one will talk to him or play baseball with him. He is the most vocal of any con with regard to racism; his objections to integration are heard loud and clear by anyone willing to listen.

Then, one day, the pride of Texas was found in an empty cell with a negro inmate, Cal Smith (AZ-1000). It would be difficult to say which one of them was the more embarrassed over the discovery—each claimed the other was giving the blow job but regardless Shortgrass's reputation is ruined.

I remark to Pappy after we continue past Simcox, "I wonder what Simcox wants with Shortgrass?"

"I can't imagine," answers Pappy. "Ever since that nigger incident they've been keeping him away from the rest of us for his own good."

Pappy and I reach the handball court and turn to start back the way we came. Ahead of us, Simcox looks around, as if in search of someone and comes off the steps into the yard proper. He starts out across the yard where he meets "Dog" Mann coming from the opposite direction.

Inmate Floyd Mann (AZ-941) is serving his second sentence in Alcatraz. Due to his ugly canine features he is dubbed "Dog". His looks would make him unpopular regardless, but he has an obnoxious personality to match so, next to Shortgrass, he is probably the next most unpopular con in the cellblock.

Dog is about ten feet beyond second base trotting out to the center field area when he passes Simcox. As their paths cross something casual is said by Simcox because Dog nods in response. Then, after passing him, Simcox whirls suddenly, grabs Dog in a strong grip with one hand, and spins him around, jerking him off balance as he does so.

I see the knife flash from the sleeve of Simcox's free hand just seconds before he plunges it into Dog's chest, up high near the collar bone. Incredulity frozen on his frightened face, Dog whimpers and squirms to free himself. Simcox's large hand rears up and strikes again forcing five or six inches of steel into Dog's chest and neck area three or four more times before he relaxes his vicelike grip and steps back confident he has completed his task.

Instead of rolling over and dying, Dog runs from Simcox. He resembles a human water fountain, blood spouting in arcs from his neck and chest wounds. Blood also gushes from his nose and mouth as he spits and yelps in a shrill voice, "Somebody help me! Help me!"

His shaggy bloody head turns desperately in every direction, but no con is about to mix in.

The yard screw arrives, uncertain of what is happening, and Dog looks to him for help with pathetic spaniel eyes. The screw calls for some cons to help take Dog up the steps to the hospital emergency room. Simcox, disinterested, stands quietly watching.

Up in the hospital, Dog sprinkles his blood over the clean white emergency ward and everyone in sight. The hospital staff takes one look at him and decides he won't live, but an orderly shoves his hand into the open gashes and ties off the blood vessels or arteries, stopping the main blood loss.

An emergency call is placed to San Francisco's Marine Hospital. A crew of specialists, crackerjack doctors from the Pacific war who have seen every kind of wound while in action, arrives on the island and saves Dog's life.

According to the cons, Dog's life was saved by fate. Purely by chance, a woman was walking her St. Bernard on the docks of San Francisco at that critical moment and the officials rushed the dog over to the island to give Dog Mann a blood transfusion that saved his life! A cruel joke but Alcatraz is a cruel place.

Simcox is taken to isolation which is exactly what he wants. He planned to kill Shortgrass but, when the Texan didn't show up on the yard that morning, he settled for Dog as second choice. It might just as easily have been me or Pappy when we passed him. Simcox staged the entire incident to ensure that he would be thrown in D block where he can learn the truth about his friend Gauvin and San Quentin Smitty.

Shortgrass, when he learns how close he came to death, insists the authorities lock him up in isolation where he remains until they send him out of Alcatraz on the next transfer back east. Dog is kept in hospital and then released on the condition he testify against Simcox in the San Francisco courts.

I can't believe the rumour just whispered in my ear—"Swope is leaving!"

Swope suddenly resigns to accept the job of Director of Prisons in the New Mexico State Prison System and takes both inmates and authorities by surprise. For us it is a pleasant surprise but the Federal Bureau of Prisons must decide, almost overnight, on a replacement. The final decision is even more exhilarating than the announcement of Swope's retirement. "Madigan will be the new warden."

Although convicts are skeptical and suspicious by nature, no one has a negative thought about Madigan. I had already decided to keep out of trouble after getting out of D block; Madigan is a bonus I hadn't expected.

Alcatraz, 1956

Smoke rises from Ringwald's cigar as he scans the papers scattered about his desk. He's so intent on his work, I have to attract his attention. "Mr. Ringwald, the warden is at the gate."

Madigan is standing outside the wire mesh separating the library from the cell house; he breaks into a smile at my recognition of his new title. It's his first trip into the cell house since becoming warden and he has come straight to the library.

As Ringwald clumsily unlocks the gate with all the flourish and fluster of a subordinate meeting his new boss for the first time Madigan steps past him with a nod and grasps my hand in a warm and steady greeting.

"Here we are!" he laughs. "How are you Ray? I hear you've had a pretty rough time."

"Now that you're back, it'll be alright. Things will simmer down pretty fast."

"We can't change what's already happened," Madigan apologizes. "But you tell the guys that even though I don't have the money allotted as yet, nevertheless, I'll start to instal radio headphones immediately.

"How's the food—good?" he asks next, knowing that I worked in the kitchen for twelve years.

"Hell no!" I respond and begin another long and detailed complaint. Ringwald is no longer disguising the astonishment spreading across his face.

"I'm glad I spoke to you, Ray, I'm having a meeting with Mr. Stoddard and his stewards today."

Just before he leaves, Madigan gives me a message to pass on. "Tell the 'old timers' I'm going to try to get them transferred to a prison where they can apply for a parole and receive it. I'll put one of them on every shipment out, starting with the lowest numbers. Waley will be the first one away—no wait—Jim Clark was here ahead of Waley. Each of you will go in sequence."

Madigan's words give me more hope than I've had for twenty years.

The next morning in the dining hall it's obvious that Madigan has returned. Breakfast includes two eggs, bacon, waffles, syrup, orange juice, milk, dry cereal, wet cereal, and cinnamon toast. Meals at Alcatraz improve.

I realize that my "pick and peck" typing is hampering my efficiency in the library so I request permission from Skinhead to buy a typing manual from my personal money kept in the front office. His response is brisk. "No, request denied!"

Ringwald, who is my boss in the library, is furious when he hears the result of the interview. When I explain to him that Franklin ordered one to improve his talents for working up in the hospital he grows angrier and explodes, "You'll have your manual!"

He orders me one from town in the name of the library and charges it to the prison. "Go ahead! Learn to type!" he says handing me the book.

It is while learning to type that I recognize the bad mental shape I'm in. I get punchy and lose my coordination after an hour of practice. I haven't used my brain for years and it's gone stagnant. I'm a mental mess! Nevertheless, I persist with the self-instruction, determined to make every effort at rehabilitation and prepare myself for the opportunity Madigan has promised with the hope of a transfer which is the first step toward a parole.

A fellow Canadian by the name of Mockford (AZ-1067) asks me to come to work in the industry office. When I point out to him that I don't know anything about accounting and bookkeeping required in such a job he simply says, "My boss is Dollison, he told me to tell you to come down—we'll teach you."

I get up this morning and go to wash. From my shelf I take my new glass mirror which has replaced the old highly polished stainless steel mirrors. "That Madigan has a lot of common horse sense," I think to myself. "He knows if you want to commit suicide, you'll do it anyways, with or without a mirror."

In the clear reflection I watch the beads of water trace the wrinkles in my forty-six-year-old face. It occurs to me that I have spent twenty years at Alcatraz. My eyes focus on my neck and I see a small puffed-up lump on the right side. Poking and playing with it, I discover it doesn't hurt. "It'll go away in a couple of days whatever it is," I conclude.

But it doesn't go away, it only grows larger each day until I am forced to see the new doctor, Wolfman, who used to be an expensive heart specialist. Told he would be dead in six months from his heavy workload and cigarette smoking, he succumbed to his wife's pleading and left a lucrative private practice. The boredom of retirement, with only the ticking of his own heart to help him measure less strenuous work in the public health service, brought him to Alcatraz.

"Do you smoke?" is his first question.

"Yeh!"

"Well listen," his tone is confidential, almost secretive, "my doctor told me if I didn't stop smoking I'd be dead within six months. Well I'm telling you the same thing!"

With a wink he takes out a cigarette and lights up. "Now what's the problem?" he coughs.

"My neck," I point to the protrusion.

"Let's take a look."

The cigarette dangles from his dry lips as he probes and pushes the enlarging growth on my neck. His breath is tickling the lump, as large clouds of smoke make my eyes water. He straightens up coughing and mutters through the cigarette, "I'm going to take some tests in the next few days. Report to the hospital tomorrow."

During my repeated visits to the hospital I have to pass the "Birdman of Alcatraz": Robert Stroud is the only prisoner who has his own entire room in the hospital wing. He is usually standing on the inside of his barred doorway when I come down the hospital corridor. It's a large rectangular room with two doors, one of wood, the other of bars. Inside he has hot and cold water but no toilet; a bed pan is emptied each morning. I usually chat with him for ten or fifteen minutes.

Today he presses a bundle of papers into my hands—it's his autobiography. He wants my opinion. As I scan his manuscript and offer polite observations I can't help but ponder what a paradox he is. His writings on ornithology have made him a recognized expert: *Diseases of Canaries* was published in 1933 and *Stroud's Digest on the Diseases of Birds* in 1943. Since arriving at Alcatraz he has mastered the French language during his long hours in isolation.

The pressure on the parole board to release Stroud increases as the book and film about him become popular. I discover a communication on Ringwald's desk in the library —Ringwald is on the classification committee at Alcatraz. Stroud is to be sent to the medical center at Springfield "to expire". The parole board refuses to bend under the weight of public pressure; Stroud is destined to die in prison.

I shall myself struggle for years with the parole board as Hoover resists all my efforts to obtain a parole out of McNeil Island. Although I hate to say anything bad about another prisoner or anything good about the parole board, I consider it a credit to them that they didn't give in to the pressure to release "The Birdman".

He had a definite mental quirk. His behaviour and statements in isolation convinced me he was dangerous. I have vivid memories of his lanky form and his unusually long arms hanging low in apelike fashion and the profanities and threats he uttered against the guards and their families rush into my mind. He hated Fatso Mitchell and would rave about how he would "eat up" the guard's little daughter before he tore her apart, giving half to each parent. His wild exclamations dwelt on how, if he were released, he would grab little boys or girls off the street, "eat them up" and then kill them. I believed him. They weren't just idle threats: he would have killed or mutilated a child. He bragged of how he would show society that they really owed him something. If I had the responsibility of deciding whether or not to release Robert Stroud, I would have reached the same conclusion as the parole board.

Each day I return to the hospital to be shot full of different antibiotics but each morning the growth on my neck is larger than ever. Finally I ask the doctor, "Look, if I had an infection wouldn't I be hurtin' there? Wouldn't I be running a fever?"

"Well, I have to agree with you," he admits. "We'll bring some specialists over from the Marine Hospital. I'm getting a little worried about this myself and I know you must be."

The specialists arrive from the Marine Hospital. Both are very young, not even thirty years old. They check me out and retire into the office for a huddle before confronting me. "Look Karpis, we don't have a lot of time so lets drop the bullshit! We don't know what's wrong with your neck. It could be just an ordinary cyst or it could be something a hell of a lot worse than that—I think you know what I mean."

I know what he means alright. I am starting to worry already that I might have cancer.

"We have to operate on you to find out! The problem is we don't know how to go about it. We could go through your throat or cut from the outside of your neck. We'll wait until we get back to the hospital to decide which."

"What's the difference?" I ask.

"If we operate from the outside of your neck it will leave a bad scar on you whereas from inside your throat there will be no scar, but we might run into complications. What's your opinion?"

"Piss on that scar! I don't care about a scar, do it the way you think would be best. If we were going to rob a bank, I would tell you how to do it, but you're the experts here."

It is six days following the operation. On the side of my neck from which they took their souvenir, there is no feeling—not in my neck, not in my face, not in my throat, not in my head—even down to my collarbone on that side there is no feeling.

"How are you now, Karpis? Are you alright?" I turn my head slowly expecting to see Wolfman, but it is Warden Madigan.

"Yeah, I think I'll be alright."

"I came up to tell you the report on the specimen we sent to the lab came back from town. You can rest sure, there is nothing malignant—it was just a cyst! You're alright! Just get yourself well.

"I have the report here. The doctor won't be here until late today so I opened it up because I wanted to know if you were alright. I came up right away to tell you what the score was."

It is not one of the obligations of a warden to take such a personal interest in informing a con of his medical condition and not the sort of behavior you expect from an average warden—but Madigan is not an average warden!

My typing improves to the point where I can handle a job in the industries office. As I sit practicing, a large hand descends on the typing manual beside me on the desk.

"I didn't authorize you to buy this book!" roars Skinhead. "Someone is going to be in big trouble!"

As he flips open the cover, his eyes rest on the official stamp "Alcatraz Library". Immediately he turns and storms over to Ringwald's desk in the library.

Ringwald is disgusted with the prison and ready to retire. He responds vehemently to Skinhead's attack. "I want Karpis to be a good typist. Why would you let Franklin have one up in the hospital but not let Karpis have one in the library? This has nothing to do with custody. Take it up with the warden or the educational department in the Bureau of Prisons!"

Skinhead stomps out of the library.

The echoes of drill hammers resound through the cell house daily now as volunteers give up their pay in the industries in an effort to have the headphones installed before the World Series begins. Madigan is a sports fan and announces that he'll call a holiday on that day so the cons can stay in their cells with earphones or sit around on the yard listening to the series over loudspeakers.

I finally apply for the work change to the industry office. Several days pass without any reply. I send in a second request. Still no reply.

I'm in the hospital getting some cocoabutter for my neck when up the steps comes Skinhead. He walks past me sitting on the bench in the hospital corridor without speaking. On his return down the corridor I interrupt him, "Say, Mr. Latimer, I've put in a couple of requests—did you get them?"

"Yeah, I got them."

"Well I want to know, do you intend to give me that work change?"

"Hell, no!"

"Why not?"

"You ain't going down there. You think you'll get a nice soft office job but you don't need any paying job. You'll never get out of here so what use will the money be to you?"

"You could have called me out and told me that."

"Get the fuck down to the library!"

The next morning Madigan stops outside my cell.

"I got your letter last night, Ray. You really want to go down to the industries, eh?"

"Yes, warden."

"When I was associate warden here a lot of people used to go over my head and Swope would change my orders. I make it a matter of policy never to interfere with the decisions of my subordinates if I can help it. I don't know what this problem is between you and Mr. Latimer but you'll go down to the industries, I promise you that."

Later that day a slip arrives at my cell from Latimer saying I'm to report to the industries in the morning.

A Tuesday Night, Fall 1956

The World Series begins tomorrow. The radio is installed. A pushwagon squeaks around the cell house depositing boxes containing headphones. Each con must sign a form agreeing not to damage or alter the headphones. Frank Davenport (AZ-913) and a few other troublemakers refuse to sign. He calls down to me from his cell. "Did you sign, Ray?"

"Yeah, I signed."

"Why did you do that?"

"Davenport, it's twenty years since my arrest. Don't tell me how to do my time. If you want to do without headphones, don't sign for them, but I've heard about how you once gave advice before about breaking up a toilet bowl then whined your way out when you were going to lose 'good time' over it."

My response meets with embarrassed silence. There are always a few Davenports in any prison, willing to stir up trouble when none is needed. He and his friends eventually end up signing for headphones.

I scrunch another ruined form into a paper ball and toss it into the wastebasket beside my typewriter with disgust. Impatiently I turn to rise from my chair only to confront Dollison. I tell him, "I think I'd better quit. I'm only holding things up."

"If you want to learn, try it a bit longer," he soothes me. "Look at all the money the government spent trying to capture you. Look at all the money they're spending now to keep you here. Did you know that each prisoner in Alcatraz costs the government about five times the normal cost in other federal prisons? They can afford the cost of a few ruined forms or slowdowns."

Dollison's logic convinces me to remain on the job but my mind is so slow from lack of practice, I can't remember figures for more than a few minutes. I acquire some books—*Beginning Bookkeeping, Advanced Bookkeeping*, and *Accounting*—and take them back to my cell every night to do some homework.

(AZ-1163) is almost thrown in the hole over his religious beliefs because he refuses to go into the mess hall to eat. The Catholic priest intercedes: "Leave this man alone! He's sincerely religious! He's on a fast!"

I have had many quiet conversations with the slender, soft-spoken Puerto Rican. He is one of the most polite and religious people I ever met. His intense black eyes are calm, his black hair neatly groomed, his dark complexion healthy for a man of thirty-five.

It's difficult to picture Miranda and two accomplices walking into the visitors' gallery of the Hall of Congress, standing up, and lobbing hand grenades, yet his picture is there in *Life, Newsweek,* and *Time.* His personality in

Alcatraz remains gentle, there is never anything to indicate violence. His actions were strictly politically motivated to achieve independence for Puerto Rico.

Alcatraz, 1957

I am given a desk in the purchasing office working under Red Smith who is the purchasing clerk for Dollison. We put out invitations to bid on the various government contracts involving the prison industries—hair for the brush factory, leather for the glove factory. Then one day Red doesn't show up for work. Dollison comes over to talk to me. "Smith ain't coming back; he's in the hole. As of today, you're the purchasing clerk. Can you handle it?"

"I don't think so. I don't understand these ledgers or business machines."

"I'll help you. All of us will."

"O.K., I'll try it."

My homework increases with my new position. Every night I'm studying for hours in my cell trying to learn accounting. Then Mockford, the cost accountant, goes to court. Dollison comes to me again.

"You can see the situation. Someone has to be the cost accountant. I want you to take the job. It's first-grade pay. It's bacon, take it!"

Shortly after my second promotion, Dollison is also promoted to the position of superintendent of industries. He is replaced by an unforgettable character who arrives with his personal custom-made chair. L. B. Davis is the fattest human I've ever seen who can still walk.

I'm working late into the night on the files, which I take up to my cell from the industries, when Father Clark pays me a visit just before Christmas. "How's it going, Ray?"

"Everything is going too good. It can't last. You know how prison life works, one day you have the chicken, the next day the feathers."

Christmas brings icy rain and sharp winds. Very few guys go to the yard. Sitting in my cell, I relax, listen to the radio which Madigan has left on for our enjoyment and think about the letter I hold in my hands.

It's from my sister in Chicago. My son, who I have never seen although he's twenty-two or twenty-three years old, is in trouble. He ignored thirty traffic violations which he accumulated in his flashy Cadillac convertible. Now the police have arrested him so he's facing a $600 fine and, because he's my son, the newspapers have picked up the story. The kid was born in 1935 and is now married to an Italian girl in Chicago. Alone, in my cell, I experience a warm sympathy for my unseen offspring.

Alcatraz, 1958

Madigan is true to his word. All the "old timers" in Alcatraz are transferred, one at a time, as each new shipment goes out to other prisons. It's February twenty-fourth when my number comes up and my name is included on the list of transfers to Leavenworth. The transfer is the most important thing in my life since I arrived on Alcatraz Island. I can apply for a parole from Leavenworth once I establish myself there.

However, on the morning I step down into the launch, shackled in the long line of transfers, I get an ominous sign. The sky is dark with rain clouds; the water whips against the small boat crowded with huddled convicts. As we churn our way toward the mainland the cold rain slashes at our bare faces, the majority of the manacled prisoners are ill and the bottom of the boat splashes a sickly green mixture of sea water and vomit. Overhead, flashes of lightning illuminate the desolate island behind us. Although I am not a superstitious person, I feel a strong sense of futility; it's as if the dark Rock is objecting to my desertion. I have a foreboding sense that nature itself is against this journey. High winds of over sixty mph cause flooding across the railroad tracks taking us out of California. "An evil omen," I think, in spite of myself.

12

Leavenworth Prison, Kansas, 1958

Cold slush soaks my shoes as I step down from the bus at the gate to Leavenworth. It's the beginning of a long, hard nightmare.

"Do you remember your last number at Leavenworth?"

"49368," I answer mechanically, as if the last twenty-two years have been compressed to as many hours. There are 3,000 inmates lost in the crowded insanity of Leavenworth, a drastic change from the two hundred familiar faces of Alcatraz.

"Where you guys from?" questions a gruff voice from under a shabby blanket below as I dump my sheets and pillow case into the top bunk.

"Alcatraz," I answer. The figure turns to me showing a toothless smile—an old, grey-haired scarecrow weighing about 100 pounds. "How's 'Old Salty'?"

"What?"

"How's 'Old Salty'?—'Salty' Johnston, the warden?"

I don't bother to inform him that Johnston is long retired. "Did you know him?"

"Hell yeah. I used to be in Alcatraz."

"What was your number?"

This question starts the delapidated old form spluttering incoherently. "When they found out I didn't have five years they transferred me out. I never got a number."

I realize instantly he's lying but I don't bother to embarrass him. Alcatraz is known as "the Prison of Prisons."

Only 1576 prisoners were ever sent there in all the years it was open from 1934 to 1963 whereas half the convicts in Leavenworth and other federal prisons brag of time done in the superprison designed to hold only "the most notorious public enemies." Aiken, the deputy warden here at Leavenworth, has a photograph behind his desk of Alcatraz Island which he uses to threaten young convicts up before him on discipline charges.

The word is soon out that I have arrived from Alcatraz. Former friends and inmates now assigned to Leavenworth flood my dormitory with cartons of cigarettes, boxes of cigars, and candy. The convict clerk who comes on duty assigns me two lockers rather than one but, even so, the spoils arriving from other prisoners overflow into the "orientation unit". I start giving them away to other cons but the flood continues. Finally the screw suggests that I send out word that I don't want anymore. By now I have enough to last me six months. I sit on my bunk, rubbing the bruise on my leg where my ankle has swelled from the days on the train when I was shackled, and sample my spoils.

Soon the insanity of the new rules begins to affect me. I can keep only ten photographs accumulated over the years from my family. I can't keep my guitar unless I donate it to the prison for general use in the orchestra. When eight or ten snapshots arrive in a letter from my sister, I'm told to pick out six and send the others back. Only six pictures every six months.

From my first interview with Aiken, it is made clear that I'm not welcome. Leavenworth has been forced to accept me. I am to be assigned to an interior cellblock, not one facing the streets of town. Guards are to keep me in sight at all times while I'm on the yard. I'm assigned a job working inside the cellblock.

One week after my arrival I'm leaning against the radiator in the dark cellblock trying to keep warm when a new screw walks up. "How do you like it here, Karpis?" he asks.

"I like it fine," I lie.

"That's too bad. They don't want you here. They say

you won't last six months. They won't let you last six months!"

Worse than the rules and the attitudes of the officials are the petty rackets run by the other convicts. If you want white sheets out of the laundry it costs you several packs of cigarettes. A haircut is worth three packs of cigarettes. If you don't want your clothes to disappear in the laundry when you go for a bath, it costs you a pack of cigarettes. A good book from the library requires a pack of cigarettes. The petty larceny crap makes me sick. I resent it.

"You're Karpis?" The guard in the visiting room has never seen me before.

"Yeah," I reply, trying not to sound excited.

"Wait here a minute!" He goes to inform my visitors that I'm here. Then I see them! It's as if I'm looking at myself in a mirror and the last quarter of a century never slipped past; he resembles me when I was younger. However, my first encounter with my son, born back in 1935, is marred by the presence of a guard. Not the regular guard watching the waiting room, but a special guard assigned to sit beside us and listen to every word.

When a man meets his twenty-three-year-old son and his daughter-in-law for the first time, there are many personal and sensitive thoughts to exchange. We are furious at the intruder sitting in our midst. No other prisoner at Leavenworth has to put up with such interference in a family visit. We complain to each other about the conditions of the visit only to have our comments interrupted by the guard. "Did you come here to visit or to criticize?"

"Don't get excited," I warn my son, who is not used to the bullshit of prisons. "Drive over again tomorrow. In the meantime I'll try to find out what this is all about."

When my son and his wife return the next day from the motel room they have rented on their trip from Chicago to visit me, I have no news for them. "I couldn't get an interview," I begin.

"I did!" intercedes my son. "I saw that dog Associate Warden Aiken." The special guard is taking note of the entire conversation.

"How did you see him?"

"After we left yesterday a screw ushered us into his office. I asked him what the hell he wanted and he asked if we had 'discussed anything about crime'. I told him to find out from the asshole of a screw who was spying on our conversation."

The guard fidgets angrily.

"This is no good for visiting! We're going back to Chicago to talk to a lawyer, then we'll be back down for a proper visit!"

I learn later that Aiken again waylaid the two youngsters on their way out of the institution, capitalized on my son's hot temper, and, after provoking him into an open row, had him banned from any further visits to Leavenworth.

Dr. Lam, who operates on a bad vein in my leg and removes a blood clot, is Chinese. Aiken calls him every day after the operation demanding to know whether he is ready to release me from the hospital.

"They want you out of here," apologizes the doctor. "Normally we would keep you until you're not limping but in this case I'm being pressured to get you back into the cell house."

During my stay in the hospital I ask the doctor if he would object to my working there. He agrees to the idea and even recommends that I be given a job in the hospital. Immediately Lam is on the carpet before Aiken trying to answer hostile questions such as, "What's your interest in Karpis?"

Afterwards Aiken interviews me. "Why do you want to transfer to the hospital?"

"I'm bored to tears in the cell house. It's the dark narrow halls, they're depressing."

"I don't care what you like. It's that cellblock or isolation. Nowhere else!"

I can't adjust to life in Leavenworth; it's driving me crazy. I feel myself becoming more desperate to get out of the cellblock I've been left in day and night. It's dark and dismal and the dirt has been accumulating for seventy-five years. It turns me despondent. The quiet is underlined by the aggravating cooing of pigeons all night which roost high in the rafters. Blackbirds seeking warmth fly blindly into the windows during the nights. Their bodies are found, by the dozens, frozen to death outside the frigid windows of Leavenworth.

I have row after row with the authorities in attempts to get a work change that will take me outside the cellblock.

A young bank robber from Canada by the name of John Machibroda from Brantford, Ontario, convinces me to ask again for a work change to the hospital where he and some others work. If he had warned me what was going on over there I never would have requested the work change.

September 10, 1958.

A con enters the cellblock from the rotunda. "They're having hell over in that hospital!" he tells me. "Two dozen screws are tearing it apart! They've found outside clothes, ropes, shivs, and hooks in the operating room where the sterilized clothing is kept packaged."

The three cons in the operating room, including Machibroda, are grabbed automatically. I find myself escorted to Aiken's office where I'm kept waiting for a long time. Finally Aiken opens the door and looks out at me, then disappears inside again. Two screws come to get me and I'm taken directly to isolation. From the hole I write a letter to a lawyer—I explain that I'm in trouble and that if he hasn't come within a week, I'll write to a judge directly assuming my letter has been ambushed. I'm soon confronted by Aiken outside my hole cell.

"You s.o.b.! You caused that food strike! You pulled the strings!"

"Is that what I'm locked up for?" He's referring to a recent strike here in Leavenworth.

"You s.o.b.! It'll be a long time before you get another crack at it! You're going back to Alcatraz, tonight!"

As the "San Francisco Chief" wails its mournful song across the country, I count up the months in Leavenworth:

March, April, May, June, July, August, the beginning of September. Goddamn! The little screw who spoke to me the first week after my arrival was right. I only lasted six months.

Bradley, the large lieutenant taking me back to Alcatraz looks half-negro. I know him only by reputation. He was transferred to Leavenworth where he reputedly beat a convict named Olli Melton to death in Atlanta. His sympathy stuns me. "I can't imagine why they sent you back," he confides. "Everyone knew you were trying to get along." For three days on the long cross-country treck, Bradley harps on the rotten deal I was given by the authorities at Leavenworth.

Throughout the return trip I'm desperately worried about the reaction of the authorities and the convicts in Alcatraz toward my return. Have I made Madigan look bad for giving me a chance? Will everyone now give me "a bad way to go"?

As I step from the back of the prison van, my fifty-year-old bones creak as loudly as the wooden planks on the jetty. The first face I see is Skinhead's—he is disembarking from the boat which will take me on its return to the island. "You know Karpis, I'm sorry to see this. I'm sorry to see you back here."

To my surprise there is a touch of sincerity in his tone which I have never heard before.

Madigan comes down Broadway immediately on his return to Alcatraz. "What in the world happened?" he asks.

"I guess they just didn't want me there."

"I know they didn't want you, I sent you there over their protests. They complained to Washington, but there was no other prison secure enough to hold you. I didn't think they'd go this far. My son-in-law is a guard at Leavenworth. I've just been visiting him and my daughter, but when I heard what they did to you, I never went inside that prison. I was disgusted!"

The classification committee at Alcatraz requests a reason

from Leavenworth for my return. The answer is that the authorities in Leavenworth decided I was a "disturbing element". They didn't accuse me of being involved in the strike and no mention is made of the hospital incident, which is understandable since I had never been allowed out of the cell house.

My sister writes a letter to the Bureau of Prisons asking for a reason. The reply comes from Acting Director Myrl Alexander who informs her that, "After your brother arrived in Leavenworth, he quickly got into serious difficulties."

Machibroda (AZ-1373), and the others involved in the hospital escape, arrive at Alcatraz. From them I learn that I was indirectly responsible for the discovery of the escape equipment in the operating room. When I applied for a work change from the cell house to the hospital, the cons in the hospital decided to stash the equipment in the operating room so that if I ever landed in the hospital, I wouldn't get blamed if the authorities discovered the assortment of tools and supplies. Ironically they were trying to protect me when they moved them. Unfortunately, a stool pigeon in the hospital saw the equipment and alerted the authorities.

Alcatraz, October, 1958

I've hardly had the opportunity to re-adjust to the industries when the wailing siren of Alcatraz announces an escape. Immediately we are returned to our cells from the various work stations around the island. I'm somewhat puzzled as I follow the long line up the hillside—it's a clear day, no fog to encourage an escape. Also, I've heard no shooting.

For four or five days all activity on the island comes to a standstill as the authorities discover only one of the escapees, Clyde Johnson (AZ-864). While they search for the second one, Burgette (AZ-991), the rest of us are confined to our cells. The captured con, Clyde Johnson, is a very efficient bank robber and escape artist. At one point in his career, before being sent to Alcatraz with a fifty-year sentence, he even escaped from the Dade County Jail which is on the twenty-seventh floor of the County Building in Miami, Florida.

The missing con, Walter Burgette, is from St. Louis and is doing twenty-five years. He and Clyde were working on the garbage truck making the rounds of the island, when they jumped the screw, tied and gagged him, then left him fastened securely to a tree. When the truck didn't show up on its scheduled route, an investigation led to the discovery of the escape. Johnson was found almost immediately hiding in one of the many caves around the water's edge of the island. After several days, the search for Burgette is given up and we return to work. It's a few weeks later that the boat travelling from the island to town veers off its course to investigate an object floating in the water by the point of the island. The body, obviously Burgette's from the prison clothing and remnants of a homemade swim fin, is beyond recognition. The face has been eaten away by crabs and the limbs are reduced to badly mutilated stubs.

Clyde Johnson tells me later of how he watched Burgette walk into the cold water, feeling he had protected himself from its temperature by wearing two undershirts with sleeves fastened tightly at the wrists by thin strips of wire and two pair of longjohns. "I was watching to see which way the current would carry him, before jumping in myself, when it was as if a huge shark nabbed him from below. He went down like a rock in the sudden grip of a swift undertow. I'd have been crazy to follow him out there!"

Dock Area, 1958

Bishop (AZ-1195) takes a long leap in the direction of a guard named Valentino standing a few feet away from him. He strikes the screw, knocking him several yards as a heavily loaded forklift charges over the spot where the officer had stood. The eyes of a frightened negro, "Wild Bill" Williams, bulge from the driver's seat of the runaway forklift.

The guard, who was in the wrong for stepping into the path of the loading vehicle without looking where he was going, thanks Bishop but doesn't file a report. When the news reaches Madigan, he is furious with the guard for not reporting the heroic action of Bishop. "I should suspend you for the sixty days which I am recommending be taken off Bishop's sentence as 'meritorious good time.'"

The "Birdman of Alcatraz," Robert Stroud, never kept birds in Alcatraz but Sam Tiblow (AZ-1265), a moon-faced happy-go-lucky Indian from Oklahoma, does.

Sam has a rare gift with all types of animals and his list of pets is legendary. At one time he was keeping a hawk in his cell and on another occasion he was forced to return a pet parakeet which had escaped from its home on the island. He always has a pet blackbird on his shoulder down by the incinerator where he works. Aside from birds, Sam has the patience to catch any animal that comes around looking for food in the garbage, even a mole on one occasion.

At this moment, however, his full attention is centered on a pet lizard which he has refused to sell to anyone at any price. He lies on the yard, near the home plate area of the baseball diamond feeding flies and bugs to his newest child. The lizard romps proudly in a large circular arc on a chain of fine copper wire out of the electrical shop, fastened to a handwoven collar of hair from the brush factory. Sam fusses paternally, hovering over the lively lizard which he has staked down on the yard.

For a careless moment Sam wanders toward a neighboring chess game to observe the play. His ancestors' instincts warn him of the danger before it strikes. He turns and dives protectively for his pet, trapped in the open yard. Too late! The seagull descends like a fighter plane snatching its prey and swooping up again to the open skies, the copper chain dangling from his triumphant beak. Sam is left in the Alcatraz dust, tears forming in the corners of his eyes.

Pappy Kyle discovers that the deputy marshal who he had been accused and convicted of killing during an escape attempt died, according to the death certificate, of natural causes. Pappy had always claimed he never struck the old deputy who collapsed at his feet during the escape attempt. Before he leaves for McNeil Island and a new court case Pappy says goodbye to me: "If I win this case, I'll only have a few months to go so they'll probably keep me at McNeil Island."

At Madigan's recommendation, Bishop is also on the transfer to McNeil Island, the only federal penitentiary without a wall surrounding it. As one of the senior citizens of Alcatraz, I watch old friends disappear more frequently from my isolated island world as 1958 comes to a close.

Alcatraz, 1959

It is clear to me that, after my return from Leavenworth, I'll have to wait two or three years before applying for another transfer out of Alcatraz. In the atmosphere of friendship and cooperation extended by almost everyone in the administration from Madigan on down, and the convict population, I relax and find the industry work more intriguing than ever.

Madigan subtly reverses Swope's policy of filling the cells with blacks in order to keep the prisoners at each other's throats. As he transfers blacks out of Alcatraz, the tension gradually relaxes.

From my office in the industry I see across the hallway directly into the dry cleaning plant which requires only one convict worker. A young kid, Jack Twining (AZ-1362) from Florida, comes to work there. Jack is a pleasant youngster about twenty-three years old doing a five-year sentence. He stands about six feet, is husky, has sandy-coloured hair, and clear blue eyes. He was sent to Alcatraz after escaping from a Florida chain gang, robbing a bank, stealing a car, and in general giving the authorities an active chase.

When Twining arrived at Alcatraz, he tried minding his own business but a "wolf" on the job with him wouldn't leave him alone. The aggressive homosexual is about thirty years old and is in strong physical condition from the manual labour he's been doing in prison. To avoid further confrontation Twining quit his job and asked for the one in the dry cleaning plant where he works alone. Not willing to take "no" for an answer the "wolf" also obtains a work change to a job in the laundry which places him on the same floor with Twining. He starts pestering the kid again.

One day I look up from my desk to see the "wolf" stalking up and down in front of the door to the dry cleaning plant where Twining works alone. He hesitates, looks around him, as if scenting the air, then "signifying" he has a knife he slips his way roughly into Twining's sanctuary.

Twining grabs for his throat and they churn about in each other's arms. As they smash to the floor, the kid pops out on top and desperately bangs his opponent's head against a valve containing chemicals and fluids for the plant. If the aggressor gets loose of the grip Twining has on his throat, the kid is no match for him. They roll from my sight.

It's a long wait. Then the kid wobbles painfully out of the room and plops down in a swivel chair, obviously exhausted and weakened. At the sight of a convict in his chair, the guard on duty is attracted from his platform perch to Twining's side. Before he can object, Twining, breathing hard, chokes in a quivering voice, "You know there's something bad happened—in there—just now."

"What?" questions the officer, but Twining is having difficulty talking, he only succeeds in moving his lips without the sounds. The screw walks to the door of the dry cleaning plant. Stretched grotesquely across the floor is the "wolf," his mouth wide open, his tongue hanging out, choked to death.

The FBI arrives at Alcatraz to investigate the murder. They interview everyone who works in the vicinity. "You're Karpis, eh?"

"Yeah."

"Were you working down here when this thing happened?"

"What thing?"

"When Twining killed the guy. You could have seen into the door of the dry cleaning plant from your office. Did you see anything?"

"No I didn't see a thing!"

"We hear you were down to Leavenworth for a short vacation but now you're back home."

Obviously objecting to the sarcasm of his partner the other agent changes the subject. "If it's any consolation to you, Karpis, your arrest has made the FBI what it is today. Anytime we've needed appropriations over the years, we bring up your name and case. There's reams of copy on you at the bureau."

"Don't you have anything to say about this Twining affair?" asks the other agent, getting back to the murder.

"Yeah, it's pretty obvious that the kid tried to avoid it. He changed jobs but the guy followed him over there. Then he charges into Twining's work area where no other convict belongs. There is no question about it, it's self-defence."

After interviewing everyone possible, the agents decide to call it a case of justifiable homicide. Twining is not even charged.

Alcatraz, 1959, Clothing Issue

Simcox, the kid who tried to kill "Dog" on the yard, is released from isolation. They put him down in the clothing issue, his old job in the basement, a few weeks after he is back in population.

At the court case in San Francisco, Simcox was declared "Not Guilty". Dog was turned loose from Alcatraz on the condition he would testify in court and he did. He stayed with relatives in San Francisco but died shortly after the court case.

Dog had always been unpopular in Alcatraz, he had an obnoxious personality and appearance. Simcox became a hero after stabbing him. Half the yard was willing to go over and testify for Simcox and make Dog out a monster. Anytime a con goes to trial in Alcatraz, the rest of the population does or says anything to get him off. The guy who got killed or the screws are the accused in any such court cases. Dog was called a pervert, a homosexual, a dangerous murderous personality who was attempting to kill young Simcox because he wouldn't have sex with him. According to the witnesses on the yard, Dog had carried the knife; young Simcox wrestled it away from him.

Simcox was acquitted without a problem. Even a dead con's best friends wouldn't help out the authorities by testifying for them. It is an unwritten law.

Simcox is placed back in population, and the rumour circulates that Gauvin will be out soon. San Quentin Smitty refuses to leave isolation.

Saturday Gauvin is let out of isolation. He is taken down to the clothing issue and shower room in the basement. His friend Simcox is back of the cage door handing him his clothing issue. He speaks calmly to Gauvin: "Glad to see you out, kid."

Gauvin takes the clothes with his number on them and goes halfway down the basement room where he places them on a bench while he takes a shower. Free from the tiny cell in isolation after many years Gauvin enjoys the freedom of a warm shower as the water trickles softly over his naked body.

A few feet away Simcox steps nonchalantly from behind the clothing issue cage. The screw has relaxed after seeing there is no friction between the two at their first encounter.

"I'd better go see my buddy to see if he needs cigarettes or anything," Simcox says casually.

Gauvin is now drying off with a towel and as Simcox approaches a few friendly words are spoken. Simcox places his hand affectionately on Gauvin's naked shoulder. The kid smiles.

Simcox's free hand sends a 12-inch steel file, ground down to a shiv, directly into Gauvin's chest. The first blow probably hits him in the heart but Simcox withdraws the weapon and plunges it several more times in and out of Gauvin's limp body before he lets him slip slowly from his grasp onto the cold cement floor of the shower room. He lies there, his blood flowing into the open drain. The kid never uttered a sound. There was no scuffle. No attempt to defend himself. He simply did not expect to die. Gauvin is not out of isolation ten minutes before he is dead.

During the trial that follows, Simcox describes how the kid had the knife stashed in his clothing issue, that the kid was trying to cut him and that he killed Gauvin in self-defence while trying to get the knife away from him. All the cons in the basement at the time testify it was self-defence.

Simcox is once again acquitted.

Skinhead leaves and a new deputy warden is chosen by Madigan. His name is Blackwell and he is a drastic change from Skinhead. He's a soft-spoken individual who is so relaxed himself, he puts everyone else at ease. His calm, grey eyes emit intelligence and even warmth while his even teeth smile a welcome to convicts brought before him for "court call". A gold bracelet decorates his wrist and an ornament hangs casually around his neck. Although his clothing is expensive and well-tailored, he rarely wears a necktie.

However, there is nothing weak about Blackwell. A bad scar runs across the bridge of his nose into the light complexion of his face giving him a rugged appearance. His broad shoulders and erect stance suggest his 180 pounds are as powerful physically as his personality is psychologically. With Blackwell and Madigan working as a team, the prison becomes as congenial as a prison can get: hot water is installed in the cells and new bunks replace the sagging antiques which date back to pre WWI. The new beds have lockers at each end.

A bulletin is sent out by Blackwell stating that he has observed only handball and baseball being played on the yard. He allows inmates to vote on sports they wish to play.

Only a handful of convicts want to continue the baseball. Overnight the yard becomes a peaceful playground where you can walk without being in danger from the flying bats and balls. New sports replace baseball on the yard: weight lifting, horseshoes, basketball, volleyball, and shuffleboard.

The radio is now left on two stations. One pumps in music constantly while the other includes talk shows and newscasts.

Ringwald retires and is replaced by a newcomer named

Schaller, who is equally as helpful and understanding as Ringwald had been. He interviews me. "You've never been up for parole. You could have applied years ago. Why didn't you?"

"You know no one gets a parole from Alcatraz. The parole board reasons that if you're so dangerous you have to be kept in Alcatraz then there's no reason to grant you a parole."

"You're right! Although it's against the law, that's the way the system works. The best thing we can do is try to get you away from here. Do you know anyone in Canada who can help you?"

After the interview I decide I'd better help the authorities to help me.

The classification committee approves the suggestion of Bayless (AZ-966) that each inmate be allowed to purchase a box of chocolates at Christmas. As we parade into the mess hall for Christmas dinner, everything seems tranquil and no one expects trouble. The Christmas tree stands in its traditional spot, ten feet in front of the steam tables in the center of the room. We file past its glittering lights and I take my seat at a table when I first hear the sounds.

"You ain't no Christmas tree!" It's the "Green Lizard" (AZ-1306) who is talking to the Christmas tree as if he expects it to answer him. He's a "bug" doing a life sentence for killing someone in the army. Everyone knows he's crazy. His one way conversation with the tree continues until, almost as if he is enraged by not getting an answer from the twinkling giant, he reaches over and jerks the electric cord instantly disconnecting the lights.

As everyone looks on in awe he drops to the floor and disappears from sight. Within seconds the decorated tree shakes and then topples to the floor only to seemingly spring alive as it moves down the aisles of tables and convicts, its branches knocking everything off the tabletops and sending guys sprawling to avoid being clobbered by the runaway evergreen.

Lieutenant Miller, a new six-foot, three-inch import from Lewisburg, chases the "bug" down the aisle hollering at him to stop. Like a disobedient pup, the tree seems to have a mind of its own as it runs faster. Eventually it's trapped in the corner of the mess hall and the Green Lizard emerges from the branches. The lieutenant's club is out and raised above his head as he descends on the Green Lizard. Immediately shouts begin from the audience in the hall: "Don't hit that guy, he's crazy!"

Miller's blows fall hard on the confused head of the culprit and they only cease when the other guards grab the lieutenant's arms and pull him off his prey. Regaining control, he is ushered quickly from the mess hall as the Green Lizard is rushed upstairs to the hospital. The riot could explode any second but it's not until everyone is back in his cell that the booing and hell-raising begins.

After a noisy and messy Christmas Blackwell sends the "Green Lizard" to Springfield and reassigns the lieutenant to a job outside the cell house where he won't have to deal directly with convicts. I am sure Miller just lost his head in the panic of the moment; he was not a vindictive person.

Alcatraz, 1960

I begin 1960 with a new job in the clothing factory. It's a big step down from the responsibility I had in the industry office but I had become a little miffed with the situation there. I'd been asked to help break Mantell (AZ-1351) into the cost accounting job; I had lots of help from others to learn the work there so I didn't mind passing the favor on. As the weeks and months continued to pass, however, it became obvious that Mantell had no intention of learning the job. He hadn't even taken the time to learn how to touch add on an Underwood. He wanted the first-grade pay, but made no consistent effort to master the job.

I wanted out—I was doing his work and mine too. By now I am less impulsive than when I first came to Alcatraz. I want out diplomatically, I had no intention of complaining about another con. When I put in my request to transfer to the clothing factory L. B. Davis waddled over to me. "Anything wrong?"

"No, all's well. I just want a change."

Now I'm standing around a table in the clothing factory pulling threads off trousers from the production lines with eight or nine other guys. It's the last operation on the cook's and baker's white pants before they are inspected and the inmates receive their money. The discovery of too many strings or other defects could cause the entire lot to be rejected by the government before shipment to the armed forces thus cancelling out the paycheques. A village idiot can do the job and most of the convicts around the table are well-suited for the work, including "Grasshopper" (AZ-959) who has a junkie's jaw and an ape's intelligence. He's very lazy and the rest of us have to carry him in spite of the simple nature of the work.

Grasshopper became one of America's most notorious public enemies when he tried to rob a bank with a bottle of piss given to him by a wino. The plan was that Grasshopper would take the bottle and a note claiming it contained nitro into the bank, obtain the money, then outside he would hand off the money to his partner so even if he was caught there would be no evidence found on him.

Grasshopper probably never doubted that his new-found partner would show up to share the loot. However, he never made it out of the bank. He has fifteen years for bank robbery although the sentence should read "for being retarded".

Only once does Grasshopper get excited and actually jump onto another convict. It's because they want to change his name to "Bollweevil" following the release of the "Bollweevil Song". He loses the fight but retains his title of "Grasshopper".

When John F. Kennedy is elected President of the U.S.A., he appoints his brother, Bobby Kennedy, as Attorney General and the changes in the federal prison system begin.

Applications for pardons are usually filtered through

the pardon attorney who picks out a few which he forwards to the attorney general. Bobby Kennedy gives orders that he wants all the applications forwarded to him, although he is still interested in the recommendations of the pardon attorney who has held the position for more than a quarter of a century. The result is that there are more pardons granted while the Kennedys are in power than in the total history of the United States. Also, those receiving the pardons are poor, friendless convicts with no political influence.

Attorney General Robert Kennedy appoints "Wizard" White, an old collegemate of his, and lawyer, to the criminal division. During a tour of Alcatraz, "Wizard" comes through the laundry. He requests two pair of denims with "Alcatraz" sewn on the pockets, one for himself and the other for Bobby Kennedy. "When we're up in Cape Cod playing touch football, we'll wear these," he explains. The cons in the clothing factory are delighted to do anything for Bobby Kennedy.

Alcatraz is the only prison where there is no recreation in the evenings. Madigan tries to institute school classes and allows inmates to bring musical instruments to their cells in the evening. I sit musing about my future, a negro is practicing the scales on his saxophone in the next cellblock. As he hesitates on difficult notes, I find myself hesitating with him.

I'm starting to think about myself now. These bastards won't get me involved in their problems again. Fuck all of them. The first twenty-five years was for them, from now on it's for me. I write to the John Howard Society in Vancouver, B.C., with the help of Schaller. Their reply states, "This agency is prepared to help any prisoner reestablish himself on the outside, provided he is not a Catholic!"

Although I'm not, nor have ever been, religious, I was baptized a Catholic. I decide I don't want anything to do with people who discriminate so I get another address and write to the Catholic Federation of Charities, Rehabilitation Branch, in Montreal. The reply, from Frank Roberts in St. Vincent de Paul, is swift and positive. It states that they are prepared to help anyone. In my first correspondence I use my real name, Karpowicz. When I reply to their invitation, I explain I am Alvin Karpis. They become more interested than previously.

Warden Madigan soon pays me a personal visit. "The people in Montreal are writing letters and asking questions about you. They want to know if you're lucid, what kind of work you can do, and I've sent them some nice letters about you.

"They aren't the only ones asking about you. The members of the federal parole board have frequently asked me why you've never applied for a parole all these years."

"They know you can't get a parole out of Alcatraz."

"I've never told you how you should do your time. You've taken a hard line—refused to go before a parole board—showed your contempt—scorned those people—probably you're the only convict in the history of the federal parole board to wait so long without asking to see them. It's time you did and you'd better figure out a good reason why you've waited so long to save *their* faces."

December, 1960

The pains come just before Christmas. They spread in sharp bursts through my chest. Thinking it may help alleviate the trouble, I stop smoking "Wing" cigarettes but the pain only increases until I have to spend a few weeks in hospital. My spine is riddled with arthritis.

One good thing comes of the experience. I never smoke another cigarette. I've been smoking since I was ten years old but from December of 1960, I never touch a smoke again. My food starts tasting better, I sleep better, my hands no longer tremble, my armpits are no longer soaked, my eyes clear up, and my sore throat disappears. I realize now what I was doing to myself; I always thought I was supposed to feel the way I did until I quit smoking.

New Year's Eve, 1960

Cigar smoke rises lazily through the tiers of cells. Every con was given a surprise present of four cigars as he left the dining hall after supper. The New Year approaches with me meditating on the changes in Alcatraz since Madigan arrived. New Year's is a good example. No hell-raising, no breakage. The radio is left on all night. The atmosphere is quiet and enjoyable. There'll be no work tomorrow.

The guards in the gun cages don't even carry weapons any longer. The theory behind Madigan disarming the screws is "no guns, no temptation to break into the gun cages." Besides, if hostages are ever taken the guards are as apt to be hit by bullets as convicts. Guns are trouble that lead to trouble, so Madigan bans them altogether.

We follow the big dance bands as they bring in the New Year across the country. We start listening to the celebrations in Times Square, New York, and then switch to the next time zone where the music comes from Chicago's "Tonight Club". When it's Rocky Mountain Time the city is Denver and by the time the magic hour hits San Francisco the music is hot from the "Hungry Eye". One song played in each location catches my fancy—it's "Heart of My Heart".

Alcatraz, 1961

We congregate by the clothing factory door waiting to go in to eat dinner. The casual atmosphere and friendly conversation give no hint of an impending attack.

Only one inch of the concealed heavy scissors extends from Buck Morris's hand (AZ-1202), as he joins the group. With the first pop out of the box he hits the Mexican in the forehead. Then, methodically, he works over face, neck, and body as he spins him around with sharp blows. Blood splatters everyone in the vicinity as Buck vindictively teaches the Mexican not to romance with his kid, a youngster named Heffington (AZ-1343). The guards and foreman watch, unwilling to enter the bloodbath—they stand at the edge of the frey like frightened kids on a hot summer day dancing nervously on the outside edge of a water sprinkler. It's another Mexican, Mendoza (AZ-1283), who breaks in and pins Buck's thrashing arm.

"You crazy? You're goin' to kill this guy!" The interference from Mendoza snaps the wild gaze from Buck's eyes. He hands the scissors over to the Mexican.

A screw rushes forward only to be stopped in his tracks by Mendoza's words of warning, "You stay out of this until we get it straightened up ourselves!"

Mendoza escorts the bloody figure in the direction of the hospital, leaving a red trail across the floor from over seventy-five wounds.

July, 1961

Madigan, Father Clark, and Schaller convince me I should go up for a parole even with the knowledge that I'll be turned down. When Washington hears that I have applied, Judge Sullivan, the usual representative of the parole board in this area, is replaced by the chairman of the board himself.

As I enter the room I find myself alone with a small man in horn-rimmed glasses setting up a recorder. He tells me, "This is the first time in the history of the parole hearings that we've used a recorder rather than a secretary."

I think to myself, a lot of people including J. Edgar Hoover will get a copy of this.

"I know I ain't going to get no parole. I'm just here to get the denial over with to please everyone around here."

"Why are you so certain you'll be refused?"

"No one ever gets a parole from Alcatraz."

"That's not constitutional."

"Do you know anyone who ever did get one?"

By now he has got his machine ready and, as he switches it on, changes the topic. "Well Karpis, you've waited a long time for this interview."

"I suppose it's been a while."

"A while! You've waited twenty-five years! Why? A lot of people besides myself are curious. We can't find any precedent in the history of the parole board."

"If I had asked for a parole after fifteen years, wouldn't it have been a big joke to everyone?"

"You might be right," he grins. "No one would have given you a parole ten years ago."

"How about now?" I look him straight in the eye.

"Maybe, possibly," he squirms, looking down at the machine.

"Also you could have deported me anytime without me asking for it. I couldn't have stopped you."

"Do you have a sponsor in Canada?"

"Yeah, Frank Roberts."

"I know Frank, he's a good man—a responsible man—the best one to have on your side. Do you have any regrets over your past life?"

"No, none!"

His jaw almost falls on his recorder. It's as if he expected the atmosphere of Alcatraz to have taught me how to be a reformed and responsible citizen scorning the violence of the past when in fact I have seen more violence and corruption inside than I ever knew in my robbing days. He ends the interview abruptly and shuts off his machine. The entire conversation takes about five minutes. The denial of my parole application arrives from Washington within ten days.

Captain Richtner leaves as predicted and the new captain arrives from Leavenworth. He is none other than Bradley, the lieutenant who had brought me back from Leavenworth.

Bradley is being shown around Alcatraz when the lieutenant escorting him stops to say hello to me. I take the opportunity to ask Bradley a friendly question. "Captain Bradley, I'll be going before the classification committee on Friday. Will you be there?"

Only an aloof grunt comes from the new captain. His response puzzles me since I recall vividly his sympathetic remarks throughout the return trip from Leavenworth.

As I walk into the classification committee the first face I see is that of the stern-looking Bradley. Madigan, Blackwell, Schaller, the chief MTA, the record clerk, the warden's secretary, and the head steward are also sitting on the committee. Madigan chairs the meeting. As I make myself comfortable, he begins, "We'd like to do something for you. We've never been satisfied with the reasons given for your return from Leavenworth."

"Maybe Mr. Bradley can help you out," I suggest, "I never knew myself. If you think I've been back long enough, I'd like to be transferred again."

"You've been back long enough. We all know you've just been turned down for a parole, maybe you'll have a better chance of obtaining one in another institution."

Thus setting the stage, Madigan invites each member of the committee to give their opinion about me. They all give me "a nice send off." Bradley, having just arrived at Alcatraz, is not asked for an opinion.

"Is there anything else you'd like to say?" asks Madigan and I reply, "Yeah, Mr. Bradley escorted me back from Leavenworth on the train and gave me a strong impression that he felt I had been unjustly dealt with. Maybe he can clear up the reason I was returned."

"We'll discuss that, but not in your presence," says Madigan and I am asked to wait outside while they deliberate. I'm left outside so long I begin to wonder what they could be discussing. When I am eventually brought back into the room, Madigan turns to Bradley.

"Mr. Bradley, is there anything you would like to say to Karpis?"

"Karpis, you play a lot of bridge, don't you?" sneers the new captain.

"No, as a matter of fact I don't know how to play bridge, I play a little gin or two-handed hearts."

"You don't play bridge?" repeats the captain, making it sound like a threat.

"No, I don't. I just told you."

The other members are all staring at Bradley who was obviously about to make a point based on my bridge playing. While there is a lull I decide to ask a question of my own. "While I'm here, didn't you tell me on the train I shouldn't have been sent back—that I did nothing to deserve being sent back?"

"I don't remember what I said on the train." Bradley is now defensive. I pursue him.

"Well, do you remember me doing anything at Leavenworth which justified me being sent back here?"

"I remember you sitting on the grandstand by the baseball diamond with guys coming up to you and walking away again." Bradley has placed a note of suspicion in his statement.

"That's not unusual," I point out.

"I know what I know!" insists Bradley.

"Well, you say so. Why don't you tell Mr. Madigan what you know while I'm here to defend myself."

"I know what I know!" repeats Bradley ominously. Madigan comes to his assistance by asking me a question.

"Is there anything else you'd like to say?"

"Yeah!" By now I'm so angry I would jump Bradley without a second thought. "It seems to me the way to get a transfer from Alcatraz is to kill a guard first." (My allusion is to "Icebox Annie" who was transferred.) "And, if you want to be made captain, all you have to do is beat a guy to death in the hole in Atlanta!"

"I think you've said too much!" comments Madigan, bringing the hearing to a close.

The sun is warm, there's no breeze, I sit on a cushion on the corner of the steps overlooking the yard consulting my own private physician, Doc Spears (AZ-1493). I know from the first advice he gave me that I could trust his word. "The worse thing people can do is ask for medical advice. Medical science is nothing! Doctors make more mistakes than convicts in Alcatraz. If we guess wrong, you're not around to complain. Don't ever place any faith in what a doctor says. We're all groping in the dark."

I'll take free medical advice from Doc Spears but I'll never take a free plane ticket from him. The sixty-year-old, chunky, medical practitioner with thick massive shoulders, steel-rimmed glasses, grey hair and red complexion seems apathetic toward the fate of his friends.

Doc had bought himself a ticket to Mexico City from Florida, persuaded his drinking companion to take the flight in his place, took out an insurance policy on himself in his wife's name, and waved goodbye to his buddy. The plane reached Texas but disappeared without a trace over the Gulf of Mexico. Doc's wife collected the insurance but they made the mistake of escaping in the victim's car. The insurance company, suspicious, located them and the car in a cottage in Arizona, but could prove only car theft.

"What the hell did you take that guy's car for?" I ask Doc Spears. He laughs at the question.

"Ray, you never asked me if I put the guy on the plane, like most people do."

"I don't have to. I know goddamn well you did it." Doc chuckles to himself as I continue speculating. "How far do you think that plane was out before it exploded?"

Now Doc is laughing openly. "Somewhere between Houston and Mexico City," is his noncommittal reply.

"What the hell did you use, nitro?"

"Oh, you old-time box-men," admonishes Doc, shaking his head. "Hell no! No one fools with that stuff anymore. It's too unstable! They've got stuff now that's like putty. You can wrap it around anything."

"What did you use?" My question returns him to the cat and mouse game we are playing.

"The only thing I didn't use was my head. I got greedy and took the car by mistake."

July 4, 1961

It is traditional to have T-bone steaks on the fourth of July at Alcatraz. It's a sign of how good things have become in recent years. A rumor spreads through the cells that there will be a riot in the mess hall. The place is reportedly going to go up with a bang because the cook prepared turkeys instead of T-bone steaks.

As we file into the mess hall, I notice the extra screws in the gun cages and realize that any day in Alcatraz can bring an end to my hopes of ever seeing the outside world again. The story of the riot obviously reached the authorities, but inside the mess hall there are no extra guards. Madigan and Blackwell stand beside the steam tables cool and calm. They chat amicably with inmates who pick up their meals. No tables are turned over, everyone eats turkey.

I know that the classification committee recommended I be sent to Leavenworth on a transfer. However, this recommendation has to be approved by the Bureau of Prisons in Washington. The longer I wait for the news, the more nervous I become.

Then the unexpected—Madigan is leaving. As suddenly as he was transferred to Alcatraz as warden, he is removed. The reason is an emergency at McNeil Island where the warden there is involved in a sex scandal and has been forced to resign. Madigan is being sent to fill the vacated post and Blackwell becomes the fourth warden of Alcatraz. Dollison is shortly promoted to associate warden.

I injure my back picking up clothing bundles and land in the hospital for a month. Schaller comforts me by whispering that the Bureau of Prisons approved my transfer.

November, 1961

Again I injure my back, this time on the yard, and return to hospital. Tension over my impending transfer causes my stomach to act up as I begin to wonder what awaits me at Leavenworth this time around.

Bennett, the Director of Prisons, while paying a visit to Alcatraz, stops outside my cell in the hospital. "How you feeling Karpis? What's wrong with your back?"

"Arthritis—it acts up."

Turning sober and changing his voice to emphasize his point Bennett snaps, "Fellow, I want you to understand! This is your last chance!" It's not necessary to ask what he refers to—it's my transfer to Leavenworth, of course.

Alcatraz, 1962

As the year 1962 begins, I'm back in the library and still anxiously awaiting the next big transfer to Leavenworth. Two prisoners approach me. They want me to get them some plaster of paris from a friend of mine who is working in the hospital. Both are trustworthy and, in fact, are brothers— John Anglin (AZ-1476) and his brother Clarence Anglin

(AZ-1485) from Montgomery, Alabama. They and two others plan an escape. I arrange for them to get their plaster of paris hoping their escapade won't occur until I'm gone on the transfer.

My stomach again acts up on me and I'm lying in hospital when the news of the Leavenworth transfer reaches me. As the date approaches my nervous system reacts more violently. With the exception of the six months when I was last sent to Leavenworth, I've been at Alcatraz since 1936, longer than any other prisoner, more than a quarter of a century.

I'm still in hospital the morning the shipment is to leave for Leavenworth. It seems as if they should have come for me and my belongings long ago.

"Hello Karpis." It's the chief MTA. "Karpis, I just don't have the heart to tell you, you've been turned down! When the authorities at Leavenworth discovered your name on the transfer list, they raised such hell Bennett was forced to change his decision."

I'm speechless. The desperate feeling that I'm destined to die in Alcatraz replaces the turbulent expectations which have plagued me.

"I hear though that you'll be going to McNeil Island on the next shipment there."

"Bullshit!" I think to myself, realizing that he is trying to cheer me up. It took a great deal of persuasion on the part of a number of people around Alcatraz to convince the Bureau of Prisons I was ready for a maximum security prison such as Leavenworth. The idea that after Leavenworth's refusal they would send me to McNeil is preposterous. I appreciate the MTA's attempt to ease the blow, but feel somewhat insulted that he thinks I am foolish enough to believe his story. I don't sleep all night.

I have a horror of dying in prison. My perseverance is mainly due to the message I sent back to Hoover when he told me I would rot to death in Alcatraz. I'm determined to spite him thus I'm depressed to hear that death claimed an old convict from the clothing factory who had heart trouble in the hospital wing. His first number had been AZ-105 but his second number when he returned to die was AZ-1246.

Mickey Cohen (AZ-1518) is the survivor of many gun fights as well as ring fights. He's a professional fighter turned "Shylock". In Alcatraz he uses up a fortune in clean bars of soap. His phobia over cleanliness is so strong, he won't even touch a bar of soap after he's used it once and he requires a fresh laundry daily. Mickey has the money to indulge his idiosyncrasy and, working in the clothing issue, he has the opportunity.

Frankie Carbo (AZ-1568), who was caught by the FBI when they recorded a telephone conversation during which Frankie was deciding who would win the next championship boxing title eighteen months ahead of the bout, confesses to me how he robbed Cohen.

"You know how scared of germs Mickey is?"

"Yeah."

"Well, when Mickey got his box of candy at Christmas he decided to keep it. I slipped into his cell one day and cut the corner out of his box. Then I told Mickey about the trouble in the cell house with mice getting into candy boxes and how they will nibble at the corners of the boxes. Half an hour later, he presented me with his candy."

It's after I've checked out of hospital that I learn the details from the warden's secretary.

Madigan had returned to pack the balance of his belongings which he abandoned in his hasty transfer to McNeil Island. He was sitting with Warden Blackwell when the message came through on the teletype to "cancel Karpis". After reading the message from Washington handed him by Blackwell, Madigan simply said, "I'm going to use your phone for a minute."

After explaining to Bennett where he was and why he was there, Madigan continued, "I just read this teletype about Karpis!" Bennett buzzed on the other end of the line, then Madigan replied, "Well I doubt if Karpis wants to be in Leavenworth any more than Warden Taylor wants him there, but we want him transferred out of here."

Again, Bennett's voice hummed on the other end of the line before Madigan spoke. "Then send him to McNeil Island—I'll be personally responsible for him; I'll take the rap for anything he does wrong!" The buzzing turned wild until Madigan culminated it with, "Will you be in your office for the next hour?"

Hanging up the receiver, Madigan explained to Blackwell, "Bennett claims he won't take the responsibility of sending Karpis to McNeil because he doesn't think your classification committee will recommend the transfer."

Less than an hour later, Madigan again called Bennett to declare that a special meeting of the classification committee at Alcatraz had just recommended that I be transferred to McNeil Island! I'm told officially that I'll be leaving for McNeil Island on April 7, 1962.

West (AZ-1335) thanks me for the plaster of paris I gave to him and the Anglin brothers. Now I'm in a constant state of anxiety hoping they don't make their break before I leave on the next transfer to McNeil Island. There is always the danger of trouble in a prison, and no place to hide from it.

To add to my misery new toilet bowls are being installed in the cells and the heavy jackhammers rumble all day in the utility corridors. My stomach vibrates with the drills, and the dust flying as the dry concrete spreads a fine film like talcum powder through the air vents into the cells. The pounding of the drills and the fine powder supersaturating the closed area in the utility corridors between the cells are obnoxious enough to drive the screw watching the convict workers out of the corridor to stand guard at the entrance. But, lying in my cell, I can't escape the effects any more than I can prevent my stomach from churning itself into the hospital again. Even when I sign out of the hospital they give me tranquilizers several times a day, which I pretend to take but actually give away to friends.

On the Yard, 1962

A youngster, Scott (AZ-1403), comes to sit beside me on the top step overlooking the yard and beyond it the water of the bay flowing treacherously between us and the city of San Francisco. He's full of questions about the tides and wants to know anything I can tell him about previous attempts to swim to freedom. My warnings of the death lurking in the undercurrents around the island only seem to make him more determined to conquer them.

Recalling the days when I was young and desperate enough to jump into the cold waters myself, I have to admire Scott's spunk although my experience tells me he hasn't any chance of swimming to freedom.

Friday, On The Yard, April 6, 1962

Tomorrow I leave for McNeil Island, today I say goodbye to my friends on the yard. Doc Spears, Bigsey, Mickey Cohen all shake my hand.

The Anglin brothers are working themselves into good physical condition on the handball court; they hang in the background nodding as I leave the yard but show enough courtesy not to be seen with me by the ever watchful guards. I'm relieved to be out of Alcatraz before they make their play. If the plaster of paris is ever connected with me, it will be the end of my transfer but there are obligations a convict has to himself and to *escape* which no one, who has never been locked in a cage, can hope to appreciate.

Saturday, April 7, 1962

The boat crossing the waters to San Francisco takes me for the last time from the dreary existence of the Alcatraz cell house into the future. I only made this trip once before, on the way to Leavenworth during a violent storm in a crowded puke-filled boat. Today, the sun shines brightly on the serene waters of the bay. Swimmers splash freely in its reflection along the beaches of San Francisco.

Alcatraz has been an exercise in survival. If I could at this moment escape successfully, I would still kill anyone in my path. If paroled at this moment, I would head straight for friends of Mickey Cohen and Frankie Carbo who would hopefully set me up in a protected position with organized crime. The rules, the regulations, the routine of Alcatraz have done nothing to reform me; reform awaits me, although I don't realize it at this moment, on McNeil Island with my friend Warden Madigan. A quarter of a century in Alcatraz has been an empty, futile experience.

EPILOGUE

Alcatraz, Cell House
June 13, 1962

"Sarge," a six-foot four-inch screw, rushes along the B block flats waking the inmates for the morning count. Bartlett used to be a master sergeant in the army, thus earning his nickname. It's not unusual to count convicts who are still asleep or in bed, if he stops to wait for everyone to stand by his door he will be late turning in the count. On the way back he again tries to shout the few late sleepers into a conscious state.

Today three prisoners are still curled up in their bunks. Swearing to himself, Sarge reaches into each of the cells shaking the pillows under the sleeping bodies. It's at the third cell that he grabs the con by the hair, prepared to jerk him awake. The head rolls from the bunk onto the hard concrete floor. Sarge screams for help, believing in the confused seconds of discovery that someone has grotesquely severed the head from its body.

A closer inspection of the object on the cell floor proves it to be a "dummy" head. Similar heads, moulded from plaster of paris, are found in the bunks of the other cells from which prisoners refused to respond to the morning call. Missing are Frank Lee Morris, age thirty-five (AZ-1441), John W. Anglin, age thirty-two, and John's younger brother Clarence Anglin, age twenty-eight.

Investigation uncovers holes dug through the back walls of each cell into the utility corridor behind. The convicts have managed to burrow through several feet of reinforced concrete, climb to the ceiling of the cell house, force their way through an air vent onto the roof outside and escape the island on an improvised raft. A fourth cell is found with a hole leading to the utility corridor. It belongs to West who baulked at the last moment.

The authorities investigate and release details to the press, including the manner in which the men dug their way from the secure cells with spoons stolen from the dining hall. Even today the literature in the pamphlets bought by tourists on the docks in San Francisco before boarding a ferry boat for the island tour reinforces the myth that the escape was accomplished with plain tablespoons. Complete bullshit! The truth is that the authorities were too embarrassed to admit that the holes were cut from the utility corridors behind the cells where the inmates had been left alone with jackhammers while the careless guards avoided the discomfort of the dust in the air.

The "dummy" heads were made lifelike by embedding real hair in them obtained from the barbershop where the Anglin brothers worked as barbers. None of the three escaped convicts are ever recaptured.

Six months later in December of 1962 two more convicts break out of Alcatraz and, outfitted with flotation gear, jump into the dark swirling waters. Earl Lee Parker (AZ-1413) is found clinging to "Little Alcatraz" 100 yards from shore; his partner John Paul Scott, actually swims successfully to the mainland where he is found two and one-half miles away, exhausted on the rocks at Fort Point.

May 15, 1963

Robert Kennedy, Attorney General for the U.S.A., reaches the conclusion that Alcatraz is an expensive relic in the Bureau of Prisons and closes its doors permanently.

Now Available!

VIDEO INTERVIEW WITH ALVIN KARPIS BEFORE HIS DEATH IN 1979.

ALVIN KARPIS: PUBLIC ENEMY #1

THIS 50 MINUTE INTERVIEW WAS PROFESSIONALLY PRODUCED BY THE **CANADIAN BROADCASTING CORPORATION**. IN IT, ALVIN KARPIS DISCUSSES HIS CRIMINAL CAREER AS PUBLIC ENEMY #1, **J. EDGAR HOOVER'S** CLAIM TO HAVE PERSONALLY CAPTURED HIM, AND HIS ASSOCIATES AND FRIENDS **(MA BARKER, BABY-FACE NELSON, PRETTY BOY FLOYD, AND JOHN DILLINGER.)** HE ALSO DESCRIBES LIFE IN ALCATRAZ AND CELL MATES SUCH AS **DOC BARKER, MACHINE-GUN KELLY, AL CAPONE**, AS WELL AS A YOUNG INMATE WHO LATER PERSUADED THE OLD GANGSTER TO TEACH HIM TO PLAY GUITAR AT THE FEDERAL PRISON ON McNEIL ISLAND, **CHARLES MANSON**.

$20.00 plus $10.00 for shipping and registration.
TOTAL $30.00 U.S.
To order the above video, please send a money order or certified cheque to...
L.B.S. Inc. Publications,
P.O. Box 84001,
1235 Trafalgar Road,
Oakville, Ontario, Canada, L6H 3J0

Other books by Robert Livesey..

Professor Livesey's other publications are textbooks designed for senior elementary students (grades 5-8) or high school students (grades 9-12)

<u>**Creating with Shakespeare**</u> (subtitle: <u>Shakin' with Willie</u>) A new and entertaining textbook designed to introduce students to Shakespeare's plays while encouraging their creative talents. Highly visual and project-driven. $15.00

<u>**Faces of Myth (Revised)**</u> This popular textbook is designed to introduce students to world mythology, past and present. Highly visual. $15.00

<u>**Footprints in the Snow: the heroes and heroines of Canada**</u> This textbook is approved by Canadian Ministries of Education. It contains short biographies and visuals of 100 famous Canadian personalities. $12.50

<u>**Coming to Canada:**</u> More than 40 new Canadians from different countries describe why they left their native lands, what they expected, what they found and how they now feel about their new home. $18.00

Discovering Canada series...

This series is based on early Canadian (North American) history. Each book is 96 pages, fully illustrated, containing many student projects and activities.

<u>**The Vikings:**</u> Stories of the Vikings who first crossed the Atlantic ocean and founded settlements in North America in 1000 A.D. $9.95

<u>**The Fur Traders:**</u> Stories of the fur traders who first explored the North American continent. $9.95

<u>**New France:**</u> Stories of the first French settlements in North America which stretched from Hudson's Bay to the Gulf of Mexico, and west to the Rocky Mountains. $9.95

<u>**Native Peoples:**</u> A description of the native tribes that existed in Canada before the arrival of the Europeans, including their myths, ways of life, and locations. $9.95

<u>**The Defenders:**</u> A description of the War of 1812 between Canada (Britain) and the United States. $9.95

Please send a money order or certified cheque and add $1.00 for shipping. Schools may send purchase orders.

For the Collector...

If you collect rare books or autographs, you may wish to obtain **Public Enemy #1**, the first book written by Alvin Karpis, which recorded his criminal activities before he was arrested and sent to Alcatraz.

There are only 8 hardcover copies of **Public Enemy #1** available.

Each copy was **personally autographed** by Alvin Karpis before his death in 1979.
cost… $200.00 U.S.

To order the above book, please write to...
L.B.S. Inc.Publications,
P.O. Box 84001,
1235 Trafalgar Road,
Oakville, Ontario, Canada, L6H 3J0

Do not send cash or cheques!
The book will be reserved in your name, if it is still available, and you will be notified by mail. At that time you will be asked to send the payment.